Studies on Entrepreneurship, Structural Change and Industrial Dynamics

Series editors

João Leitão
University of Beira Interior, Covilhã, Portugal

Tessaleno Devezas
University of Beira Interior, Covilhã, Portugal

The 'Studies on Entrepreneurship, Structural Change and Industrial Dynamics' series showcases exceptional scholarly work being developed on the still unexplored complex relationship between entrepreneurship, structural change and industrial dynamics, by addressing structural and technological determinants of the evolutionary pathway of innovative and entrepreneurial activity.

The series invites proposals based on sound research methodologies and approaches to the above topics. Volumes in the series may include research monographs and edited/contributed works. Please send the completed proposal form downloadable from this page (see "For Authors and Editors") to the series editors.

More information about this series at http://www.springer.com/series/15330

Francesca Grippa • João Leitão • Julia Gluesing •
Ken Riopelle • Peter Gloor
Editors

Collaborative Innovation Networks

Building Adaptive and Resilient Organizations

Springer

Editors
Francesca Grippa
Northeastern University
Boston, Massachusetts, USA

João Leitão
University of Beira Interior
Covilhã, Portugal

Julia Gluesing
Industrial and Systems Engineering
Wayne State University
Detroit, Michigan, USA

Ken Riopelle
Industrial and Systems Engineering
Wayne State University
Detroit, Michigan, USA

Peter Gloor
MIT Center for Collective Intelligence
Massachusetts Institute of Technology
Cambridge, Massachusetts, USA

ISSN 2511-2023 ISSN 2511-2031 (electronic)
Studies on Entrepreneurship, Structural Change and Industrial Dynamics
ISBN 978-3-030-08957-3 ISBN 978-3-319-74295-3 (eBook)
https://doi.org/10.1007/978-3-319-74295-3

Softcover re-print of the Hardcover 1st edition 2018

Printed on acid-free paper

This Springer imprint is published by the registered company Springer International Publishing AG part of Springer Nature.
The registered company address is: Gewerbestrasse 11, 6330 Cham, Switzerland

Preface

In today's unpredictable world, demonstrating resilience and responding to external shocks is becoming a key imperative. At the individual and organizational level, collaboration and collective actions provide an important advantage to bounce back from adverse situations. Most of the organizations rely on sophisticated collections of strategies, tools, and processes to manage risks and reduce the impact of external threats. Yet, any strategic dashboard or individual effort might be inadequate if changes are as unpredictable as the ones we are witnessing with climate change, social change, and global terrorism.

Highly networked individuals, teams, and communities sustain positive relationships with others and use their social capital to master turbulence. Collaborative Innovation Networks (COINs)—as self-organizing emergent social systems—are primary building blocks of innovation for coping with external change. As small cyberteams of intrinsically motivated individuals, COIN members get together to innovate in domains they are passionate about and to respond to unexpected events and opportunities. Developing and supporting networks has been recognized in literature as a key process to minimize excessive risks and reduce the stress on the system.

The interdisciplinary nature of the book offers a unique opportunity to frame the discussion around resilience using a multiplicity of perspectives, including social innovation, anthropology, leadership, change management, and big data applications. The book and its nineteen chapters describe how COINs enable resilience in four sections: Entrepreneurship, Healthcare, Society and Culture, and Open Dialogue and Creativity.

The Entrepreneurship section covers topics such as the impact of U.S. venture capital on start-up success and the importance for Chinese entrepreneurs to connect with foreign and domestic venture capitalists.

The Healthcare section discusses how COINs of team of patients, family members, doctors, and researchers support patients with chronic diseases and how infant mortality can be reduced by forming groups of mothers, social workers, doctors, and policy makers who work together.

The Society and Culture section includes contributions on the role of COINs in promoting food sharing networks, protecting bird species in New Zealand, analyzing the evolution of world cultures through epic stories and finding the "Truth of Tribes" through social media.

Last, the Open Dialogue and Creativity section explores the impact of peer learning on creativity and the role of story writing to improve daily conversations and generation of new ideas. Combined these sections provide the reader with specific, concrete examples of COINs in action around the world and the real impact they are having today.

Resilience is particularly important in healthcare. For example, COINs of patients, family members, doctors, and researchers are formed to develop together new, innovative ways of dealing with chronic diseases and improving patient and caregiver quality of life. Another area in healthcare where COINs build resilience is reducing infant mortality by forming COINs of mothers, social workers, doctors, and policy makers to provide mothers with the support necessary to give their newborns a better future than they had themselves. In internal healthcare processes, COINs act as an enabler for process change, representing a novel approach to human resource management by nurturing free exchange of ideas and a rotating leadership style.

A second area for resilience is in industry, where COINs can strengthen adaptability and transformability to leverage uncertainty as a competitive advantage. Inside large corporations, COINs can form spontaneously and with minimal management intervention to creatively react to new risks and external threats. COINs might appear in well-established firms as a bottom-up response to find new applications for emerging technologies, thus flexibly adapting to change and anticipating competitors' next moves. COINs will also be tremendously useful to start-ups, offering new self-organizing and entrepreneurial forms of leadership, where all stakeholders, including founders, early employees, customers, suppliers, and business partners, collaborate to develop new and innovative products, services, and business models for an ever-changing environment.

Resilience through COINs is also necessary in social innovation and sustainable entrepreneurship. COINs can help align practice with policy and provide leadership in seeking funding from diverse sources. In urban areas such as for example Detroit and other postindustrial cities, social innovation through COINs has turned crisis into opportunity as cities become a source of inspiration and solutions for other challenged American cities looking for innovative new models of urban governance.

Creating COINs of students will build resilience in an educational setting, where self-organizing student teams might collaborate over long distance to solve complex problems. Students might also engage in rotating leadership behavior inside the classroom, thus increasing resilience against bullying and for better learning. Similarly, COINs of faculty and researchers promote resilience and reshape the higher education environment by reimagining the future of collaborations across departments and institutions.

Boston, MA	Francesca Grippa
Covilhã, Portugal	Joao Leitão
Detroit, MI	Julia Gluesing
Detroit, MI	Ken Riopelle
Cambridge, MA	Peter Gloor

Acknowledgments

This volume combines selected contributions presented at the 7th International Conference on Collaborative Innovation Networks held in Detroit from September 14 to 17, 2017. Scholars and practitioners discussed how to build resilient systems through collaborative innovation networks across a variety of disciplines, including health, business, social innovation, entrepreneurship, and education. We would like to thank the sponsors of the conference who helped bring together international scholars, researchers, and practitioners to discuss how to improve resilience in large and small organizations, communities, and territories. These include the Global Data Insight & Analytics Group at Ford Motor Company, Wayne State University, the MIT Center for Collective Intelligence, Illinois Institute of Technology/Stuart School of Business, Aalto University in Finland, and The Pontifical Catholic University de Chile.

We are also grateful for the valuable insights provided by the Conference Program Committee members and to the many reviewers who provided precious feedback and constructive criticisms.

Contents

Part I
Entrepreneurship

Analyzing VC Influence on Startup Success: A People-Centric Network Theory Approach

Beth Hadley, Peter A. Gloor, Stephanie L. Woerner, and Yuhong Zhou

Abstract We study the impact of venture capitalists on startup success using social network analysis. Using multiple sources, we compile a unique dataset of 3199 US-based technology startups and their board members, from which we generate and analyze the interlocking directorates network (formal network) and the Twitter activity network (informal network). We define three metrics of success: startup funding (collected from Crunchbase), annual sales (collected from OneSource), and return-on-investment (annual sales/funding). We find that startups with more VCs on their board are more centrally located in the formal network, tend to receive greater funding, have greater annual sales, yet a smaller return-on-investment. We also find that VCs are significantly more central in the Twitter network than non-VCs, and they have greater Twitter popularity (number of followers/number of people they follow). Interestingly, VCs tweet significantly less than non-VCs. Our results indicate that VCs carry a significant amount of capital, both financially as well as socially, which they transmit to the startups they become involved with, yet they tend to invest disproportionately to startup revenue (hence lower ROI).

B. Hadley (✉)
MIT Department of Computer Science, Cambridge, MA, USA
e-mail: bhadley@mit.edu

P. A. Gloor
MIT Center for Collective Intelligence, Cambridge, MA, USA
e-mail: pgloor@mit.edu

S. L. Woerner
MIT Sloan School of Management, Cambridge, MA, USA
e-mail: woerner@mit.edu

Y. Zhou
South China University of Technology, Guangzhou, China

MIT, Cambridge, MA, USA
e-mail: yuhongz@mit.edu

F. Grippa et al. (eds.), *Collaborative Innovation Networks*, Studies on Entrepreneurship, Structural Change and Industrial Dynamics,
https://doi.org/10.1007/978-3-319-74295-3_1

1 Introduction

There is much uncertainty involved with early stage startups. Venture capitalists are faced with literally million dollar questions as they seek to evaluate startups, to determine the potential of an investment. Likewise, entrepreneurs are faced with equally valuable questions as they seek venture capitalists from whom to not only gain funding, but also support and mentorship.

Fundamentally, we aim to investigate the question of how venture capitalists influence the success of a startup, and how this is manifested in people-centric networks. To answer this broad question, we adopt a network theory approach, in which we construct social networks of the board members of each startup. We choose to study the board of directors of a startup, as board directors have a great deal of influence over a startup due to their financial, intellectual, and social capital resources. Furthermore, board members often sit on multiple boards, and therefore may share their resources with multiple startups. The resulting network formed by board membership represents a communication network, through which critical resources flow.

Collaborative Innovation Networks (COINs) are self-organizing social systems in which self-motivated individuals collaborate to achieve a common goal (Gloor 2005). We believe the board membership network bears some similar traits to a COIN network—within this network, multiple players, namely VCs and entrepreneurs, strive to create something new—a new venture and financial gain. That said, it remains an open question the extent to which such a network is actually "collaborative", and specifically, to what extent the venture capitalists in this network contribute to the overall success of the entrepreneurs and their startups.

To investigate these questions, we first construct a formal network, an interlocking directorates network composed of companies (the nodes) and links between two companies who share at least one board member (Mizruchi 1996). We look at the position of successful startups in this network and compare this to the position of startups with many VCs on their boards. Secondly, we construct an informal social network composed of the Twitter activity of the individuals in our formal network, and look at the behavior of venture capitalists in this network. By looking at venture capitalists' influence in these networks, we develop evidence that informs our response to the ultimate research question—how do venture capitalists influence the success of startups.

2 Background and Related Work

Venture capital (VC) is well established as one of the key driving forces in the American entrepreneurial ecosystem. According to the National Venture Capital Association, in 2015 nearly $60 billion in venture capital was deployed across 4380 deals. More than 30% of those deals were to companies receiving venture investment for the first time (Franklin and Haque 2016). That said, research studies have not provided consistent conclusions regarding the impact of VC investments on entrepreneurial firms, and whether this impact is a net positive or negative. Although the answer is likely, "it depends", the question is worthy of continued rigorous analysis.

Advocates for the positive influence of VCs claim that VCs serve three main roles to identify and promote successful startups:

1. "Screening": VCs choose to invest in high quality companies with promising potential. They are experienced at selecting for certain criteria that predict success, such as technical expertise and founder commitment (Chan 1983; Amit et al. 1998).
2. "Monitoring": VCs track the status of their portfolio companies, comparing investments with market trends and opportunities. They protect the value of their investments by adding credibility and prestige to those companies they invest in (Lerner 1995; Kaplan and Strömberg 2003).
3. "Coaching": VCs provide advice and support to their portfolio companies with the intent of improving their chances of success and, in return, the return on their investment. This may include connecting the firm with resources (networking), assisting with recruitment, and providing experience, advice, and mentoring (Hellmann and Puri 2002; Hellmann 2000).

Multiple studies have demonstrated the correlation between VC involvement and startup success: VC-backed firms have faster growth, faster times-to-market of their products, more patents, higher productivity, greater innovation, higher efficiency, and are more to have a successful exit (IPO or acquisition) (Wright and Robbie 1998; Bernstein et al. 2015; Chemmanur et al. 2008). That said, many studies fail to disentangle the influence of the VC themself on the startup, as it is often difficult to decouple the effects of screening from those of monitoring and coaching (Lahr and Mina 2016).

However, reasons and explanations abound which indicate just the opposite; that venture capitalists can and do have a negative influence on startups and their entrepreneurs. Foremost, a large body of research exists regarding conflicts between startup entrepreneurs and VCs. Prior research has identified three main areas of VC-CEO conflicts: conflicts of interests and unfavorable attributions, conflicts of inefficient collaboration, and conflicts of VC-CEO mismatch (Khanin and Turel 2013). Conflict does not necessarily have a negative impact on the success of a startup (Higashide and Birley 2002). However, at high levels of occurrence and intensity, conflict is generally considered to be costly to those involved (Reve and Stern 1989). Furthermore, the negative impacts of VC investments have been demonstrated analytically for a number of geographies external to the US, including China, France, and Singapore (Xi and Su-Sheng 2016; Pommet 2017; Wang et al. 2003), although to the authors' knowledge no studies in the US have reached similar conclusions. Furthermore, there seems to be a growing sentiment emanating from Silicon Valley that entrepreneurs must be dubious, or at a minimum cautious, of venture capitalist investment (Mullins 2014).

In this research, we attempt to disentangle the conflicting messages coming from academia and industry regarding the impact of VCs on startup success. By applying a unique approach, namely a network theory analysis of the board membership network and Twitter social network, we believe our work provides a unique contribution to the literature.

3 Data and Methods

3.1 Network Construction

To construct and analyze our VC-startup networks, we compiled a unique dataset from multiple sources. We limited the scope of our study to tech startups founded in the US in the past 5 years. We extracted 3199 startups from the S&P Capital IQ database (https://www.capitaliq.com), including a list of the board members of each startup as well as whether each individual was a VC or not. We constructed the interlocking directorates network based on the 8474 total board members, resulting in a network with 3199 nodes (1 per startup) and links between startups that share at least one board member. We used the Condor software tool (www.galaxyadvisors.com) to calculate three centrality measures on this network: betweenness, degree, and closeness.

We also constructed an informal social network with which to compare against the formal network, as well as inform our understanding of VC communication behavior. We chose Twitter as the source of this network as Twitter is the social media platform most extensively used by startups and investors, and broadly used by the business community (Wu et al. 2015). We foremost wrote python scripts to query Twitter's Search API to identify the corresponding Twitter handle (ID) for the 8474 people in our formal interlocking directorates network. Our query searched for users by name who included one of their associated company names in their Twitter description or included the keywords "vc", "capital", or "partner". This resulted in 1271 matched individuals, whose accuracy was manually verified on a 10% sample and found to be 87.4% accurate. We found that 15% of the interlocking directorates network was composed of VCs, whereas 23% of the Twitter network was composed of VCs. We believe this representation of VCs is reasonably similar, and relatively realistic.

We used Condor to automatically generate the Twitter network. Links in this network exist between a person who has tweeted to another person, or a person who has retweeted another person's tweet. We limited the network construction to only the users' past 100 tweets. This produced a network of 45,521 nodes and 168,326 links. We analyzed the Twitter network using standard centrality algorithms including betweenness, degree, closeness, and reach-2 (the number of nodes the ego can reach in 2 steps).

3.2 *Startup Success Metrics*

We defined three metrics of success as the dependent variables with which to evaluate startup success. Foremost, we collected information about the total amount of funding (venture capital or otherwise) that the startup has received since its founding using Crunchbase (www.crunchbase.com). Secondly, we collected information about the startup's annual sales from OneSource (www.onesource.com). We found total funding information for 1514 of the startups extracted from Capital IQ, and annual sales information for 525 of these startups. Finally, we defined our third success metric as return-on-investment, or annual sales/total startup funding. This is effectively a measure of the efficacy of a startup in transforming dollars of investment into revenue. We consider these three success metrics separately, however we did observe a positive correlation between startup funding and annual sales ($c = 0.513$, $p = 1.166\text{E-}36$, $n = 525$). We observed no significant correlation between ROI and total funding.

Note that one of the fundamental challenges of conducting this kind of study is not only in determining a good metric of startup success, but also acquiring accurate data. We acknowledge that our metric choices (startup funding, annual sales, and return-on-investment) are not absolute measures of startup success, yet we are confident in the accuracy of our data and we are also confident that they at least partially reflect overall startup success in a meaningful way.

4 Results

Using the dataset previously described, we conducted an analysis to measure the impact of VC networks on startup success. We discuss a number of research questions to inform our investigation of this question.

4.1 *VCs in the Formal Interlocking Directorates Network*

Foremost, in order for us to make any conclusions regarding startup success, we needed to locate successful startups within our networks. Therefore, we investigated the question: are more successful startups more centrally located in the interlocking directorates network?

To answer this question, we looked for correlations between the various centrality measures and our three dependent variables (funding, annual revenue, and ROI). We observed strong positive correlations between total funding and annual sales and all three centrality measures (see Table 1).

Startups central in the interlocking directorates network have board members who are highly connected, likely highly connected venture capitalists sitting on multiple

Table 1 Correlations between centrality measures and funding and sales in formal network

	n	Log of total funding	n	Log of annual sales
Betweenness	1514	0.217**	525	0.232**
Degree	1514	0.312**	525	0.298**
Closeness	1514	0.220**	525	0.197**

**p < 0.001

Table 2 T-Tests on formal network centrality measures: VCs vs. Non-VCs

	VCs	Non-VCs	n	p-value
Mean betweenness centrality	1662.56	149.8	7350	9.13E-11
Mean degree centrality	3.40	2.87	1124	6.79E-09

boards. We tested this hypothesis using a standard Pearson's t-test and did indeed find VCs to be more central than non-VCs in our network (see Table 2).

VCs not only have on average more connections, but also much higher betweenness centrality than non-VCs. Combined with our earlier observation regarding successful startups being more centrally located, we therefore made the hypothesis that the more VCs on a startup's board, the more successful the startup in terms of total funding and sales. Indeed, we found positive correlations between VC board membership and total funding ($c = 0.29$, $p = 6.02E\text{-}12$, $n = 525$) and between annual sales ($c = 0.21$, $p = 1.99E\text{-}06$, $n = 525$). This is not surprising, as venture capital firms that invest in startups often negotiate for board representation, so a correlation between total funding and VC board membership is to be expected.

We then looked at VC board membership and ROI, defined as the ratio of revenue to funding. Surprisingly, we observed a negative correlation between board membership and ROI ($c = -0.10$, $p = 0.02$, $n = 525$). We verified these results with a Welch Two Sample t-test, where we broke the dataset into two groups: startups with VCs on their board, and startups without. All t-tests proved statistically significant with $p < 0.005$. We found that startups with VCs on their board earn on average \$6.81M more annually in revenue than startups without VCs on their board, and receive \$15.7M more in funding. However, startups without VCs conclusively experience higher ROI, on average 191% higher than startups with VCs. When sorted by ROI, the top 20% of startups have on average 18% VC board membership, whereas the bottom 20% of startups have on average 31% VC board membership. This is statistically significant (t-test $p = 0.0037$, $n = 525$)

On the other hand, startups with high ROI seem to have less VC members on their board. These startups likely did not receive large amounts of funding, yet are generating a disproportionately large amount of sales. Because they did not receive a large amount of startup funding, they were not in a position to need to accept VCs onto their board. This does seem to lead to the logical conclusion that startups without VCs—and therefore without VC funding—seem to do better in terms of ROI, at least in the first 5 years. This concept has been written about in a number of entrepreneurship blogs and articles, with the underlying recommendation (as one article put it): "If you are looking towards more measured growth for your startup, want to keep control or you're simply not established yet, you probably want to avoid VCs" (Jee 2016). The evidence is clear—avoid VC investment if possible.

4.2 VCs in the Informal Twitter Social Network

We now turn to an analysis of the informal network, the Twitter network, as we hypothesized that by analyzing a different, more informal, network of communication, we would likely reach new insights regarding the influence of VCs on the success of startups.

We began our analysis by first comparing the formal network with the informal network, as both networks were composed of the same people. Interestingly, we found little to no statistically significant correlations between these two networks, neither in terms of centrality measures nor in terms of overlap of core individuals (only three people were among the most central in the top 100 of both networks ranked by betweenness centrality and degree centrality). These top three individuals (Jon Sakoda: New Enterprise Associates, Roger Lee: Battery Ventures, Peter Levine: Andreessen Horowitz LLC) are all venture capitalists with a long history in the tech startup industry, sit on 12 or more boards (as compared to the average number of boards someone sits on in our dataset which is 3.92) and have an above-median number of Twitter followers.

Our comparison of the formal network with the informal network demonstrated that the two are very different networks, with no clear correlation between individuals' position within each. That said, in our continued attempt to ascertain the influence of venture capitalists on the success of startups, we reasoned that an investigation of venture capitalists' behavior and location in the Twitter network would inform our understanding of their communication patterns and influence on startup success.

From our previous study, we found venture capitalists to be centrally located in the interlocking directorates network. This held true for our smaller network composed of only the 1271 people we found Twitter usernames for. We expected venture capitalists to be centrally located in the Twitter network as well.

Using a two-tailed unequal variance t-test, we observed VCs are indeed more central in the Twitter network. We measured statistically significant differences in a number of centrality measures among VCs and non-VCs, with the VC group consistently more central than the non-VC group (see Table 3).

Given our observation that VCs are more central in the Twitter network, we were curious to determine what about their Twitter behavior—and by extension their communication behavior—influenced their network centrality.

We conducted t-tests between VCs and non-VCs on a number of Twitter usage characteristics, including the number of followers the user has, the number of public lists the user is on, the number of tweets the user has made, and the number of people the user is following. To prevent distortion from outliers with very many and very

Table 3 T-Tests on formal and informal network centrality measures: VCs vs. Non-VCs

n = 1271	p-value T-Test	Mean for VCs	Mean for non-VCs
Betweenness centrality (ID network)	4.19416E-06	4298.5847	614.7755
Degree centrality (ID network)	2.4368E-07	4.3431	3.0514
Closeness centrality (ID network)	4.78385E-16	0.0001	0.0001
Betweenness (Twitter network)	0.012260342	2243375.0498	1980369.7281
Closeness (Twitter network)	0.029473497	0.0036	0.0035
Degree (Twitter network)	0.011655465	65.8159	60.2025
Reach 2 (Twitter network)	2.48729E-07	918.0084	670.8886

Two-tailed unequal variance t-tests are reported

few followers, we performed our analysis on a truncated mean dataset sample (we sorted the dataset by number of followers, and removed the top and bottom 5%). As a measure of the "popularity" of the user, we took the ratio of the number of users the person is following to number of followers the user has. The lower this number, the more followers the user has in proportion to the number of users the user is following, and thus the more "popular" the user.

The results of this analysis are provided in Table 4. Generally, we discovered that VCs truly are more "popular" than non-VCs (the popularity ratio differs by 23% between the two groups, with a significance of 0.012). Furthermore, VCs have 22% more followers than non-VCs (although this result only has a statistical significance of 0.077). Additionally, VCs appear on 31% more public lists than non-VCs.

VCs appear to have greater social capital on Twitter than non-VCs. Interestingly, VCs tend to tweet less than non-VCs (VCs post and repost 38% less than non-VCs). However, they have a strikingly higher Twitter popularity ratio as compared to non-VCs (a higher ratio indicates lower popularity). This means that VCs truly do—at least in the digital social networking space—have a higher social capital than non-VCs.

4.3 Network Centrality and Financial Success

These results lead us to the conclusion that VCs are truly popular people—guardians not only of money but also social status and information. Clearly, this bears implications on the success of the startups they fund and sit on the boards of. To this end, we wondered if we could determine a clear correlation between centrality in the Twitter social network and some measure of financial success—either their personal income and/or the funding of the startup(s) they are affiliated with.

Table 4 T-Tests on Twitter characteristics: VCs vs. Non-VCs

Description	T-test	Mean (VCs)	Mean (non-VCs)
The number of followers this account currently has	0.0773	4032.16	3302.95
The number of public lists that this user is a member of	0.0127	194.05	148.48
The number of tweets (including retweets) issued by the user	0.0004	1844.6	2963.41
The number of users this account is following	0.3864	794.3	681.26
Twitter popularity (# following/# followers). Lower number is more popular	0.0119	0.454	0.5875

4.3.1 Network Centrality and Income

Foremost, we investigated the correlation between an individual's' position in the network and their income, as measured by the average income of their residential zip code (we extracted this data from the public US IRS dataset from 2014[1]). We looked at both the formal and informal networks. We found that generally, the more central someone is located in either the formal or informal network, the higher his or her income. This was especially true with the measure of reach-2 in the Twitter network ($r = 0.14$, $p = 0.000$) (Table 5).

This would imply that VCs, who are generally more central in both networks, tend to have greater income. That said, we did not find a statistically significant difference in income between VCs and non-VCs (t-test $p = 0.25$, $n = 830$). Clearly, VCs are not the only individuals in our networks who are generating personal wealth.

Additionally, from our earlier analysis, we demonstrated that VCs have a significantly higher social capital than non-VCs. We reasoned that perhaps this ratio would correlate with residential income. Indeed, we found just that. We found a significant negative correlation between an individual's' income (on the logarithmic scale) and their ratio of # following/# followers. Because this ratio is inversely proportional to social capital, the greater someone's Twitter social capital, the greater their income ($c = -0.105$, $p = 0.00018$, $n = 1172$). Therefore, by transitive reasoning, we conclude that VCs are not only socially prominent people—their prominence is rewarded financially.

Our analysis so far enabled us to determine that as individual VCs are more central in both the formal and informal networks, which correlates with greater income and a higher social capital.

[1]https://www.irs.gov/uac/soi-tax-stats-individual-income-tax-statistics-2014-zip-code-data-soi

Table 5 Correlations between network centrality measures and somone's income

Correlation with	Log of average income r	p
Betweenness (Twitter network)	0.079**	0.005
Closeness (Twitter network)	0.038	0.173
Degree (Twitter network)	0.079**	0.005
Reach 2 (Twitter network)	0.145**	0.000
Betweenness centrality (ID network)	−0.012	0.670
Degree centrality (ID network)	0.053	0.061
Closeness centrality (ID network)	0.066*	0.018

*$p < 0.05$
**$p < 0.01$

4.3.2 Network Centrality and Startup Funding

Next, we investigated whether an individual's' position in the Twitter network was indicative of the financial success of the startup to whom that person is affiliated. We hypothesized that those individuals who are more central in the network—those with higher personal income—would be affiliated with more highly funded startups.

The CapitalIQ database contained a listing of all the companies each individual is affiliated with—either as a board member or employee. If a person was affiliated with a startup we analyzed in our dataset of 1514 startups (from the formal interlocking directorates network), we had a funding amount for that startup. In total, we found funding information for at least one affiliated company for 830 people in our dataset. Less than 10% of these people were affiliated with another startup for which we had funding data, so we decided an accurate and comparable measure would be to take the maximum startup funding of all startups for which we had data for each person. We looked at the correlation between our centrality measures and the log of the maximum affiliated startup funding for the 830 people with such data. We found significant positive correlations between centrality measures and startup funding, as seen in Table 6.

All centrality measures except closeness exhibit a significant positive correlation with their max affiliated startup funding. However, reach-2 displays the largest correlation, at 0.24. A possible explanation for this is that in real life, people are very likely to share leads and opportunities with their close friends (1 degree) and their friends of friends (2 degree). Degree is correlated (at 0.109) with funding, but significantly less correlated than reach 2 (which is 0.24). We reason that degree is less strongly correlated than reach 2 because people really do use their friends-of-friends network and don't depend merely on their closest contacts. Using simply degree to indicate funding misses out on the real-world events that happen due to friends-of-friends. Thus, the friends-of-friends network (reach-2) is really a much better representation of how information and opportunities spread throughout the network. It's not who you know that counts, it's who your friends know. This finding is supported by the academic world; in fact, the strength of weak ties (indirect

Table 6 Correlations between Twitter centrality measures and someone's max startup funding

Twitter network centrality measures n = 830	Log of startup funding	p
Betweenness	0.098	0.005
Closeness	0.063	0.070
Degree	0.109	0.002
Reach2	0.244	0.000

connections, or friends-of-friends) was first presented in Granovetter's seminal work "The Strength of Weak Ties" (1973). With over 40,000 references to date, in his paper Granovetter presents his theory regarding the prevalence of weak ties and their efficacy in a variety of contexts. Our research appears to affirm that the VC-startup context is yet another domain where weak ties dominate.

5 Conclusion

In our study of the influence of venture capitalists via formal and informal networks, we have determined that VCs play a central role in the success of a startup. Startups with VCs as board members are consistently more central in the networks, and startups central in the network receive more funding and have greater revenue. That said, startups with more VCs have lower ROI, which bears implications on the startups' long-term success. We found that people central in the formal network are not necessarily central in the informal network, although VCs in general have greater centrality in both. VCs can be considered the keepers of funding and information, and therefore hold considerable power and influence in the tech startup ecosystem.

References

Amit, R., Brander, J., & Zott, C. (1998). Why do venture capital firms exist? Theory and Canadian evidence. *Journal of Business Venturing, 13*, 441.

Bernstein, S., Giroud, X., & Townsend, R. R. (2015). The impact of venture capital monitoring. *The Journal of Finance, 71*, 1591–1622.

Chan, Y. S. (1983). On the positive role of financial intermediation in allocation of venture capital in market with imperfect information. *Journal of Finance, 35*(5), 1543–1568.

Chemmanur, Thomas J., Krishnan, K., & Nandy, Debarshi K. (2008). *How does venture capital financing improve efficiency in private firms? A look beneath the surface*. US Census Bureau Center for Economic Studies Paper No. CES-WP-08-16.

Franklin, B., & Haque, M. (2016, March). *National Venture Capital Association yearbook*. New York: Thomson Reuters.

Gloor, P. A. (2005). *Swarm creativity: Competitive advantage through collaborative innovation networks*. New York: Oxford University Press.

Granovetter, M. S. (1973). The strength of weak ties. *American Journal of Sociology, 78*, 1360–1380.

Hellmann, T. (2000). Venture capitalists: The coaches of Silicon Valley. In W. Miller, C. M. Lee, M. G. Hanock, & H. Rowen (Eds.), *The Silicon Valley edge: A habitat for innovation and entrepreneurship* (pp. 267–294). Stanford, CA: Stanford University Press.

Hellmann, T., & Puri, M. (2002). Venture capital and the professionalization of start-up firms: Empirical evidence. *The Journal of Finance, 57*, 169–197. https://doi.org/10.1111/1540-6261.00419

Higashide, H., & Birley, S. (2002). The consequences of conflict between the venture capitalist and the entrepreneurial team in the United Kingdom from the perspective of the venture capitalist. *Journal of Business Venturing, 17*(1), 59–81.

Jee, C. (2016, July 25). Why you should avoid venture capitalists. *Techworld* (Web).

Kaplan, S. N., & Strömberg, P. (2003). Financial contracting theory meets the real world: An empirical analysis of venture capital contracts. *Review of Economic Studies, 70*(2), 281.

Khanin, D., & Turel, O. (2013). Conflicts between venture capitalists and CEOs of their Portfolio companies. *Journal of Small Business Strategy, 23*(1), 31–54.

Lahr, H., & Mina, A. (2016). Venture capital investments and the technological performance of portfolio firms. *Research Policy, 45*, 303–318. https://doi.org/10.1016/j.respol.2015.10.001

Lerner, J. (1995). Venture capitalists and the oversight of private firms. *Journal of Finance, 50*, 301–318.

Mizruchi, M. S. (1996). What do interlocks do? An analysis, critique, and assessment of research on interlocking directories. *Annual Review of Sociology, 22*, 271–298.

Mullins, J. (2014, November 05). VC funding can be bad for your start-up. *Harvard Business Review*. https://hbr.org/2014/08/vc-funding-can-be-bad-for-your-start-up

Pommet, S. (2017). The impact of the quality of VC financing and monitoring on the survival of IPO firms. *Managerial Finance, 43*(4), 440.

Reve, T., & Stern, L. W. (1989). The relationship between interorganizational form, transaction climate, and economic performance in vertical interfirm dyads. In L. Pellegrini & S. K. Reddy (Eds.), *Marketing channels: Relationship and performance*. Lexington, MA: Lexington Books.

Wang, C. K., et al. (2003). Effects of venture capitalists' participation in listed companies. *Journal of Banking and Finance, 27*, 2015–2034.

Wright, M., & Robbie, K. (1998). Venture capital and private equity: A review and synthesis. *Journal of Business Finance & Accounting, 25*(5–6), 521–570.

Wu, A., Jin, F., & Hitt L. (2015, July). *Social is the new financial: How startups' social media activities influence funding outcomes* (Working Paper).

Xi, Y., & Su-Sheng, W. (2016). Do venture capital firms play as supportive mentors or free-riders? Evidence from China. *Journal of Commercial Biotechnology, 22*(4), 3–18.

Resilient Community and Economic Development Through Collaborative Innovation Networks

Jacob Leppek, Jen Bruen, and John Schweitzer

Abstract A single organization or individual is almost always unable to provide completely satisfactory solutions to a community problem. Collaborative Innovation Networks (COINs) provide a method in which entities capitalize on existing human capital to spur cooperative innovation in community and economic development. This report details the successful experience of the U.S. EDA University Center for Regional Economic Innovation (REI) at Michigan State University in utilizing a COIN as a resilient economic and community development strategy. This method is successful as it allows for the resilience and adaptability of decentralized networks while retaining access to a large resource base.

1 Introduction

During Michigan's recovery from the 2008 recession, the U.S. Economic Development Administration funded a University Center for Regional Economic Innovation (REI) at Michigan State University for a 5-year period from 2011 to 2016. REI's stated mission was to build a new economic development ecosystem in Michigan by leveraging higher education assets to support the creation and application of innovative economic development strategies to yield high-growth entrepreneurship and job creation throughout the state.

These goals were accomplished through the creation of a Collaborative Innovation Network (COIN). Named the REI Network, this model is successful in overcoming the usual obstacles to economic and community development by creating a resilient self-organizing system that can operate in any environment. Networks allow for growth to transcend organizational boundaries, encourage inclusive social innovations, and build on local knowledge to create efficient solutions (Van Dijk 2012).

J. Leppek (✉) · J. Bruen · J. Schweitzer
Michigan State University, EDA University Center for Regional Economic Innovation, Lansing, MI, USA
e-mail: LeppekJ@michigan.gov; bruenjen@msu.edu; schweit1@msu.edu

F. Grippa et al. (eds.), *Collaborative Innovation Networks*, Studies on Entrepreneurship, Structural Change and Industrial Dynamics,
https://doi.org/10.1007/978-3-319-74295-3_2

This report details how collaborative innovation networks can operate successfully in the community and economic development industry by crowdsourcing innovation while retaining access to a resource base to facilitate action. Within the bourgeoning field of research on social innovation, this analysis seeks to remedy the lack of literature applying social innovation techniques to the ecosystem of economic development and individual empowerment, and to encourage future studies on the topic. This report is also meant to provide further quantitative evidence on the topic of how a mission of social innovation is applicable and successful in economic development, and that collaborative innovation networks are an excellent method to achieve that goal.

Furthermore, this report advances a method to utilize COINs in the context of community and economic development. This report also describes the structure of the REI Network to relate how this facilitation process works. It offers an overview of how REI utilizes its network to find and fund research. Methods of communication and implementation are reviewed to understand how ideas flow from conception to publication. Lastly, it reviews the results of REI's first grant cycle (2011–2016).

2 Background

REI operates within a context of community and economic development on local, regional, and state levels. It is necessary to understand the various objectives and obstacles to fully appreciate how COINs offer a resilient solution to typical barriers faced by community and economic development organizations.

2.1 Community and Economic Development in Michigan

Michigan's economy was severely damaged by the 2007–2009 recession, and it still had not fully recovered due to the loss of jobs, lack of qualified candidates, not enough incentives for companies to operate in Michigan, and several other supplementary factors by 2011 (Chiteji and Danziger 2011). While the overriding objective for the development industry is to spur Michigan's recovery and future growth, multiple methods exist to accomplish each organization's primary aim.

Community development and economic development are overlapping categories; the former utilizing an empowerment, resident-centric approach whereas the latter generally increases the tax base. Each of these approaches has strengths and weaknesses. Community development emphasizes internal growth, capitalizing on existing resources and strengthening human capital. Economic development organizations create an enticing environment for incoming and new businesses. These approaches require a wealth of knowledge and expertise, leading to limited coordination between the two as organizations became more specialized.

Michigan is a fairly diverse state in terms of community and economic development needs. With a population of nearly 10 million people, the state has a high rate of income inequality, large rural areas, and many economically distressed urban areas.

This has resulted in a massive number of development organizations which specialize in certain aspects of development with varying scopes. Public agencies affiliated with cities, municipalities, townships, regions, and the state are frequently working toward parallel objectives as third-party non-profit organizations. Smaller scopes are seemingly more manageable, especially with limited funds and actors, whereas large scopes improve coordination across geographical areas or resources, among other aspects. Larger cities, such as Detroit, Grand Rapids, or Lansing, typically have a higher concentration of development organizations, while rural areas receive less attention. As an example of differing aims, some organizations focus exclusively on singular skill-based development, and others more generally on improving workforce competitiveness of Michigan. This results in overlapping initiatives in which collaboration does not always occur.

2.2 *Common Obstacles to Development*

What is important to understand is the current patchwork of community and economic development organizations and public agencies in Michigan often target different communities, geographical areas, and aspects of economic development, simply because of limited resources. Limited funds force organizations to operate with few full-time staff members, instead relying on volunteers. Grant funding is incredibly competitive, and private donations are an inconsistent source of funding. This prevents many non-government funded organizations from achieving concrete goals. While objectives of these organizations and communities frequently overlap, communication is often lacking, resulting in a knowledge, access, and sustainability gap. The infrastructure for communication between the large number of development organizations is lacking, creating high costs in finding community leaders, activists, and knowledgeable experts. It is quite possible that two organizations could be working on the same issue in different areas without knowing, and the chances that solutions and strategies are shared among community members is low. Top-down solutions are limited in their ability to spur economic development.

A major issue in community and economic development is empowering the locals by providing resources necessary to achieve certain goals, and coordinating these goals to encourage inclusive growth (Wilson 1996). While locals better understand what is lacking in their communities, it is often necessary to provide them with monetary funds, methods to fix the problem, and connections with experts.

2.3 Understanding Innovation in Collaborative Networks

Collaborative networks have been applied in many settings to great success. Collaborative Innovation Networks are virtual groups of intrinsically motivated actors that collaborate on specific issues, bringing differing perspectives, knowledge, and abilities to solve problems (Gloor 2006). It has been demonstrated that innovation is spurred and facilitated through interorganizational cooperation, especially in research and development activities (Enkel et al. 2009; Faems et al. 2005). Research networks that linking diverse actors together have been shown to create innovation clusters (Liyanage 1995). Clusters like these, based around similar locations or issues, have been suggested to play a large role in an increasingly globalized economy (Porter 2000). Yet successful innovation depends on the nature of the actors involved (Barzi et al. 2015; Marinucci 2012). By connecting actors with varied skill sets and sufficient motivation, a COIN creates a space for collaborating, creating, and sharing.

These models can be applied to complex community, and even global, problems (Sawhney 2003). Social innovation can be broadly defined as interdisciplinary innovations with broad impact which contribute to the diffusion of knowledge (Mulgan et al. 2007; Westley and Antadze 2010). Despite some doubt of whether social innovation is a useful term for analysis or not, the term has proved sustainable, and does seem to play a valuable role in determining how to facilitate such innovation (Pol and Ville 2009). Through connecting various individuals working in different fields of study and application, it is apparent that networks allow for a wider spectrum of results (Nieto and Santamaría (2007). In other words, large, diverse groups allow for interdisciplinary approaches to problems.

Networks increase the capacity of nonprofits to address challenges through social capital (Keyes et al. 1996). The collective impact model, for example, demonstrates the benefits of collaboration across organizations (Kania and Kramer 2011). These are often composed of organizations with similar target demographics and project goals, focused on sharing resources to implement in their respective communities. For example, networks of disaster relief organizations demonstrate opportunities for knowledge sharing and sharing of responsibilities for a successful response (Matsuda 2016). Innovation centers, such as business incubators, are based around the idea that these social hubs engender innovation through collaboration, funding, and knowledge exchange (Ziemer and Long 2009).

Concerning the public sector, it has been argued that multi-actor collaboration that involves the private sector is more robust than that of top-down governance (Sørensen and Torfing 2011). More recently, Birkner et al. (2017) concluded that universities have a "prominent role in the creation of new innovation ecosystems, particularly in a well-defined geographical area." Universities are vital to knowledge transfer, economic growth, and research support, even as barriers exist to connecting these resources with industries (Bramwell et al. 2012). Community-based participatory research (CBPR) has long been studied with strong favorable findings, demonstrating that involving community members and experts in the decision making and research process is a robust method of action (Israel et al. 2006). With the funding of REI by the U.S. E.D.A. and Michigan State University, the REI Network is one of the first attempts by a university to use a COIN to promote regional economic innovation, decrease barriers to knowledge transfer, and create sustainable and resilient partnerships.

3 The REI Network

Utilizing a COIN is an attempt to capitalize on the best attributes of development organizations while empowering individuals to create growth for their own communities, which means lower costs of communication, quicker problem identification, and increased collaboration.

REI's Network is uniquely resilient to changing social and political circumstances by crowdfunding ideas drawn from the network itself. Not only does this allow for the economic and community development strategies to adjust to new ideas, but for the *framework* of discussion to change. Topics of research are directly relatable to what is happening at the time, and are free to adjust according to demand. This signaling approach is a massive improvement in researching and solving the challenges in terms of efficiency because it allows for direct communication and collaboration among residents and experts with decreased organizational or geographical concerns, similar to prices in a market (Hayek 1945). COINs facilitate quicker identification of trends through the wide variety of participants at the local level (Gloor and Cooper 2007). After identification, the collaborative nature of the REI network often allows for access to a person with knowledge of these topics. In other words, a uniform approach through a COIN engenders diverse solutions which best fit the environment. It is a dynamic approach that is constantly identifying emerging problems, which allows it to remain resilient in response to changing economic conditions.

Whereas regional hubs of economic development provide a more centralized, goal-alignment service, REI is oriented toward individual and local-specific efforts. The Michigan Economic Development Corporation, for example, brings together public agencies, non-profit organizations, and private entities to streamline and coordinate ongoing economic development efforts. REI, however, focuses on solving the communication and funding gap for individual research projects by providing access to networks on par with larger regional organizations. This adaptable approach encourages active investment on a local level while producing findings that are accessible and applicable to a variety of situations. Rather than top-down coordination efforts, the requisite coordination to solve community problems emerges in the act of collaboration (Bruns 2013).

3.1 Scope of the REI Network

As identified by Gloor (2006), integral characteristics of COINs are innovation, collaboration, and communication. The REI Network both facilitates and builds on these aspects by retaining access to a large resource base despite its decentralized network.

The REI Network is a community of over 1000 individuals from the public and private sectors who participate in a facilitation and solicitation process to identify, create, and promote innovations in research to catalyze growth in their regional economies. As an open innovation community, these members are motivated to participate through a variety of mechanisms, including monetary funding, cooperative partners, and increased access to resources such as project support and research. This approach of constituent outreach, one which is not limited to already-established organizations or government entities, has shown promise in achieving collaboration and inclusive input (Girouard and Sirianni 2014). Intangible factors like feelings of engagement and connections with a community are also appreciated, as evidenced by internal surveys and social science research; REI's strategy is similar to successful consumer-centric models for firms (Antikainen et al. 2010).

REI also maintains a Consultative Panel, a group of experts drawn from a variety of fields to advise on and guide program objectives. The Consultative Panel acts as a supportive dialogue to the REI Network by providing an ethical framework, professional advice, and acting as a knowledge resource. These parallel networks allow for an active exchange of ideas and statewide multidisciplinary interaction, encouraging innovation and participation on a local and regional level (Fig. 1).

REI is crowdsourcing community and economic development to encourage innovation. Two primary avenues (*Co-Learning Plans* and *Student-Led, Faculty-Guided Technical Assistance*) were utilized in its 2011–2016 grant cycle, with a third (*Co-Implementation Plans*) developed for its second round of funding in 2016–2021. *Co-Learning Plans* are a collaborative effort in which practitioners, decision-makers, community leaders, entrepreneurs, scholars, or other stakeholders research innovative economic development tools, models, strategies, policies, and practices and produce recommendations for other practitioners, policy-makers, and the public. These applications are drawn from REI Network members which ensures access to expert knowledge. *Student-Led, Faculty-Guided Technical Assistance* projects are collaborative efforts between university students and Michigan communities to complete local or regional development initiatives, while being supervised by experienced faculty members. *Co-Implementation Plans* are REI's attempt to further implement the products of its network. This initiative seeks to put the tools, models, and policies identified in *Co-Learning Plans* into practice in communities around Michigan.

REI supports communication between Network members by providing easily accessible platforms, events, and information. The results of all projects are posted online at REI's website and other platforms. REI utilizes various social media networks to encourage convenient collaboration and to spur casual discussion

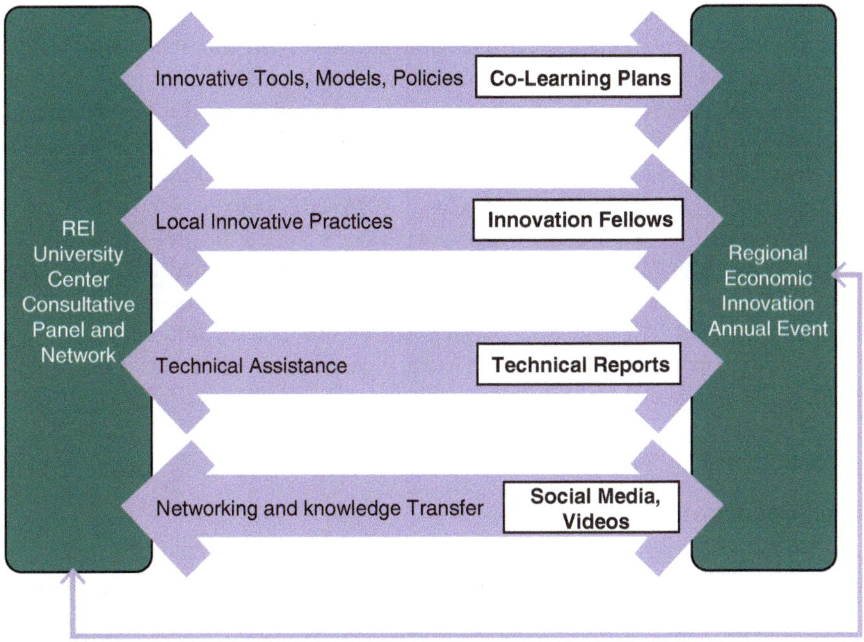

Fig. 1 How the REI Network facilitates development. Reprinted with permission from the MSU University Center for Regional Economic Innovation

between partners. The self-organizing nature of the REI Network allows for communication through local, regional, and state levels.

3.2 *Results of the REI Network*

Over 100 REI projects have generated an estimated $8,288,000 in public investments, $50,675,806 in private investments, and $505,500 in other investments throughout Michigan. These projects ranged from skill-based workshops to technical assistance projects and the development of policy recommendations. In addition, REI partners believe the most important impacts of projects and events to be the opportunities to gain knowledge about issues pertinent to their work and innovations in economic development, and to network with people working towards similar goals. In some cases, Network members were also able to secure additional funding through their work with REI. One of REI's partners, the Northern Initiatives, reported that they secured over $200,000 from various sources. In addition, 154 individuals received eight or more hours of technical assistance from REI.

Additionally, REI successfully disseminated new knowledge through the creation and sharing of 29 webinars and over 25 project videos; these informational videos on products of the REI Network have reached almost 9000 views. Presenting information this way, in multimedia and storytelling format, is accessible to a more diverse audience and increases engagement (Brown and Wyatt 2010). REI has hosted more than 65 in-person presentations at five Innovate Michigan! Summits, held yearly. REI regularly engages with its community over social media; its Twitter page has more than 1600 followers; Facebook, about 700 likes; and hosts a LinkedIn group of nearly 500 members. In the fall of 2015, REI was recognized as a finalist in the University Economic Development Association's Awards of Excellence program. An internal REI Network survey conducted in 2016–2017 demonstrated that roughly 75% of respondents found a REI-supported partner's work to be useful in their own projects. Moreover, 68% of Network members have implemented the knowledge and ideas developed by other members. It has been reported that the knowledge disseminated from REI helped its partners connect to their communities too. "We learned how to ask better questions and become partners, not an outside organization looking in," said one respondent.

4 Conclusion

Approaching community and economic development through a COIN-based framework allows for broader application to industry issues while maintaining the benefits of local knowledge. It encourages coordination through a unified approach, but recognizes and supports diverse actors.

This is a resilient approach to community and economic development, especially in regards to encouraging social innovation. The REI Network closes the gap between professional and local knowledge. Furthermore, it identifies and empowers residents while providing the necessary resources. A COIN then offers a natural avenue to disseminate and publicize these results for other community members and development organizations to utilize in their work. REI's strategy of developing others' solutions with monetary and research support allows for a successful open innovation strategy, as it provides encouragement for active participation by qualified community members.

This model will be increasingly important in the future. Concepts such as "smart cities" will need collaborative networks, and creating strategies which facilitate individual and non-profit organization partnerships is key (Schaffers et al. 2011). Facilitating social innovation through collaborative networks can create a larger impact on economic outcomes (Westley and Antadze 2010). Rather that imposing top-down solutions on increasingly globalized, diverse, and complex communities, COINs allow communities to create and adapt personalized solutions which best fit their needs.

Encouraging the growth of human capital in communities is emerging as the dominant model of economic development. REI has successfully implemented a Collaborative Innovation Network to produce resilient economic development strategies that serve local and regional needs. No longer should economic development organizations operate independent of each other, as the social innovation which occurs through collaborative networks produces excellent results.

References

Antikainen, M., Mäkipää, M., & Ahonen, M. (2010). Motivating and supporting collaboration in open innovation. *European Journal of Innovation Management, 13*(1), 100–119.

Barzi, F., Cortelezzi, F., Marseguerra, G., & Grazia Zoia, M. (2015). Cooperative innovation: In quest of effective partners. Evidence from Italian firms. *Innovation, 17*(3), 281–307.

Birkner, Z., Máhr, T., & Berkes, N. (2017). Changes in responsibilities and tasks of universities in regional innovation ecosystems. *Naše gospodarstvo/Our Economy, 63*(2), 15–21.

Bramwell, A., Hepburn, N., & Wolfe, D. A. (2012). *Growing innovation ecosystems: University-industry knowledge transfer and regional economic development in Canada.* Knowledge Synthesis Paper on Leveraging Investments in HERD. Final Report to the Social Sciences and Humanities Research Council of Canada.

Brown, T., & Wyatt, J. (2010). Design thinking for social innovation. *Development Outreach, 12* (1), 29–43.

Bruns, H. C. (2013). Working alone together: Coordination in collaboration across domains of expertise. *Academy of Management Journal, 56*(1), 62–83.

Chiteji, N., & Danziger, S. (2011). *Family finances after the great recession – Evidence from the Michigan recession and recovery study.* National Poverty Center Working Paper Series #11.

Enkel, E., Gassmann, O., & Chesbrough, H. (2009). Open R&D and open innovation: Exploring the phenomenon. *R&D Management, 39*, 311–316.

Faems, D., Van Looy, B., & Debackere, K. (2005). Interorganizational collaboration and innovation: Toward a portfolio approach. *Journal of Product Innovation Management, 22*(3), 238–250.

Girouard, J., & Sirianni, C. (2014). *Varieties of civic innovation: Deliberative, collaborative, network, and narrative approaches.* Nashville: Vanderbilt University Press.

Gloor, P. A. (2006). *Swarm creativity: Competitive advantage through collaborative innovation networks.* Oxford: Oxford University Press.

Gloor, P. A., & Cooper, S. M. (2007). *Coolhunting: Chasing down the next big thing.* New York: AMACOM.

Hayek, F. (1945). The use of knowledge in society. *American Economic Review, 35*(4), 519–530.

Israel, B., Krieger, J., Vlahov, D., Ciske, S., Foley, M., Fortin, P., Guzman, J., Lichtenstein, R., McGranaghan, R., Palermo, A., & Tang, G. (2006). Challenges and facilitating factors in sustaining community-based participatory research partnerships: Lessons learned from the Detroit, New York City and Seattle Urban Research Centers. *Journal of Urban Health, 83*(6), 1022–1040.

Kania, J., & Kramer, M. (2011). Collective impact. *Stanford Social Innovation Review, 9*, 36–41.

Keyes, L., Schwartz, A., Vidal, A., & Bratt, R. (1996). Networks and nonprofits: Opportunities and challenges in an era of federal devolution. *Fannie Mae Foundation, 7*(2), 201–231.

Liyanage, S. (1995). Breeding innovation clusters through collaborative research networks. *Technovation, 15*(9), 553–567.

Marinucci, M. (2012). *A primer on R&D cooperation among firms.* Bank of Italy Occasional Paper No. 130. SSRN Electronic Journal.

Matsuda, Y. (2016). Networking of disaster relief volunteer organizations as a knowledge-sharing platform-A comparative study between US and Japan. *Journal of Natural Disaster Science, 31* (1), 1–10.

Mulgan, G., Tucker, S., Ali, R., & Sanders, B. (2007). *Social innovation: What it is, why it matters, and how it can be accelerated.* London: Basingstoke Press.

Nieto, M. J., & Santamaría, L. (2007). The importance of diverse collaborative networks for the novelty of product innovation. *Technovation, 27*(6), 367–377.

Pol, E., & Ville, S. (2009). Social innovation: Buzz word or enduring term? *The Journal of Socio-Economics, 38*(6), 878–885.

Porter, M. (2000). Location, competition, and economic development: Local clusters in a global economy. *Economic Development Quarterly, 14*(1), 15–34.

Sawhney, N. (2003). *Cooperative innovation in the commons: Rethinking distributed collaboration and intellectual property for sustainable design innovation*. Thesis, Massachusetts Institute of Technology.

Schaffers, H., Komninos, N., Pallot, M., Trousse, B., Nilsson, M., & Oliveira, A. (2011). Smart cities and the future internet: Towards cooperation frameworks for open innovation. In J. Domingue et al. (Eds.), *The future internet. FIA 2011, Lecture notes in computer science* (Vol. 6656). Berlin: Springer.

Sørensen, E., & Torfing, J. (2011). Enhancing collaborative innovation in the public sector. *Administration and Society, 43*(8), 842–868.

Van Dijk, J. (2012). *The network society*. London: Sage.

Westley, F., & Antadze, N. (2010). Making a difference: Strategies for scaling social innovation for greater impact. *The Innovation Journal, 15*(2), 1–19.

Wilson, P. (1996). Empowerment: Community economic development from the inside out. *Urban Studies, 33*(4-5), 617–630.

Ziemer, N., & Long, S. (2009). *Collaborative networks as innovation accelerators*. IIE Annual Conference Proceedings, pp. 391–396.

Resilience Through Collaborative Networks in Emerging Economies: Evidence from Chinese Venture Capital

Yuhong Zhou, Peter A. Gloor, and Stephanie L. Woerner

Abstract The high-speed growth of emerging economies attracts the attention of global investors, but the uncertain institutional environment in emerging and transitional economies makes investors uneasy. Using China's venture capital (VC) data, this article examines the performance consequences of differences in ownership between foreign and local investors, and network position established when VC firms (VCs) syndicate portfolio company investments. There is a phenomenon of separate institutional settings between China's local VCs and foreign VCs in China, which makes ownership significantly affect investment performance. The VCs' positions in the collaborative networks can play a mediating role; foreign VCs have better investment performance because of their more central-network position. Better-networked VCs can supplement or replace formal institutions in transitional economies.

1 Introduction

Since the first venture capital firm was founded in the 1940s, global VC has presented two characteristics. First, with a wealth of experience, VCs founded in developed countries are looking for investment opportunities on a global scale, and favor emerging economies that are growing. However, the unstable and immature institutional environments of transitional economies present challenges for foreign VCs (Ahlstrom and Bruton 2006; Prijcker et al. 2012; Zhang and Pezeshkan 2016). Foreign VCs are unfamiliar with the specific problems of transitional economies, for example, tax policy. Therefore, they are investing in emerging economies by

Y. Zhou (✉)
South China University of Technology, Guangzhou, Guangdong, China
e-mail: yuhongz@mit.edu

P. A. Gloor · S. L. Woerner
Massachusetts Institute of Technology, Cambridge, MA, USA
e-mail: pgloor@mit.edu; woerner@mit.edu

F. Grippa et al. (eds.), *Collaborative Innovation Networks*, Studies on Entrepreneurship, Structural Change and Industrial Dynamics,
https://doi.org/10.1007/978-3-319-74295-3_3

registering offshore firms to avoid the negative impact caused by unstable institutions (Fuller 2010). Second, the governments are speeding up the development of the domestic VCs in emerging economies and welcome the foreign VCs (Bruton et al. 2009; Ahlstrom and Bruton 2006). For example, China's VC[1] industry experienced rapid growth, especially in local VCs, and related policies and regulations improved over time. For the first time, local Chinese funds, mostly RMB-denominated funds, led over USD-denominated foreign funds both concerning the number of funds and fundraising amount in 2009. From then on, local Chinese investment became the dominant force in China's VCs. At the same time, foreign VCs in China still play an important role; 98.39 % of foreign VCs are from developed countries, and 53.77 % are from the United States.[2] To avoid the changes and constraints of the institutional environment in China, foreign VCs often adopt a way of registering offshore firms to participate in China's VC investment, which results in a separate institutional phenomenon between foreign-owner and Chinese-owner VCs (Fuller 2010). While the literature documents the conception of the separate institutional settings between foreign VCs and Local VCs, the performance consequences of this independent ownership remain largely unknown. This paper investigates the impact of this phenomenon on performance. Controlling for other known determinants of VCs' performance, we find that foreign VCs outperform local ones.

How do foreign VCs achieve better investment performance in China than local VCs? Social network theory has built a bridge between macro and micro levels of sociological theory (Granovetter 1973). More specifically, collaborative innovation networks (COINs, Gloor 2006) provide a potential solution. Under the existing institutional environment, in addition to passively accepting the system, enterprises can also expand their invisible collaborative relationship border, facilitate trust formation between partners (Sorenson and Stuart 2008; Meuleman et al. 2017), reduce transaction costs, and thereby enhancing performance (Hochberg et al., 2007, 2015). Any VCs can be actively or passively involved in the network environment. They will draw on their networks to seek investment opportunities, share the risk, help the start-ups succeed, and improve their own performance (Hochberg et al. 2007, 2015; Abell and Nisar 2007; Ewens 2010). Prior research has studied the performance effect of VC networks, but the important intermediary role VC networks play between the macro system and microenterprises is still unknown. This paper examines the important mediating role of collaborative networks between ownership and investment performance of VCs. Our paper suggests that, besides passively accepting the system, VCs can increase resilience through collaborative networks to thrive in uncertain institutional environments in transitional economies.

[1]Here, China's VC refers to the VC which has invested in Chinese mainland start-ups. Foreign VC firm is defined as the ownership of the firm is outside the Chinese mainland. A Chinese local VC firm is defined as the ownership of the firm is in Chinese mainland.

[2]Author is compiled from the data of CVsource database.

2 Theory and Hypothesis

2.1 Ownership and Investment Performance

Prior research has examined the impact of ownership on enterprise performance and shows that the performance of foreign owned enterprises is better than local enterprises in emerging and transitional economies (Aydin et al. 2007). Foreign owners have global managerial experience and can bring the latest and advanced technology and management that improves enterprise efficiency (Aydin et al. 2007). But few researchers have conducted empirical research on the impact of ownership on investment performance in the VC industry. In China, there is a significant amount of foreign VCs, 98.39% of them are from the developed countries. There are many differences between local VCs and foreign VCs, including registration, applicable law, sources, and exiting.

Fuller (2010) uses the grounded theory to analyze the institutional separation of VCs in emerging economies. He believes that the government dominates one set of institutional arrangements while foreign VCs, through foreign direct investment, link their Chinese activities to a set of more market-based institutions located offshore. Most foreign VCs invest in Chinese start-ups by registering and exiting at offshore locations, while making substantial investments in the China region (Zhu 2015). Specific steps are as follows. The first step is registering a limited partnership at an offshore location at a tax haven (e.g., Virgin Islands, Cayman Islands). The second step is setting up offices in China, and searching for investment projects. The third step, when foreign VCs decide to invest in a Chinese start-up, they will ask Chinese start-ups to register a special purpose company in the tax haven, and then invest in the special purpose company. In the last step, the special purpose company raises money from other investors through an initial public offering (IPO) of its shares on a stock market outside China and foreign VCs exit the company. Thus, foreign VCs do not have to pay the income tax in China, practicing reasonable tax avoidance. However, local VCs must abide by the rules defined by the Chinese government and have been under a high tax burden and other restrictions. For example, without the legal entity status of a limited partnership in China before June 2007, local VCs had to be structured as corporate VCs and had to bear the burden of double taxation compared to corporate VCs and venture investors.

From the source of VC funds, foreign VC is mainly funded by pension funds, insurance funds, banks, large corporations, governments, wealthy individuals and families and so on. They have strong financial support-systems.[3] Chinese local VC funds mainly come from the government fiscal budget and state-owned institutions. In 2006, the government budget and state-owned institutions accounted for 82.97% of the total, compared to 62.54% in 2010 (Feng 2012). When high-risk VC and scarce resources combine, it is prone to government rent-seeking which would lead to worse investment performance (Lu et al. 2012; Hain et al. 2016). In July 2010,

[3]From *Annual Statistics of China Venture Capital 2016*.

insurance funds were allowed for private equity investment in China but had been prohibited in the business of VC until 2014. Due to policy restriction, large capital sources are outside the reach of the Chinese local VCs. Thus, Chinese local VC's strength is much weaker than foreign VC's. The average total management funds of Chinese VCs was $202.93 million, compared to $4.5 billion of foreign VCs.

In addition, the exit channels of foreign VCs are more diverse than of local VCs in China. The best exit way of VCs from start-ups is through an IPO (Hochberg et al. 2007, 2015). According to the data of CVsource database, only 2.60% of Local VCs exit via an IPO out of China's mainland securities market, compared to 22.3% foreign VCs exiting via an IPO in China mainland A-share bourses, 30.54% of foreign VCs exit via NASDAQ, 20.10% via NYSE. Foreign VCs can exit from the China security markets, as well as other global securities markets. But for local VCs, it is difficult to exit out of China. Besides, M&A and trade resale are also important exit channels for VCs. Foreign VC can take advantage of the global multi-level capital market. However, Local VCs have to depend on the immature capital markets in China.

With all the differences between the different ownership VCs, we find that foreign VCs have distinct advantages. Thus, we hypothesize as follows:

Hypothesis 1: In China's VC market, VCs with different ownership have significantly different performance, and foreign VCs achieve better investment performance.

2.2 The Mediator Effect of VC Network Position

The first Chinese local venture capital firm was founded in 1993, almost 50 years later than in the U.S. With 98.39% of Chinese foreign VCs coming from developed countries, foreign VCs' investment experience is much better than Chinese local VCs and they know the importance of the benefits of network position in the collaborative networks. Foreign VCs leverage their advantages of experience and financial strength to attract local VCs to co-invest in syndicates (Hopp 2010), and overcome entry barriers by cooperation with local VCs (Hochberg et al. 2010). Because more densely networked markets of VC experience fewer new entrants (Hochberg et al. 2010), we find that many foreign VCs had established better positions in the network in the early 2000s, when most Chinese local VCs did not pay much attention to it (Keil et al. 2010; Zhou and Song 2014). Therefore, at the very beginning, many foreign VCs have become the incumbents in the Chinese VC networks and built their more central network position by repeating interactions with other VCs to facilitate trust among them (Meuleman et al. 2017). Subsequently, foreign VCs used the externalities of the network to prevent the entry of new entrants (Hochberg et al. 2010; Zhou and Song 2014). Thus, they consolidated their central network positions.

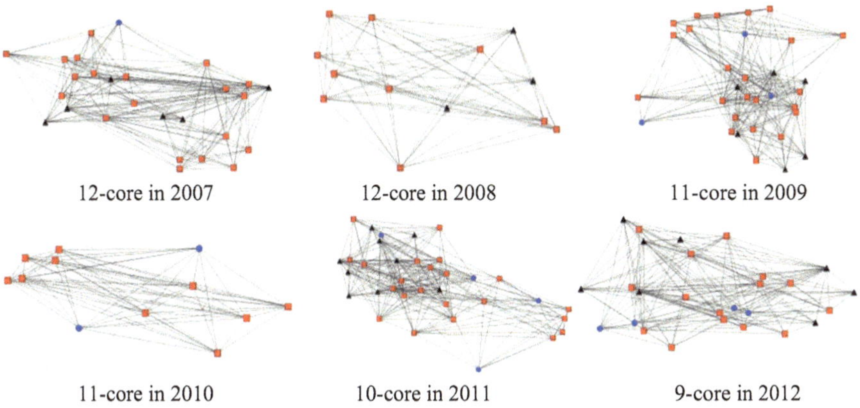

Fig. 1 Largest K-cores of China's VC networks, 2007–2012. The figure shows the largest K-core of the network that were established when VCs syndicate portfolio company investments. A blue dot is a China local VC, a red square is a foreign VC, a black triangle is a joint VC, a gray point is a missing item

Figure 1 shows the largest K-cores of China's VC networks from 2007 to 2012. A k-core is a maximal group of actors, all of whom are connected to some number (k) of other members of the group.[4] If K is larger, the member is more central in the network. Figure 1 illustrates that in the core part of China's VC networks, foreign VCs are most numerous, joint VCs followed, very few local VCs are part of the core network.

From the above information, we state that VCs with different ownership have different experience, consciousness, and motivation to set up their positions in the collaborative networks. Thus, we hypothesize as follows:

Hypothesis 2: In the Chinese market, VCs with different ownership will have different positions in the collaborative networks, and foreign VCs have more central positions in the network.

VCs tend to syndicate their investments with other VCs, rather than invest alone (Anne et al. 2016). Based on trust, they are bound by their current and past co-investments in the collaborative networks with other VCs (Hochberg et al. 2007, 2010, 2015; Abell and Nisar 2007; Ewens 2010; Zhou and Song 2014). Trusted networks can reduce transaction costs that exist in the market without the need to increase transaction costs within the organization due to the size of the firm (Carney 1998). VCs are diseconomies of scale in the industry, so it is an important way to reduce transaction costs through collaborative networks.

Local VCs are familiar with the local culture, politics, economy and institutional system, and are more likely to obtain information on investment businesses and to withdraw from the local secondary securities market. On the contrary, foreign VCs

[4] http://faculty.ucr.edu/~hanneman/nettext/C11_Cliques.html#kcore

are not so familiar with the Chinese environment, and they have the liability of being foreigners in China (Barnard 2010; Geleilate et al. 2016). At the same time, foreign companies have the advantage of experience, financial strength, and can more easily achieve favorable exits through an IPO on a global scale. Therefore, VCs prefer to cooperate with other VCs to complement each other. After fundraising, VCs have started an overlapping cycle of investment processes, including searching for promising start-ups to invest in, post-investment management and value-added services, and then reaping the rewards. Syndication networks based on trust are a critical source of information and investment opportunities (Bygrave 1988). VCs invite others to co-invest in their promising deals for future returns. Through collaborative networks, VCs can share human resources, professional skills, and specialized knowledge to evaluate start-ups more accurately (Hopp 2010). Regardless of their financial strength, VCs can be combined into a larger pool of investment via VC networks (Hochberg et al. 2007) and share many of the risks associated with new start-ups with co-investing partners (Zhou and Song 2014). This is more practical for the underfunded local VCs. Because of the transitivity of the collaborative network, VCs can transmit their own certification of start-ups through the network (Large and Muegge 2008). They can also help start-ups recruit executives by networking (Carvalho et al. 2008), and transfer part of their social capital through the network to start-ups. All these opportunities, such as selecting promising start-ups, adding value to start-ups and achieving better exit rates, are main drivers of a VC's performance. Therefore, we hypothesize as follows:

Hypothesis 3: The network position of VCs is the mediator between VCs ownership and VCs investment performance. VCs with different ownership get better investment performance through a dominant network position.

3 Methodology

3.1 Sample and Data

The data for our analysis comes from the CVsource database of China Venture group. Some of the missing data was complemented by the Z database.[5] We concentrate solely on the VC investment rounds which had been done at Chinese mainland start-ups before December 31, 2008.[6] We distinguish between VC firms. Our sample begins in 1989 and extends through 2008, with firm exit information

[5]CVsource database and Z database are the only professional private equity databases in China. CVsource website is http://www.chinaventuregroup.com.cn/database/cvsource.shtml. Z database can be refered to http://www.pedata.cn/jsp/software/smt_win.jsp

[6]In order to focus on the study of Chinese venture capital, we only study the venture capital (VC) events, and exclude the Angles, PE-Growth, PE-Buyout, PE-PIPE, Bridge/Mezzanine events.

updated through 2016.[7] We construct the multiple regression models of unbalanced panel data and test the three hypotheses. The estimation data sets contain 1593 VCs that participated in 7151 investment rounds involving 5069 start-ups. Excluding 455 missing investment data points, we finally collected 6696 rounds of VC events and 108,416 connection relationships; 26.146% of the investment rounds and 38.651% of sample start-ups involve syndicated funding.

In addition, the data used to construct the VC network dates from before December 31, 2012. Networks are not static. Relationships may change, and entry to and exit from the network may change each VC's position in the network. To capture this dynamic change, we use the co-investment relationship in the 5 years before the investment happened to build the annual network (Hochberg et al. 2007, 2010, 2015). The actor in the network refers to the VC firm, and the tie refers to the co-investment relationship between the VCs in each investment round (Hochberg et al. 2007, 2010; Abell and Nisar 2007; Ewens 2010). In this paper, we construct a directed network and a non-directional network for every year. The directed network is used to distinguish between the leading syndicate VC and VC invited to co-invest in the portfolio company. The leading syndicate VC is the VC with the largest amount at this round of investment. Since there were fewer investment rounds before 1996, the VC network of 1996 consists of 50 investment rounds involving 29 VCs from 1989 to 1996. But from 1997 to 2012, we use the 5-year window, including the base year to build the annual network.

3.2 *Variables*

3.2.1 Dependent Variable: Investment Performance

Most prior researchers use the exit rate as the investment performance of VCs (Hochberg et al. 2007, 2015; Abell and Nisar 2007; Nahata 2008). For this paper, we also use the successful exit rate defined as the investment performance of VCs. The successful exit rate of a VC firm in a year is measured as the fraction of portfolio companies invested in the year that VCs successfully exit via IPO or a sale to another company or receipt of follow-on funding.

3.2.2 Independent Variable: The Ownership of VCs

The ownership of VCs can be divided into local VCs, foreign VCs, and joint VCs. As the proportion of joint ventures in Chinese VCs is very small and the average ratio is 9.94%, in the past 17 years, it will cause a high degree of multilinearity if the

[7]Most VC funds are structured as closed-end, often 8-year in China. We close the sample period at the end of 2008 and use the following 8-year for measuring investment performance.

foreign capital and the Chinese capital ownership are introduced into the model simultaneously. Therefore, we use the foreign ownership (foreign) and joint venture ownership (CO) as a dummy variable to distinguish the three types of ownership of VCs.

3.2.3 Mediator: Network Position

For measuring the network position of VCs, we follow rules of Hochberg et al. (2007), Abell and Nisar (2007) and use five different centralities to capture five different aspects, including degree, indegree, outdegree, betweenness and closeness. To ensure comparability of networks with different size, we normalize each measure (Freeman 1979). To avoid strong multi-collinearity, we introduce the five different centralities in different models.

3.2.4 Control Variable

Our benchmark model mainly replicates Hochberg et al. (2007) and Nahata's (2008) model. We take the former research results of VCs' performance as the control variable, including the investment experience of VCs, investment risks, competition in the VC industry, and investment opportunities in the market. We will build the panel data model and focus on the impact of VC ownership and network position on investment performance.

3.3 *Model Specification*

To test the hypothesis 1, we set the regression model as (1)

$$Performance_{it} = \alpha + \beta Foreign_i + \gamma co_i + \sum_{j=1}^{k} \delta_j Control_{jit} + \varepsilon_{it} \tag{1}$$

This model focuses on the impact of the ownership of VCs on investment performance, which controls the investment experience, investment risk, industry competition, and investment opportunities of VCs.

We introduce Baron and Kenny's three-stage models to test hypothesis 2 and hypothesis 3. We use models (1), (2), (3) to test the mediator effect of the network position of VCs between VCs' ownership and VCs' investment performance.

$$Centrality_{it} = \alpha + \beta Foreign_i + \gamma co_i + \sum_{i=1}^{k} \gamma_i Control_{it} + \varepsilon_{it} \tag{2}$$

$$Performance_{it} = \alpha + \beta Foreign_i + \gamma co_i + \eta Centrality_{it} + \sum_{j=1}^{k} \delta_j Control_{jit} + \varepsilon_{it} \tag{3}$$

4 Results and Discussion

After the LM test and Hausman test, we choose the unbalanced panel model with random effects. We use the three-step regression method to demonstrate how VC network position mediates the impact of ownership on investment performance. The results are shown in Tables 1 and 2.

Models 1–5 in Table 1 illustrate that the ownership of VC has a significant impact on network position. Models 1–4 show that foreign and joint VCs are associated with more central-network positions, including degree, outdegree, indegree and closeness. In Model 5, foreign ownership is not significant to betweenness, but joint ownership is very significant, indicating that joint VCs have the function of a "bridge" instead of foreign VCs in Chinese VC network. These results support hypothesis 2, ownership of VCs significantly impacts VCs' network position, and foreign VCs have more central position in the networks.

Model 6 in Table 2 shows that foreign VCs are associated with significantly better investment performance, and Hypothesis 1 has been supported. In Models 7–11, we add the five measures for network position respectively to model 6. The results show that foreign VC's significant positive impact on investment performance either completely disappeared or weakened. Results in models 7, 9, and 10 shows that the ownership is non-significant when we add network positions to model 6, including degree, indegree and closeness. Thus, these three network centralities are full mediators of the relationship between ownership and investment performance. The coefficients of ownership in models 8 and 11 are smaller and weaker than in model 6, which explains that the network position measured by outdegree and betweenness are partial mediators of the relationship between ownership and investment performance. In the five mediator variables, closeness has the biggest influence on investment performance. A one-standard-deviation increase in closeness is associated with a 13.898% point increase in successful exit rate. Degree and indegree come next. Outdegree and betweenness have relatively small effects economically.

In summary, the results in Tables 1 and 2 illustrate that the VC network position is a mediator variable between the relationship of ownership and investment performance and that foreign VCs have better investment performance because of their advantages of network position. Hypothesis 3 is confirmed.

Table 1 The impact of VCs' ownership on VCs' network position

	Network position: centrality				
	(1)	(2)	(3)	(4)	(5)
Variables	nrmdegree	nrmoutdeg	nrmindeg	ncloseness	nbetween
Ownership					
foreign	0.1386***	0.0734***	0.0574***	8.8844***	−0.0413
	(0.024)	(0.015)	(0.012)	(2.305)	(0.107)
co	0.1990***	0.1252***	0.0892***	11.0046***	0.6319***
	(0.029)	(0.018)	(0.014)	(3.054)	(0.132)
VCs' experience					
norounds	0.0053***	0.0046***	0.0029***	0.0470	0.0252***
	(0.001)	(0.001)	(0.000)	(0.044)	(0.004)
lnfirinvdays	0.0007	0.0003	0.0018	0.1063	0.0398
	(0.008)	(0.005)	(0.004)	(0.478)	(0.035)
Investment risk					
lngrowdays	0.0142	0.0011	0.0045	1.6278***	0.0035
	(0.011)	(0.007)	(0.005)	(0.492)	(0.045)
vcseries	−0.0038	−0.0034	−0.0037	−0.2130	−0.0670
	(0.017)	(0.011)	(0.009)	(0.797)	(0.071)
avstage	−0.0119	0.0272**	−0.0071	0.1707	0.1374
	(0.022)	(0.014)	(0.011)	(0.998)	(0.090)
Competition					
lninvsize	−0.1633***	−0.1306***	−0.0828***	3.1704***	−0.2619***
	(0.017)	(0.011)	(0.008)	(0.807)	(0.069)
lnvcinflows	−0.0005	0.0028	0.0050	−0.3581	−0.0272
	(0.018)	(0.011)	(0.009)	(0.709)	(0.073)
Investment opportunities					
mk_pe	0.0031***	0.0026***	0.0015***	−0.2303***	−0.0009
	(0.001)	(0.000)	(0.000)	(0.030)	(0.003)
Constant	1.0364***	0.7853***	0.5029***	11.5914**	2.0358***
	(0.118)	(0.075)	(0.059)	(5.612)	(0.491)
Observations	868	868	868	868	868
NO. of VC	319	319	319	319	319

Standard errors in parentheses. We use ***, **, and * to denote significance at the 1, 5, and 10% level (two-sided), respectively

5 Conclusions

With the full data of China's VCs, we examine the performance consequences of enterprise's ownership and collaborative networks' position. To the best of our knowledge, this is the first study to examine the relation between ownership, collaborative network, and performance among VCs. Our findings are as follows.

Due to the separate institutional environment in Chinese VC (Fuller 2010), different ownership of VCs leads to significantly different investment performance.

Table 2 Mediator effect of VCs centrilities

		Investment performance: exit rate					
		(6)	(7)	(8)	(9)	(10)	(11)
Variables		su_rate	su_rate	su_rate	su_rate	su_rate	su_rate
Ownership							
foreign		0.1035**	0.0631	0.0874*	0.0713	0.0191	0.0923**
		(0.046)	(0.047)	(0.047)	(0.047)	(0.047)	(0.046)
co		0.0585	0.0111	0.0452	0.0282	−0.0337	0.0378
		(0.058)	(0.059)	(0.058)	(0.058)	(0.058)	(0.058)
Network position							
nrmdegree			0.1237***				
			(0.035)				
nrmoutdeg				0.0619*			
				(0.037)			
nrmindeg					0.1775***		
					(0.054)		
ncloseness						0.0059***	
						(0.001)	
nbetween							0.0296**
							(0.012)
VCs'experience							
norounds		0.0003**	0.0002	0.0001	−0.0005	−0.0003	−0.0008
		(0.002)	(0.002)	(0.002)	(0.002)	(0.002)	(0.002)
lnfirinvdays		−0.0722	−0.0843***	−0.0737**	−0.0772**	−0.0777***	−0.0726**
		(0.030)	(0.030)	(0.030)	(0.030)	(0.030)	(0.030)

(continued)

Table 2 (continued)

Variables		Investment performance: exit rate					
		(6)	(7)	(8)	(9)	(10)	(11)
		su_rate	su_rate	su_rate	su_rate	su_rate	su_rate
Investment risk							
lngrowdays		0.0550***	0.0539***	0.0520***	0.0504***	0.0562***	0.0530***
		(0.017)	(0.017)	(0.017)	(0.017)	(0.017)	(0.017)
vcseries		0.0911***	0.0827***	0.0909***	0.0903***	0.0836***	0.0923***
		(0.022)	(0.022)	(0.022)	(0.022)	(0.022)	(0.022)
avstage		−0.0465	−0.0446	−0.0436	−0.0467	−0.0525*	−0.0463
		(0.032)	(0.032)	(0.032)	(0.032)	(0.032)	(0.032)
Competition							
lninvsize		−0.0513*	−0.0181	−0.0435	−0.0275	−0.0912***	−0.0430
		(0.027)	(0.029)	(0.028)	(0.028)	(0.028)	(0.028)
lnvcinflows		0.0204	0.0213	0.0291	0.0314	0.0136	0.0232
		(0.024)	(0.024)	(0.024)	(0.024)	(0.024)	(0.024)
Investment opportunities							
mk_pe		0.0002	0.0003	0.0003	0.0003	0.0004	0.0002
		(0.001)	(0.001)	(0.001)	(0.001)	(0.001)	(0.001)
Constant		0.8232***	0.6462***	0.7085***	0.6046***	1.0539***	0.7444***
		(0.223)	(0.227)	(0.228)	(0.230)	(0.230)	(0.227)
Observations		616	614	614	614	614	614
NO. of VC		252	252	252	252	252	252

Standard errors in parentheses. We use ***, **, and * to denote significance at the 1, 5, and 10% level (two-sided), respectively

Foreign VCs have better investment performance in China than local VCs. Their network centrality mediates performance and eliminates the effects of being a foreign or a local VC. Foreign VCs' more central network position is the reason why foreign VCs can have better investment performance. In certain institutional environments, VCs can expand their advantage and make up for their deficiencies through enhancing their network relationships, so as to achieve better investment performance.

In emerging economies, institutional theory is more powerful than traditional economic theory (Ahlstrom and Bruton 2006). For the first time, combining the macro-institutional environment, the meso-network position, and the micro-enterprise performance, this paper presents a way that micro-enterprises can adapt to the unstable environment through better-networked position. VCs can enhance their collaborative network positions to achieve complementary advantages instead of being completely passive in the face of the institutional environment.

Acknowledgments We are grateful to two anonymous reviewers and Pamela Siska at MIT WCC. We thank the Chinese Government Scholarship (CSC NO. 201606155079), the Humanities and Social Science Fund of Education Ministry of China (NO. 13YJC630248) and the Central Universities Fundamental Research Grant in China (NO. 2015ZDXM01).

References

Abell, P., & Nisar, T. (2007). Performance effects of venture capital networks. *Management Dicision, 45*(5), 923–936.

Ahlstrom, D., & Bruton, G. D. (2006). Venture capital in emerging economies: Networks and institutional change. *Entrepreneurship Theory & Practice, 30*(2), 299–320.

Anne, L., et al. (2016). The best of both worlds: The benefits of open-specialized and closed-diverse syndication networks for new ventures' success. *Administrative Science Quarterly, 61*(3), 393–432.

Aydin, N., Sayim, M., & Yalama, A. (2007). Foreign ownership and firm performance: Evidence from Turkey. *International Research Journal of Finance and Economics, 11*, 103–111.

Barnard, H. (2010). Overcoming the liability of foreignness without strong firm capabilities: The value of market-based resources. *Journal of International Management, 16*(2), 165–176.

Bruton, G. D., Ahlstrom, D., & Puky, T. (2009). Institutional differences and the development of entrepreneurial ventures: A comparison of the venture capital industries in Latin America and Asia. *Journal of International Business Studies, 40*, 762–7785.

Bygrave, W. D. (1988). The structure of the investment networks of venture capital firms. *Journal of Business Venturing, 3*(2), 137–157.

Carney, M. (1998). The competitiveness of networked production: The role of trust and asset specificity. *Journal of Management Studies, 35*(4), 457–479.

Carvalho, A. G., Calomiris, C. W., & Matos, J. A. (2008). Venture capital as human resource management. *Journal of Economics and Business, 60*(3), 223–255.

Ewen, M. (2010). *Venture capital returns, new firms and social networks*. San Diego: University of California.

Feng, Z. (2012). The top 10 characteristics of China's venture capital industry in 2011. *Science and Technology Entrepreneurship, 1*, 17–19.

Freeman, L. C. (1979). Centrality in social networks: I. Conceptual clarification. *Social Networks, 1*, 215–239.

Fuller, D. B. (2010). How law, politics and transnational networks affect technology entrepreneurship: Explaining divergent venture capital investing strategies in China. *Asia Pacific Journal of Management, 27*(3), 445–459.

Geleilate, J.-M. G., et al. (2016). Home country institutional effects on the multinationality–performance relationship: A comparison between emerging and developed market multinationals. *Journal of International Management, 22*, 380. https://doi.org/10.1016/j.intman.2016.06.001

Gloor, P. A. (2006). *Swarm creativity: Competitive advantage through collaborative innovation networks*. Oxford: Oxford University Press.

Granovetter, M. (1973). The strength of weak ties. *American Journal of Sociology, 78*(6), 1360–1380.

Hain, D., Johan, S., & Wang, D. (2016). Determinants of cross-border venture capital investments in emerging and developed economies: The effects of relational and institutional trust. *Journal of Business Ethics, 138*, 743–764.

Hochberg, Y. V., Ljungqvist, A., & Lu, Y. (2007). Whom you know matters: Venture capital networks and investment performance. *The Journal of Finance, 62*(1), 251–301.

Hochberg, Y. V., Ljungqvist, A., & Lu, Y. (2010). Networking as a barrier to entry and the competitive supply of venture capital. *The Journal of Finance, 65*(3), 829–859.

Hochberg, Y. V., Lindsey, L. A., & Westerfield, M. M. (2015). Resource accumulation through economics ties: Evidence from venture capital. *Journal of Financial Economics, 118*, 245–267.

Hopp, C. (2010). The evolution of inter-organizational networks in venture capital financing. *Applied Financial Economics, 20*(22), 1725–1739.

Keil, T., Maula, M. V., & Wilson, C. (2010). Unique resources of corporate venture capitalists as a key to entry into rigid venture capital syndication networks. *Entrepreneurship Theory and Practice, 34*(1), 83–102.

Large, D., & Muegge, S. (2008). Venture capitalists' non-financial value-added: An evaluation of the evidence and implications for research. *Venture Capital, 10*(1), 20–53.

Lu, H., Tan, Y., & Huang, H. (2012). Why do venture capital firms exist: An institution based rent-seeking perspective and Chinese evidence. *Asia Pacific Journal of Management, 30*(3), 1–16.

Meuleman, M., et al. (2017). Venturing into the unknown with strangers: Substitutes of relational embeddedness in cross-border partner selection in venture capital syndicates. *Journal of Business Venturing, 32*(2017), 131–144.

Nahata, R. (2008). Venture capital reputation and investment performance. *Journal of Financial Economics, 90*, 127–151.

Prijcker, S. D., et al. (2012). The influence of experiential, inherited and external knowledge on the internationalization of venture capital firms. *International Business Review, 21*, 929–940.

Sorenson, O., & Stuart, T. E. (2008). Bringing the context back in: Settings and the search for syndicate partners in venture capital investment networks. *Administrative Science Quarterly, 53* (2), 266–294.

Zhang, J., & Pezeshkan, A. (2016). Host country network, industry experience, and international alliance formation: Evidence from the venture capital industry. *Journal of World Business, 51* (2), 264–277.

Zhou, Y., & Song, G. (2014). The dynamic evolution of venture capital network in China. *Systems Engineering – Theory & Practice, 14*(11), 2748–2759.

Zhu, Q. (2015). *Research on the tax system of private equity fund of limited partnership*. East China University of Political Science and Law.

Enhancing Social and Intellectual Collaboration in Innovation Networks: A Study of Entrepreneurial Networks in an Urban Technological University

Christine Miller, Jacqueline Verrilli, Teesta Jain, and Nik Rokop

Abstract This article documents a pilot study of the social networks of faculty, staff, and students at the Illinois Tech (IIT), an urban technical university located in Chicago. The focus of our study is the Entrepreneurship Academy (EA) Council, a university-wide, academically focused organization with an overall goal of fostering a community of entrepreneurs that transcends schools, departments, and units. In this pilot study, we used Condor, a dynamic social network (SNA) tool, to map and analyze the visual representations of the email accounts of several EA Council members. In a second phase of the project we plan to introduce the EA Council to how they might use dynamic SNA to build and enhance resilient networks connecting students, faculty, staff, alumni, corporate partners, government, and entrepreneurial advocates to foster the creation a new generation of high impact entrepreneurs. We will present the results of this pilot study to the EA Council members with the aim of stimulating strategic conversations about the role of social networks in collaboration and innovation and about how they can use dynamic SNA to further the development of IIT's entrepreneurial ecosystem.

1 Introduction

This project was initiated in response to interest in exploring the potential for social network analysis (Wasserman and Faust 1994) to generate insights about the entrepreneurship and innovation at Illinois Tech (IIT), an urban technical university in Chicago. IIT has a rich history of innovation, design, and global entrepreneurship and a strong commitment to transforming graduate and undergraduate education for the twenty-first century. However, like many organizations, including higher education institutions, silos and entrenched networks create invisible barriers to change.

C. Miller (✉) · J. Verrilli · T. Jain · N. Rokop
Illinois Institute of Technology, Chicago, IL, USA
e-mail: cmille31@stuart.iit.edu; jverril1@hawk.iit.edu; tjain8@iit.edu; nrokop@stuart.iit.edu

F. Grippa et al. (eds.), *Collaborative Innovation Networks*, Studies on Entrepreneurship, Structural Change and Industrial Dynamics,
https://doi.org/10.1007/978-3-319-74295-3_4

The Entrepreneurship Academy (EA) Council was founded in 2014 in an effort to overcome silos across the campus. Comprised of students, faculty, deans, and staff the EA Council is an academically focused university-wide body that reports to the provost. The goal of the EA Council is to foster a community of entrepreneurs by raising awareness of resources, entrepreneurial activities, and promoting collaboration.

In 2016, the EA Council published a comprehensive report of entrepreneurial activities, projects, events, and initiatives across the university. One of the EA Council's strategies is "establishing a collaborative network with alumni, corporations, government and entrepreneurial advocates that fosters a university-based entrepreneurial ecosystem."[1] We were interested to explore how social network analysis (SNA) might be used to visualize such a network and monitor its development.

Collaborative innovation networks, or COINs, have been defined as groups of self-motivated individuals from various parts of an organization or from multiple organizations who, driven by a common vision, work together on a new idea (Gloor et al. 2003). COINs are recognized as an essential element in fostering innovation. Powell et al. (1996) referred to these "networks of learning" as the locus of innovation:

> When the knowledge base of an industry is both complex and expanding and the sources of expertise are widely dispersed, the locus of innovation will be found in networks of learning, rather than in individual firms. (1996: 116)

In a University environment, individual colleges are analogous to individual firms that may include individuals interested in collaborating on a particular innovation. Universities are characterized by dispersed expertise and complex and expanding knowledge bases. An additional element is the diverse student population: individual students have self-selected into tracks that allow them to gain employment or create career paths for themselves. The diverse terrain of the university presents both opportunities and significant challenges, which the EA Council was tasked to address. One of the challenges facing the EA Council is that many collaborative pursuits are only known to those who are directly involved in them. Although the EA Council publishes an annual report of collaborative activities, these reports are not effective in reaching the majority of the university community. We think that using dynamic social network tools to visualize existing collaborative networks would be a more effective way of engaging people in discussions about nascent networks and exploring possibilities for enhancing network connectivity.

Given the EA Council's stated interest in collaboration networks, the questions that this exploratory project seeks to address are (1) how might visualizing the current social networks of key EA Council members generate strategic conversations around ways to build and sustain collaborative networks that foster innovation and

[1]From the Entrepreneurship Academy Council 2015/2016 Annual Report.

entrepreneurship? (2) Could utilizing dynamic social network analytic tools to visualize the structures of existing networks lead to ideas about how to improve connectivity and change network structures to increase the potential for innovation and entrepreneurship?

In this pilot exploration, we envisioned resilient social networks as a way of framing the EA Council goal to foster innovation and entrepreneurship within the university and among its external stakeholders. We understand resilience as the capacity to recover quickly from upheaval and to adapt to discontinuous change (Luthar et al. 2000). In the university context resilience includes

- Engaging a complex set of diverse stakeholders, including faculty, students, staff, administrators, alumni, community members, industry, and funding entities
- Adapting to a constantly changing student body that
  - Has different expectations than previous generations
  - Engages in various new technologies for the pursuit of social and professional goals
  - Learns in non-traditional ways that are less text-based and more experiential
- Adapting to rapidly changing technology that impacts all fields of study, knowledge creation, and organization
- Adapting to changes in political and policy regimes that affect enrollment and funding

To discover existing collaborative innovation networks, we chose to use Condor, a dynamic SNA software tool to map ego-centered networks of key EA Council members. Specifically, we were interested to use Condor's Fetch Mailbox Menu to create a visual map of a person's connections in her or his email network, which they can view as an animation to see how their social network has evolved over time. Analyzing the network views resulting from individual Fetch Mail queries revealed existing network structures and allowed us to identify how existing structures indicated when collaboration was probably happening and where there were untapped opportunities to enhance the social and intellectual collaborations that foster entrepreneurship and innovation. We wanted to see if sharing the existing network visualizations with the EA Council would stimulate their interest in Virtual Mirroring (Gloor et al. 2017) and *Virtual Mirror-based Learning* (Raad and Nakamoto 2017). Recent studies has suggested that Virtual Mirror-based Learning (VMBL), a method whereby individuals reflect on communication patterns mirrored back to them through visual representations of network maps, can be used as a vehicle for learning. Our goal was to use the visualizations of email accounts of key EA Council members to show how VMBL might be used to intentionally enhance social networks within the university and among its stakeholders and foster collaboration, innovation, and entrepreneurial activity.

2 Methods

This research employs the use of the dynamic social network analysis (SNA) software Condor. Using Condor, we collected six email accounts filtered for EA Council communication from: the Executive Director of the EA Council, the Chairman of the EA Council, the Director of the Knapp Center of Entrepreneurship, a business school faculty of innovation, and two entrepreneurial students. In this paper, we focus on three primary research subjects: the EA Council chair, the director of the entrepreneurship center, and one of the students associated with the EA Council. The Condor analysis provided a snapshot of the total communication for "All Mail" in the email accounts associated with the university IP addresses for each subject. We then merged the datasets from the six individuals to assess the status of the EA as a COIN. The snapshots are color-coded by domain that indicates the node type (a university constituent such as student, faculty, or staff of the university). We conducted the three main Centrality calculations—Between-ness, Closeness Centrality, and Degree Centrality (Wasserman and Faust 1994; Borgatti 2005)—in Condor to map the current state of the network using the EA Council executive director and the EA Council chair as the primary research subjects.

3 Analysis

Figure 1 depicts the archetypical model of a Collaborative Innovation Network (COIN) and its ancillary domains: Collaborative Learning Network (CLN) and Collaborative Interest Network (CIN) (Gloor 2006). Dynamic exchange among and between domains characterize the COIN Model. Collaboration is the key to innovation. However, because collaboration tends to develop organically, it is difficult to know when it is happening and exactly who is involved. The network view provided by dynamic SNA allows us to view large networks and to identify existing clusters where collaborative innovation might be occurring. The high-level view of the virtual terrain shows the nodes that are connected and the nature of their connection and suggests possibilities for connecting to other nodes and clusters. We will use the COIN model as a framework to stimulate discussions about strategy, activities, resources, matchmaking (between resources, goals and value) and connections that need to be in place for innovation to occur.

Fig. 1 COIN Model

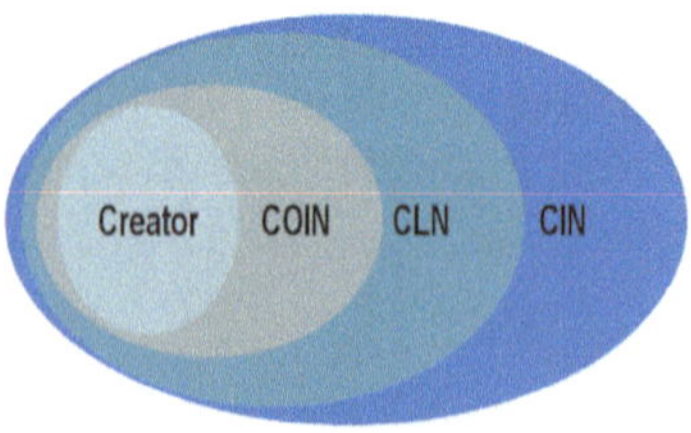

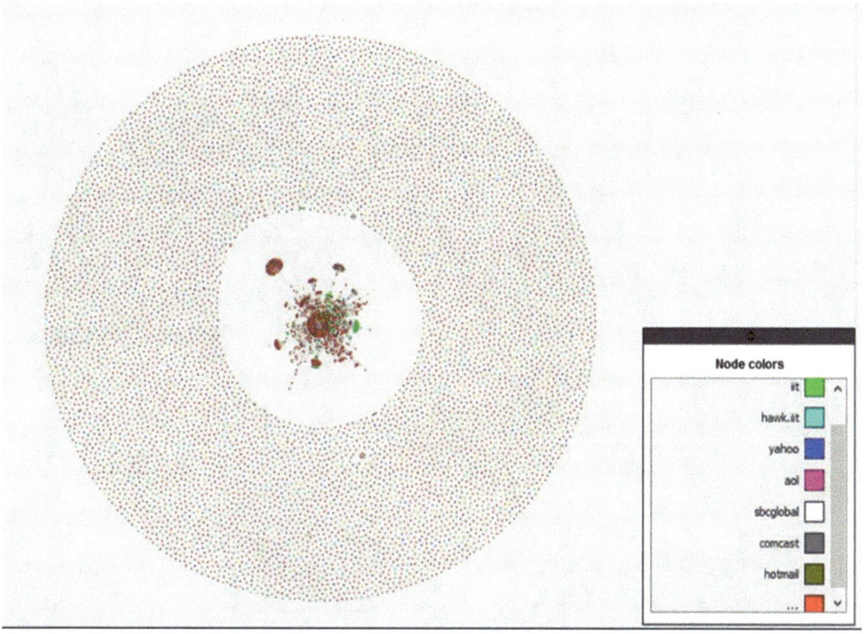

Fig. 2 Entrepreneurship Center director

Large-scale innovation requires collaboration among the private sector, governmental organizations, academia, and entrepreneurs in the small business and start-up worlds. Three vital and interrelated processes are required for innovation to take place: collaboration, innovation, and problem solving.[2]

The visual map in Fig. 2 illustrates the email network of the director of the entrepreneurship center. The green nodes represent IIT and the red nodes EA Council members. The "halo" of the ancillary nodes surrounding the main communication network are likely names on a distribution list or mass mailing to faculty, students or other groups, significant in showing the entrepreneurship director's indirect reach. In the middle is a network of individuals that frequently exchange email with the director.

The extreme enlargement in Fig. 3 shows the entrepreneurship center director's email network to highlight more densely connected and central nodes. Degree Centrality ranges from 0.0 to 1399.0. This section of the network shows that each node is interacting with other nodes and is interacting with the central node—the entrepreneurship center director—to form a densely connected web. Tracking these nodes might give us an indication of some of the important people and roles required to sustain the structure of densely connected and networked nodes. Isolated nodes might indicate which people and roles should be more closely connected. The

[2]3-GKI_Top-10-Tools-for-Collaborative-Innovation.pdf

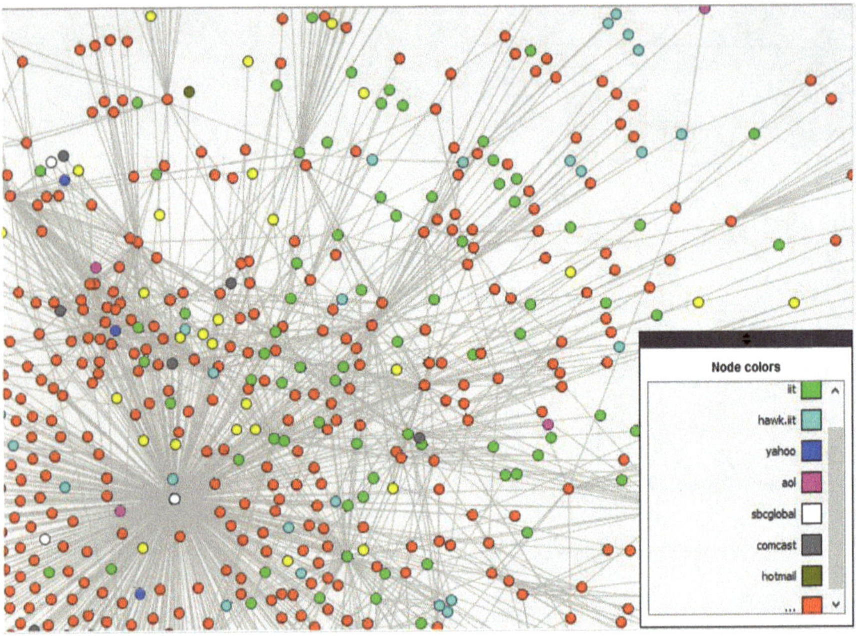

Fig. 3 Enlargement of Entrepreneurship Center director's email network

structure of the networks shows critical nodes that act as bridges that sustain the larger network. If critical nodes leave the network, the network structure will be vulnerable as important connections are lost.

Figure 4 shows two views (Fig. 4b is an enlargement) of the EA Council executive director's email to members of the EA Council during the 2016–2017 academic year. Degree Centrality values range from 3.0 to 22.0. The executive director's node is depicted in white and Degree Centrality value is 22.0. Domains in the map are color-coded. The ego-centered network views of key EA Council members are very dense, complex, and robust, which is what you would expect to see in the network of individuals who would likely serve on the EA Council. These network views show "galaxy" structures. Exploring the existing but tenuous connections between these galaxy structures might reveal opportunities for increasing collaboration.

In contrast, at the EA Council level we see a classic "star". The star configuration indicates that information is going out. There is no indication of interaction between the nodes in this view.

Figure 4b (bottom network view) is the enlargement of EA Council director's email map. Note there is a galaxy to the slight upper left of the chair's node indicating a densely connected network that suggests frequent interaction between the nodes is occurring.

In Fig. 5 the EA Council chair's overall network shows galaxy configurations on the periphery connected by bridging nodes and dense network on the inside

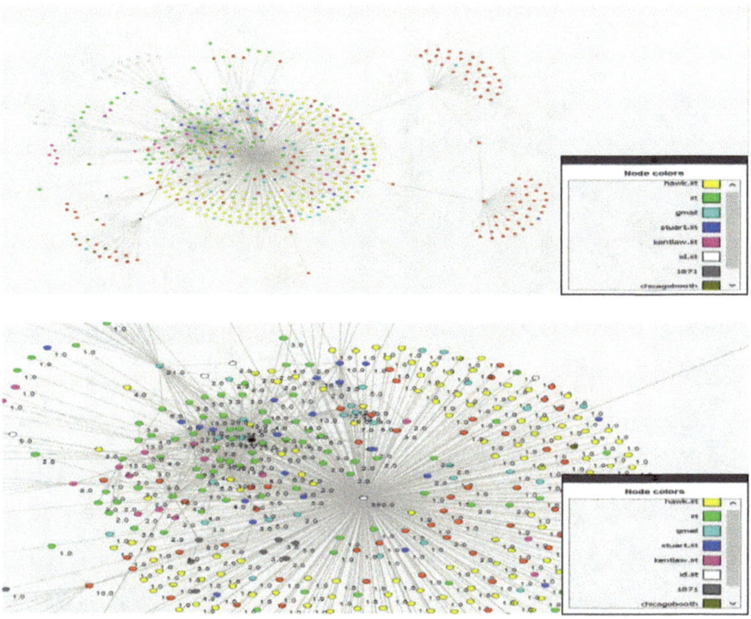

Fig. 4 EA Council director: egocentric network view [Top (**a**); Bottom (**b**)]

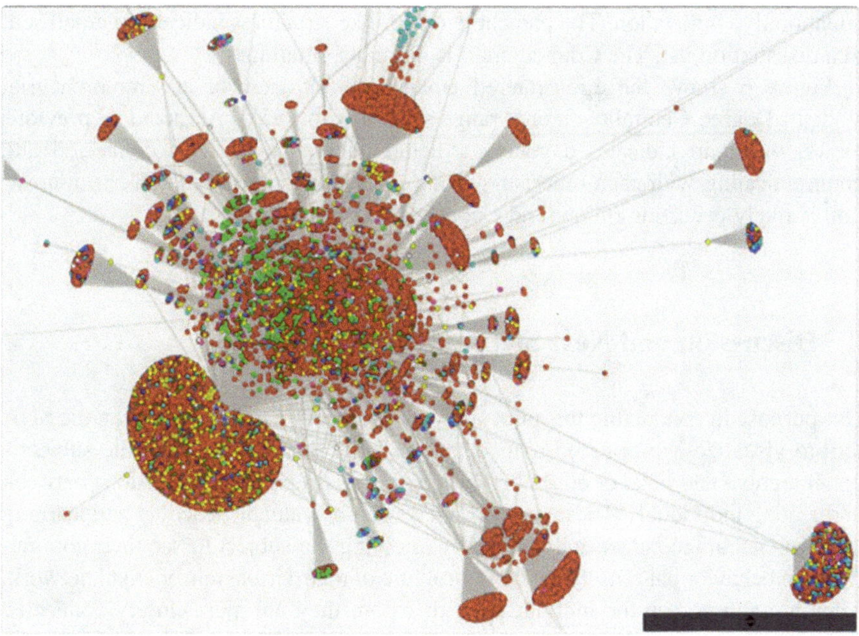

Fig. 5 EA Council chair overall network

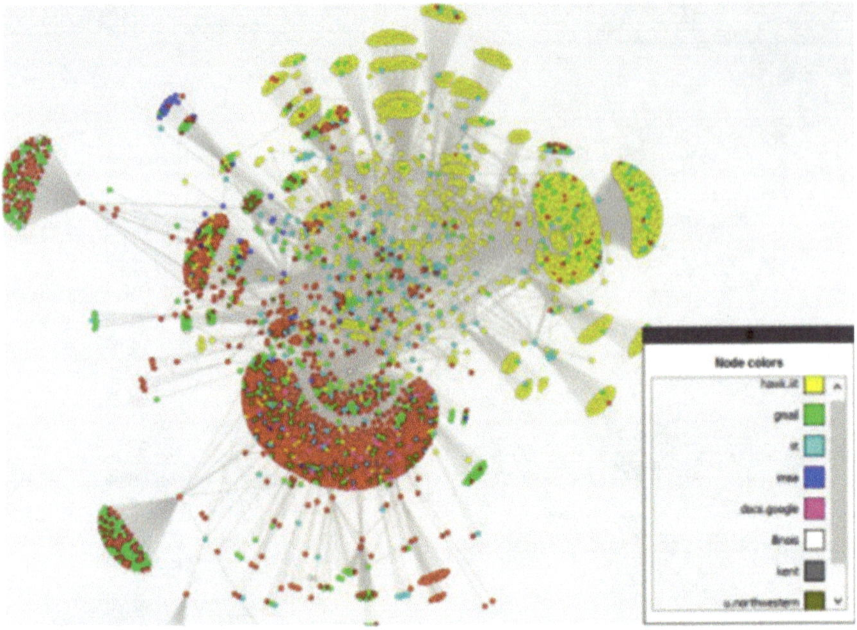

Fig. 6 Entrepreneurial student's email map

depicting frequent network communication that is indicative of and favorable for collaborative innovation. The parachute or fan-like structures indicate an email sent to a distribution list. The Council chair is on many email lists.

Figure 6 shows the ego-centered email network view of an entrepreneurial student. Degree Centrality figures range from 1.0 to 995.0. As noted in previous views, this map indicates a galaxy structure where nodes were connected and communicating with each other suggesting that collaboration favorable to innovation is likely occurring (Gloor and Cooper 2007).

4 Discussion and Next Steps

Our purpose in conducting this pilot study was to explore the use of a dynamic SNA tool to visualize ego-centered maps showing individuals as nodes in the subject's email archive and links or edges between nodes that represent connections between and among individuals. These network views can be valuable teaching and learning tools to encourage behavioral change by allowing the subject to see their communication behavior patterns through the structure of their virtual mirror email network. They are able to see the individuals with whom they are most closely connected through frequent email exchange, nodes that bridge COIN-like clusters of nodes to individuals within their network, and people with whom they might want to be more closely connected.

This process is referred to as Virtual Mirror-based Learning (VMBL) (Raad and Nakamoto 2017). In their pilot mirroring study, Raad and Nakamoto describe *enterprise resilience* as "the capacity for an enterprise to survive, adapt, and grow in the face of turbulent change." They argue, "a resilience gap has developed in the business world as organizations did not adequately adapt in the face of increasing turbulence in their environment." Citing Gloor et al. (2008) they describe virtual mirroring as "the process of showing people their communication behaviors" and suggest that this process can lead people to change their communication behaviors. We believe that the EA Council can apply Virtual Mirror-based Learning to initiate discussions about how to make network structures more *galaxy-like* to increase collaboration among Council members, the university at large, and external entities. In contrast, the current "star" structure of the EA Council director's network view indicates that even though the director is part of robust collaborative networks, the overall communication behavior with EA Council members depicts a one-way pattern and little or no interaction among individuals in the EA Council network (Gloor and Cooper 2007).

We hypothesize that positive changes in communication behaviors would have positive consequences on the network's resilience via a feedback loop of communication back into the network. The mechanisms of this positive feedback loop would be enhanced sources for collaboration and knowledge sharing, external opportunities, intrinsically motivated individuals and reputation. Positive feedback loops are known as "virtuous cycles" (Zahra 2008). We envision the virtuous cycle as a dynamic exchange "where discovery enriches creation which, in turn, fosters the discovery of new opportunities." (2008: 243) Activities such as client sponsored research, university sponsored hackathons, and competitions generate external opportunities that result in collaboration and knowledge sharing and in turn attract intrinsically motivated people, all of which builds reputation. Figure 7 suggests how

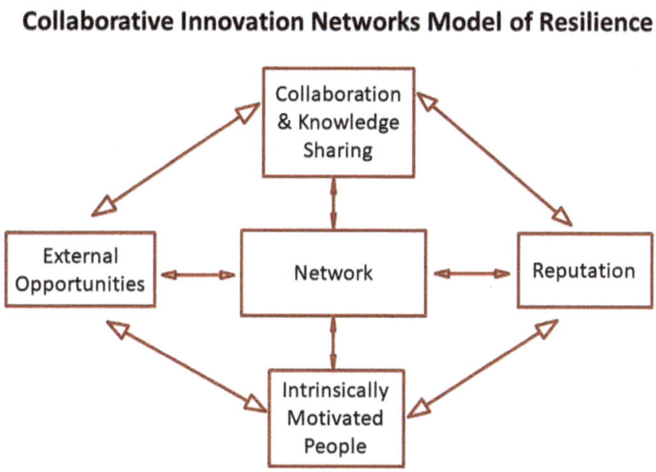

Fig. 7 EA Council model of resilience through network feedback loops

together these activities constitute a model of resilience for the university. VMBL can increase the capacity of the EA Council to actualize the potential of this model. Creating the opportunity for members to reflect on visualizations of their existing networks and communication behaviors allows for imagining how changing behaviors can open new avenues that energize and animate a resilient virtuous cycle.

In the next phase of this project we will present this pilot study to the EA Council and propose how Virtual Mirror-based Learning might be used to stimulate discussions related to networks and communication behaviour. We are interested to continue this study to learn how individually and collectively the process of VBML might change the way people collaborate both within the university, with community partners, and with external entities.

References

Borgatti, S. P. (2005). Centrality and network flow. *Social Networks, 27*(1), 55–71.

Gloor, P. (2006). *Swarm creativity: Competitive advantage through collaborative innovation network*. New York: Oxford University Press.

Gloor, P., & Cooper, S. (2007). *Coolhunting: Chasing down the next big thing*. New York: AMACOM.

Gloor, P. A., Laubacher, R., Dynes, S. B. C., & Zhao, Y. (2003). *Visualization of communication patterns in collaborative innovation networks: Analysis of some W3C working groups*.

Gloor, P., Oster, D., Raz, O., Pentland, A. S., & Schoder, D. (2008). The virtual mirror: Reflecting on your social and psychological self to increase organizational creativity. *International Studies of Management and Organization, 40*. https://doi.org/10.2139/ssrn.1327521

Gloor, P., Colladon, A. F., Giacomelli, G., Saran, T., & Grippa, F. (2017). The impact of virtual mirroring on customer satisfaction. *Journal of Business Research, 75*, 67–76.

Luthar, S. S., Cicchetti, D., & Becker, B. (2000). The construct of resilience: A critical evaluation and guidelines for future work. *Child Development, 71*(3), 543–562.

Powell, W. W., Koput, K. W., & Smith-Doerr, L. (1996). Interorganizational collaboration and the locus of innovation: Networks of learning in biotechnology. *Administrative Science Quarterly, 41*(1), 116–145.

Raad, N., & Nakamoto, K. (2017). The impact of virtual mirroring on collaboration patterns and project performance. In *Collaborative Innovation Networks Conference (COINs 2017)*, Detroit, MI.

Wasserman, S., & Faust, K. (1994). *Social network analysis: Methods and application*. Cambridge: Cambridge University Press.

Zahra, S. A. (2008). The virtuous cycle of discovery and creation of entrepreneurial opportunities. *Strategic Entrepreneurship Journal, 2*(3), 243–257.

“German Association or Chinese Emperor?” Building COINs Between China and Germany

Yang Song, Matthäus P. Zylka, and Peter A. Gloor

Abstract This paper describes our experience teaching a distributed virtual course with teams made up by students from China and Germany. It is based on a distributed course about Collaborative Innovation Networks (COINs) which has been successfully taught for the last 12 years to students from Germany, the US, Finland, and Switzerland. In this course, students form teams from different locations and languages, and together complete a complex project analyzing online social media. In 2016–2017, we applied the same course framework to participants from China and Germany. To gather insights from the course, we follow a mixed method study design by analyzing qualitative interviews with course participants and quantitative communication data of course participants. We find that combining members from China and Germany into the same team poses a set of unique intercultural challenges, overcoming language and behavioral differences. We present key lessons learned to inform future courses combining participants from the East and the West.

1 Introduction

In the age of globalization, understanding and learning from cultural diversity is important for scholars and practitioners the like. People who work with culturally different colleagues need to know the cultures with which they are interacting and must appreciate their intercultural colleagues' natures, skills, experiences and

Y. Song (✉)
Jilin University, Changchun, China

M. P. Zylka
University of Bamberg, Bamberg, Germany
e-mail: matthaeus.zylka@uni-bamberg.de

P. A. Gloor
MIT Center for Collective Intelligence, Cambridge, MA, USA
e-mail: pgloor@mit.edu

F. Grippa et al. (eds.), *Collaborative Innovation Networks*, Studies on Entrepreneurship, Structural Change and Industrial Dynamics,
https://doi.org/10.1007/978-3-319-74295-3_5

behaviors. Rising dependence on intercultural teams in the modern workplace calls for growth in understanding of working and communication processes necessary to develop well-performing teams. To improve this understanding, numerous studies were published in the context of intercultural issues in global teams in the past years (e.g. Connaughton and Marissa 2007; Gloor and Paasivaara 2013; Gloor et al. 2016; Krishna et al. 2004; Nicholson and Sahay 2001; Ochieng and Price 2010; Stahl et al. 2010). This paper contributes to this research on work and communication in intercultural teams by presenting the recent experiences we made in teaching an intercultural course on Collaborative Innovation Networks (COINs). This paper describes the extension of an intercultural course on COINs, where students from different countries work together and innovate as distributed virtual teams. They solve complex social media analysis problems, coolhunting for trends and trendsetters on the Internet, doing prediction based on social media archives, or developing new tools for analyzing communication and collaboration. In addition, this is the first time we mix the East and West students together remotely, our experiences and teaching method will provide insights for further collaborations for Eastern and Western universities. We will provide more opportunities for students from the East to have an international studying experience without having to go abroad.

2 COINs Course Overview

The basic framework of the course has been developed and fine-tuned over 12 years with participants from different European countries, and universities in the US such as MIT (Massachusetts Institute of Technology), SCAD (Savannah College of Art and Design), and IIT (Illinois Institute of Technology). The course consists of an introductory block course, where the basics of the method are taught, and a 3-month project part where students form distributed teams. The teaming process is by now well established, with bi-weekly checkpoints, where all student teams have to present to the plenary in class, with the different classroom connected by Web conferencing. These mandatory checkpoints are complemented by at least once-per-week fixed-time meetings where participants from the different locations are meeting face-to-face using Skype or another Web conferencing tools such as WeChat. As part of the course, students also use the social media analysis tool Condor (Gloor 2017), which automatically analyses all types of online communication archives such as e-mail, Twitter, Wikipedia, Facebook, and blogs. We put big emphasis on pro-active communication, encouraging students to be upfront and tell their team members as soon as it becomes obvious to them that they can not deliver a milestone at the agreed-on time.

There is now also a detailed course manuscript available with detailed step-by-step instructions for the students, both describing the theoretical foundations as well as the technical aspects of the Condor tool which is used for online social media analysis (Gloor 2017).

In an increasingly global world, working in distributed virtual teams becomes a crucial capability. While this capability has been taught in previous versions of the COINs course mostly for mixed German-US teams, China is becoming an increasingly active participant in the global economy. Improving the internationalization level of a Chinese university is one of the critical requirements for future high-level Chinese universities. Opportunities to build bridges between the East and West are thus getting more and more important. We therefore, in winter 2016, extended the COINs course for the first time with participants from Jilin University, Changchun, China. Teams consisted of four to seven members, where always at least two students had to be from both Germany and from China. They were all Masters' students; their majors were in business informatics, computer science, economics, and digital humanities. At the universities participating in Germany, University of Cologne and University of Bamberg, this course has been well established over the last 11 years, with the students knowing what to expect, and a large group of alumni who assist newcomers in the course. For the Chinese students, it was their first experience collaborating with Western peers, also they had no cohort of previous-year colleagues to ask questions for second-level support. The course included 27 students from China and 30 students from Germany working in nine different teams on tasks such as developing a smartwatch-based "happimeter", and coolhunting about sports, political trends, diseases, and sustainability.

3 Methods

To analyze the success of this year's course, we followed a triangulation multilevel mixed method study design (Creswell et al. 2003). Therefore, we collected different types of data to represent the different levels of analysis within the course with the intent of forming an overall interpretation of the course performance. In detail, we conducted interviews with 11 students (out of 57 participants) from Germany and China after the course was finished, allowing us to get a representative subset of the student population. During the interview, students were asked about their experiences working and communicating in a globally distributed multi-disciplinary group by listing their biggest challenges and successes in teamwork and project tasks. They were also asked about intercultural problems and issues, as well as about the communication tools and meeting frequency. In a second interview part, they were asked about the most valuable lessons they had learned during the course regarding working in multicultural virtual teams, and what they would do differently next time. In the end, we also asked them for suggestions on how to improve the course.

Further, we did a social network analysis of the e-mail archive of the e-mail communication among course participants. This archive was collected by asking the students to cc all their mails to dummy mailboxes, which were at the end of the course analyzed with the dynamic semantic social network analysis tool Condor (Gloor 2017).

4 Interview Results

We conducted a total of 11 interviews, with 4 German, and 7 Chinese students. During the course, we also got feedbacks about collaboration and communication issues mostly from German students. This already illustrates the key different in culture, with the Germans being pro-active, and telling the Chinese what to do, and the Chinese much more passive, waiting for instructions. This is also one of the typical characteristics of Chinese students as most of the courses are given to a large group (above 100 students). In general, we found that compared to previous years, where the background of the participants was more homogeneous and firmly embedded in Western culture, this year's course was much more challenging. As the most positive lesson from the course, the students appreciated the opportunity to learn about working together with team members from radically different cultures. They noticed that in the beginning they had misunderstandings because of different cultural contexts and language issues, which they learned to cope with over the duration of the course. Students also noticed the crucial role of face-to-face communication in Skype to work out misunderstanding arising in e-mails.

Chinese/German teamwork was supported by similarities in culture that supported collaboration—for instance, the attitude towards being reliable and predictable in German and Chinese culture is similar, and people were on time for virtual meetings, and they also mostly delivered on promises made to their team members. For instance, the Chinese students appreciated what they called the "rigorous attitude" of the Germans: "I feel the rigorous attitude of the Germans which is deserved learning"—Chinese student 6.

They also felt that the Germans were more pro-active with regards to innovation, and were impressed by their willingness to try out new ideas and deviate from the well-trodden paths. The students in China and Germany also appreciated the opportunity to make new friends from a different culture, whom they would not have a chance to meet otherwise. The students were appreciative of the efforts of the teachers, who made themselves available and approachable.

> From the course, I learnt the knowledge about social network and the most valuable thing is how to cooperate with others—Chinese student 1.

> The project offers us a chance to communicate with foreign students which has great significance—Chinese student 1.

> There are some communication challenges, but I didn't feel the cultural differences—Chinese student 2.

> Cooperation with foreign friends is completely different. We need to learn to learn from others—Chinese student 2.

> Our foreign teammates have a high efficiency all the time which is something also we should learn. In the meantime, they have a strong logic when they do anything—Chinese student 2.

One main difference between the German and Chinese students was their attitude towards leadership. While the Germans were—in the spirit of COINs—working in self-organizing sub teams, the Chinese were looking for a strong leader:

> I think we need a leader as a team. Each team needs a leader to organize everyone to meet, and division of labor, so that everyone can participate in this event. A rudderless team will reduce efficiency, according to Chinese student 3.

> Our Chinese colleagues were much more observing. Sometimes we were not sure if they understood everything or listening. We were talking like all the time. We have some people in our group who would like to talk as well. Sometimes we didn't know if our colleagues in Jilin did understand everything or felt confident to ask something. They were very quiet. But they also did a good job.—German student 1

> German students always say: "we want to do". Chinese students are not saying what they want to do, they are waiting to be assigned. This got better over time.—German student 2

All the team projects were chosen based on the mutual interests of students. There were two teams working on the same task, one team with an appointed project manager (a German student) whose sole task it was to manage the team, the other with three informal leaders (two Germans, one Chinese) who took turns depending on skills and tasks. We evaluated the final project paper, the team with rotating leadership far outperformed the team with the rigid leadership structure.

In the interviews of both Chinese and German students a list of problems was brought up: The English language skills of the Chinese students were quite varied. While some students spoke and wrote excellent English, the English language capabilities of many Chinese students were rudimentary, which made communication extremely challenging. This is also because most of the university courses are given in Chinese. The percentage of English speaking students is very low. Therefore, Chinese students have no chance to use their English skills. Our course provides an opportunity for Chinese students to communicate with international students at no costs for students who are not able to study abroad.

The Chinese students encountered technology problems doing the Web analysis for the Coolhunting projects, which were chosen by most of the teams. This is because our course involves more social science students than computer science and engineering students. Coolhunting projects are more relevant for social science students. In particular, for those students, there were two technical problems, (1) Internet connectivity and (2) Chinese language support. The Chinese students had connectivity issues because of restricted Internet access in China to Twitter, Facebook and Google search, which form the backbone of analysis for doing social media coolhunting projects in Germany and the US. While there are other systems in China, such as Baidu, and Sina Weibo, there would still be a lot of Internet content in Chinese available in Twitter and Facebook, but the "great firewall" blocked this access for automated data collection with Condor. The second issue was the missing Chinese natural language processing capabilities of the Condor tool (which only supports Western languages such as English, German, French, Italian, Spanish and Portuguese). In the end, Condor was the coolhunting tool predominantly used by the German students. The Chinese students ended up using simpler Chinese tools such as manual searches with Baidu, and directly collecting data from Sina Weibo, the Chinese equivalent of Twitter.

There were also technology problems in video conferencing between China and Germany, and one instructor frequently participating from the US. We started using Adobe Connect, hosted on a server in Germany. In the beginning, we had big connectivity issues, and so we started experimenting with WebEx and Skype, however we found that using the right settings, and asking for a high-speed connection at Jilin University solved these issues. In the second half of the semester Adobe Connect provided a satisfactory teleconferencing experience.

Despite these obstacles, the overall assessment of the students was quite positive, and they recommended keeping this seminar as a regular offering in the future:

> "We liked"…"the method of collecting foreign data. The precious experience of communicating with foreign friends is also valuable."—Chinese student 4.

> This teaching method is novel, it can be in line with international standards, so that we broaden our horizons.—Chinese student 5.

5 Knowledge Flow Analysis Through E-Mail

In addition to the interviews, we also did an e-mail based social network analysis with Condor. During the teamwork phase of the course, all students were asked to cc their e-mail communication to a different e-mail address per team, which was then collected for analysis with Condor. Figure 1 illustrates the e-mail activity over time, peaks in activity before each bi-weekly in-class meeting are clearly noticeable. This nicely illustrates the need for these meetings, because otherwise students would defer all work to the end of the course.

Figure 2 illustrates the sentiment, complexity, and emotionality of the e-mail content. Sentiment (the blue line in Fig. 2) is positive and above 0.5 most of the time. Sentiment of 0.5 would denote neutral language, values below 0.5 denote negative sentiment. We find that right before Christmas sentiment drops somewhat to 0.4, which might be because of coordination problems between Germans and Chinese students during the vacation time. At the same time, emotionality (the green line) is jumping up, illustrating the same more emotionally charged discussion style. Complexity (the yellow line) is quite high, illustrating the complex technical topics discussed by the different teams. Complexity is measured as the probability of distinctive words in individual messages compared to the occurrence of these words in all other messages (Gloor 2017). Emotionality (the green line) is measured as standard deviation of sentiment.

Figure 3 illustrates the word cloud, most words are in green, denoting the positive context of the words. Only words such as "problem", or "app", which was the product of one of the teams, are shown in red, indicating negative sentiment. The most popular words were "presentation", "meeting", "time", and "peter", the first name of one of the instructors. This illustrates that students were working from one

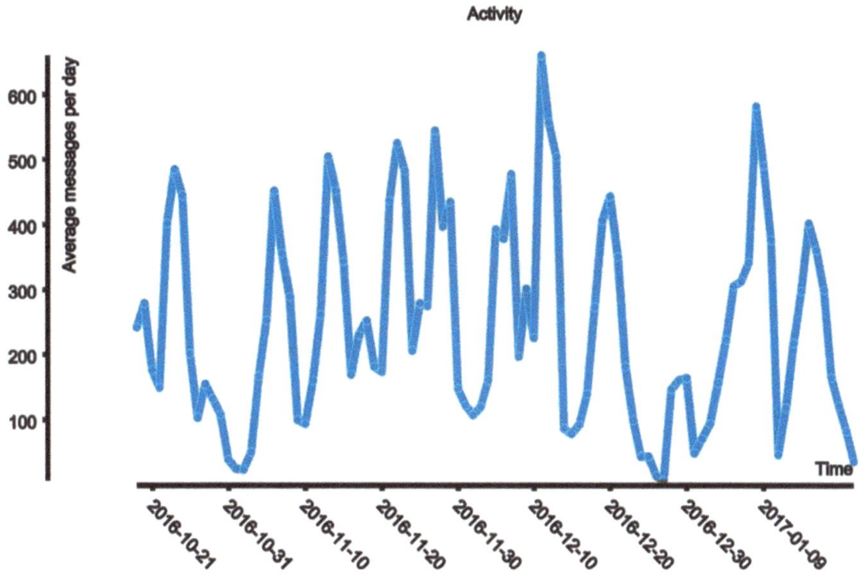

Fig. 1 Activity of E-Mail over time

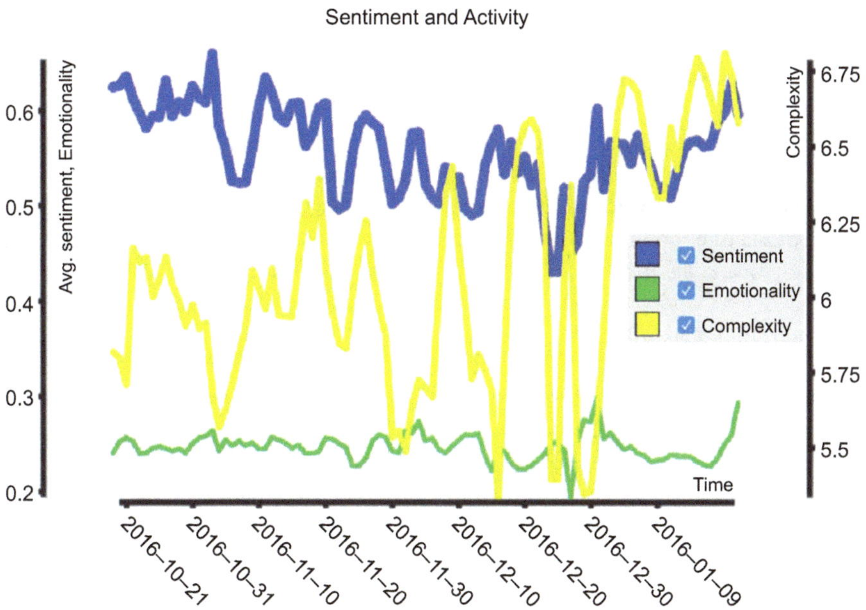

Fig. 2 Sentiment, emotionality, and complexity over time

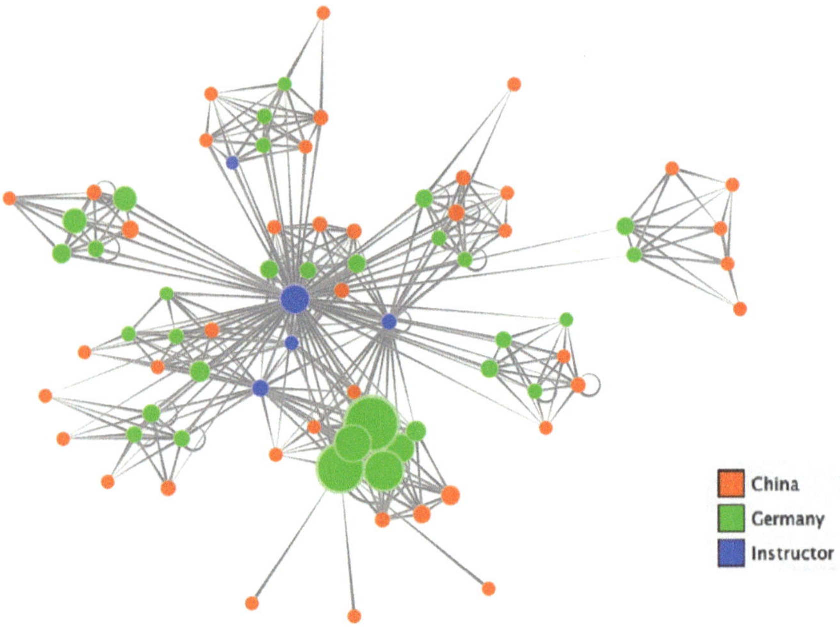

Fig. 3 Word cloud of contents, the greener the text, the more positive is the context of a word

bi-weekly presentation to the next, and discussing who would be presenting next at the meeting.

Figure 4 shows the social network, constructed by the e-mails exchanged among the students and instructors. Nodes are colored by location. We find that the German students (in green) are closer to the center and the instructors (in blue), indicating the more pro-active communication style of the Germans. The Chinese students (in orange) are all much more peripheral. The nodes are sized by influence as calculated by Condor. Condor measures influence by tracking who introduces a new word first, and who picks up this word next. We find the German members of one team, which was building a smartwatch based communication-tracking system to calculate happiness of wearers of the smartwatch, to be most influential. As the students are from very different fields, for each team, the topic they chose was also very different, most of the students prefer to work as a team instead of communicating with other teams. However, during our interview to students, they would like to communicate with the teams that have a similar topic.

Figure 5 illustrates the temporal social surface. In this representation, the x-axis shows the different people, the y-axis shows time, and the z-axis shows betweenness centrality of each person. The more this picture looks like a "stormy sea", with changing betweenness curves for each person, the more creative is the group. In Fig. 5 we see four major spikes. The first one, in the back, shows the central role of the main instructor (Peter) in kicking of the course, by exchanging e-mails with many different students. The second spike illustrates the first bi-weekly project status

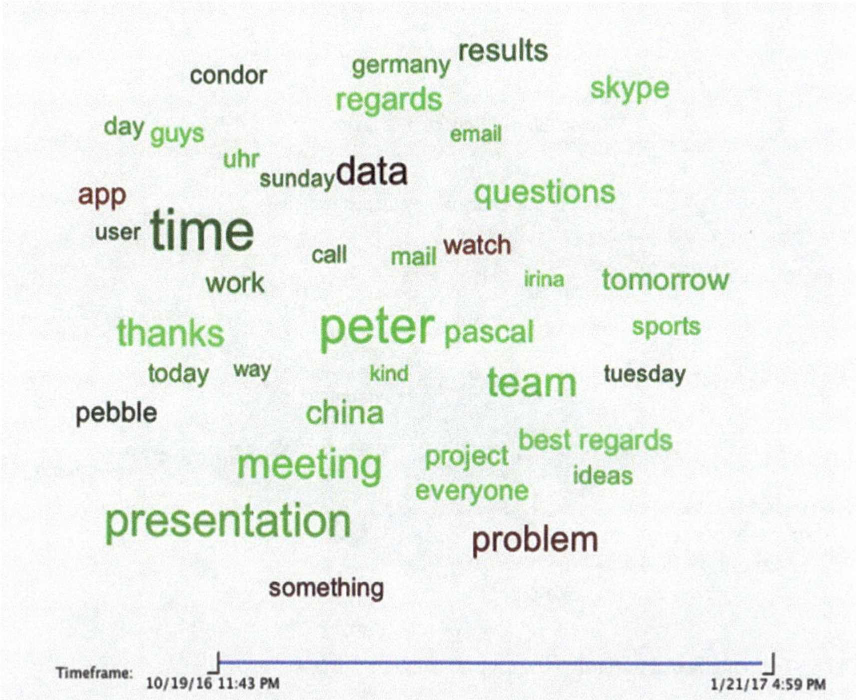

Fig. 4 Social network of class, node size by influence

meeting, where again Peter is exchanging e-mails with many different students. After this initial phase, the communication becomes much more decentralized, with many different students assuming leadership roles, resulting in many smaller spikes over the rest of the course.

Figure 6 illustrates the contribution index, which shows how pro-active a participant is. Each dot in Fig. 6 is a person, the farther to the right a person is, the more she sends or receives e-mail messages. The higher up the person, the more she sends. If a dot is at the top ($y = 1$), she only sends e-mails, if she is at the bottom ($y = -1$), she only receives e-mails. The large red oval illustrates the same team 9 as discussed in Fig. 4. We find that the German students in team 9 (the green dots) are the most active participants in the course, sending the most e-mails. We also find that the yellow dots (the Chinese students) are more passive, as they are farther to the left, and farther down, than the German students, confirming our findings from the interviews.

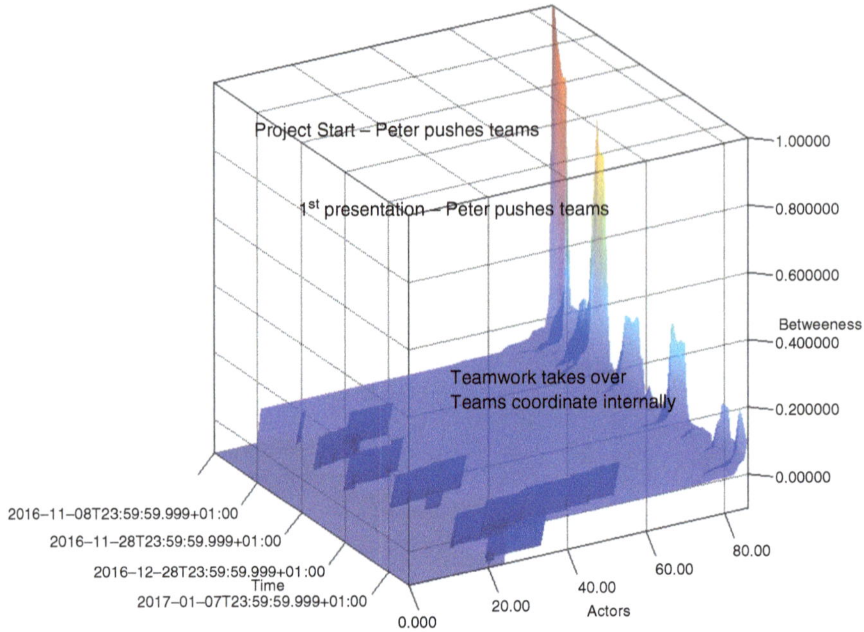

Fig. 5 Temporal Social Surface

6 Lessons Learned and Conclusion

While we still have much to improve, we found the existing COINs course framework robust enough to teach distributed virtual teamwork to participants from cultures as different as Germany and China. Table 1 below lists our key insights.

Even though we found that the Chinese students were more passive during the collaboration phase of the project, most of the Chinese students gave positive feedback about the course. Based on interviews with the students, they were attracted by the novelty of the framework of the course, which was totally new to them. First, most of the classes in Jilin University are given in Chinese, there are only 4% courses are given in English. Second, the university is collaborating with a large number of international universities. However, the students haven't gotten enough chances to work with international students yet. Thirdly, the students have never collaborated with another international university through virtual meetings. Finally, most of the Chinese students are used to sitting in a class and passively listening to the lecturers' presentation. The learning efficiency is very low. This teaching method requires the students to work together in a team, which drastically improved their productivity.

While the goals of the team projects were challenging, students were motivated to finish their assignments, as they did not want to "loose face". During the learning process, most of the Chinese students reported that they learned new behavior and

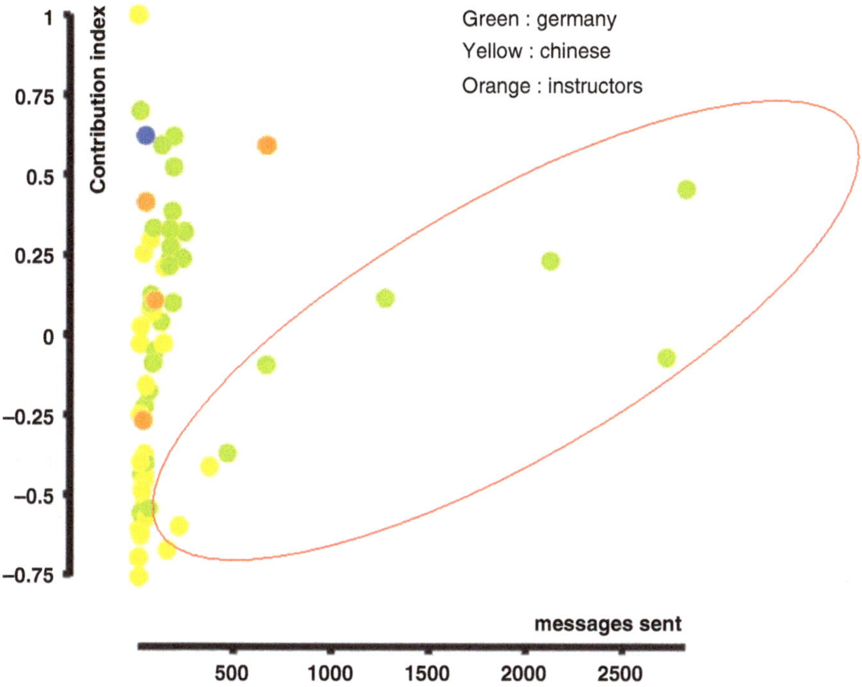

Fig. 6 Contribution index

Table 1 Key Lessons learned

Issue	Recommendation
English language skills	Make it crystal clear that English language skills are a prerequisite (particularly in China)
Passive work style of Chinese	Constantly encourage Chinese to ask questions and speak up
Long-distance project management	Encourage students to have clear deliverables for each milestone for each student
Self-organizing work style of Germans	Encourage them to allocate tasks to Chinese students
Non-aligned holidays	Encourage students to share their mutual holidays (e.g. Chinese New Year, Western New Year, Carnival in Cologne)
Not loosing face	Encourage students to ask questions and inform their peers about what they do not know
Attitude towards paper writing	Make it very clear the copying text from the Internet for the final paper is plagiarism.

processes never experienced before. First, as the course is based on international collaboration, Chinese students were forced to present to the whole group every other week through virtual meetings. To prepare their presentation, they needed to communicate with each other occasionally. Secondly, they learned a lot from the

German students such as their working attitude and time management. "It is a good opportunity for us to do a work with the students from a different cultural background although there are many challenges. We can learn many things from our teammates, such as the way of thesis writing. The students form Germany has high efficiency but are also a little stubborn...", according to Chinese student 3. Chinese students are used to be "assigned" and keep "silent". After experiencing the course, they became more critical than they used to be and started expressing their own opinions. Thirdly, most Chinese students are good at English exams rather than using English as a language for communication. The course provides students an opportunity to break the wall between Chinese and German students. They had to find a solution to communicate with each other first.

As for German students, they were surprised by the much more passive initial attitude of the Chinese students. As German behavior is more pro-active, they ended up assigning the team tasks to individuals and coordinating the projects. Also, as on average they had better English skills, they ended up writing most of the final papers. There were two main reasons why the Chinese students contributed very little to writing the final papers: (1) their English skills were not sufficient to write a scientific paper, and (2) they did not get enough credit from their university to invest large amounts of time into writing the final papers.

While the German students expressed some frustration, their overall assessment was quite positive, as they reported a unique experience not possible otherwise. To close with a quote from a German student: "Overall, the project was an amazing experience, and over long periods of teamwork we had a lot of fun interacting with our Chinese colleagues."—German student 2.

In response to what we have learned from the fall semester course described in this paper, we improved our teaching methodology in the spring semester for both Chinese and German students. In the new COINs course, the local instructor asked the Chinese students to take the initiative in the team meetings. The preliminary results show that the Chinese students can be more active when being guided. The quality of team communication has also been improved. The local lecturer has reported to the university to change the general regulation so the Chinese students can be motivated to take a more active part in the team projects in the future. We therefore think that this course framework provides a unique learning environment to both students from East and West.

References

Connaughton, S. L., & Marissa, S. (2007). Multinational and multicultural distributed teams: A review and future agenda. *Small Group Research, 38*(3), 387–412.

Creswell, J. W., Plano Clark, V. L., Gutmann, M. L., & Hanson, W. E. (2003). Advanced mixed methods research designs. In A. Tashakkori & C. Teddlie (Eds.), *Handbook on mixed methods in the behavioral and social sciences* (pp. 209–240). Thousand Oaks, CA: Sage.

Gloor, P. A. (2017). *Sociometrics and human relationships: Analyzing social networks to manage brands, predict trends, and improve organizational performance*. Bingley: Emerald.

Gloor, P. A., Paasivaara, M. (2013). COINs change leaders – Lessons learned from a distributed course. In *Proceedings of the 4th International Conference on Collaborative Innovation Networks COINs 2013*, August, 11–13, Santiago de Chile.

Gloor, P. A., Paasivaara, M., Miller, C., & Lassenius, C. (2016). Lessons from the collaborative innovation networks seminar. *International Journal of Organisational Design and Engineering, 4*(1/2), 3–25.

Krishna, S., Sahay, S., & Walsham, G. (2004). Managing cross-cultural issues in global software outsourcing. *Communications of the ACM, 47*(4), 62–66.

Nicholson, B., & Sahay, S. (2001). Some political and cultural issues in the globalisation of software development: Case experience from Britain and India. *Information and Organization, 11*, 25–43.

Ochieng, E. G., & Price, A. D. F. (2010). Managing cross-cultural communication in multicultural construction project teams: The case of Kenya and UK. *International Journal of Project Management, 28*(5), 449–460.

Stahl, G. K., Maznevski, M. L., Voigt, A., & Jonsen, K. (2010). Unraveling the effects of cultural diversity in teams: A meta-analysis of research on multicultural work groups. *Journal of International Business Studies, 41*(4), 690–709.

Part II
Healthcare

Dynamically Adapting the Environment for Elderly People Through Smartwatch-Based Mood Detection

Antonio Capodieci, Pascal Budner, Joscha Eirich, Peter Gloor, and Luca Mainetti

Abstract The ageing population and age-related diseases are some of the most urgent challenges in healthcare. This leads to an increasing demand in innovative solutions to afford a healthy and safe lifestyle to the elderly. Towards this goal, the City4Age project, funded by the Horizon 2020 Programme of the European Commission, focuses on IoT-based personal data capture, supporting smart cities to empower social/health services. This paper describes the combination of the smartwatch-based Happimeter with City4Age data capture technology. Through measuring the mood of the wearer of the smartwatch, a signal is transmitted to the Philips Hue platform, enabling mood-controlled lighting. Philips Hue allows the wireless remote control of energy-efficient LED light bulbs. Thus, measuring the mood through the Happimeter, the living environment for elderly people can be dynamically adapted. We anticipate that by changing colors and brightness of light bulbs using the Philips Hue platform, their quality of life can be improved. A validation test will be done in the context of the City4Age project, involving 31 elderly people living in a Southern Italian city.

A. Capodieci (✉) · L. Mainetti
Università del Salento, Lecce, Italy
e-mail: antonio.capodieci@unisalento.it; luca.mainetti@unisalento.it

P. Budner
University of Cologne, Cologne, Germany
e-mail: pbudner@smail.uni-koeln.de

J. Eirich
University of Bamberg, Bamberg, Germany
e-mail: joscha-friedrich.eirich@stud.uni-bamberg.de

P. Gloor
MIT, Cambridge, MA, USA
e-mail: pgloor@mit.edu

F. Grippa et al. (eds.), *Collaborative Innovation Networks*, Studies on Entrepreneurship, Structural Change and Industrial Dynamics,
https://doi.org/10.1007/978-3-319-74295-3_6

1 Introduction

The early detection of risks related to a specific health condition can help clinicians to enact appropriate interventions that can slow down the progression of the condition, with beneficial effects on both patients' quality of life and treatment costs. A disease, which is diagnosed late, in addition to decreasing the chance of recovery, also increases the cost of treatments borne by the community. In this work we try to avoid diseases by detection depression and emerging pain early, tracking the mood of elderly people, and initiate action if the mood drops.

Mood is very important for the health of a person (Mainetti et al. 2016a, b). Light intensity and color affect and alter the mood (Gloor 2017) and reduce or even avoid depression altogether. In addition there exists a ripple effect of positive emotional contagion, where group members experience improved cooperation, decreased conflict, and increase perceived task performance (Olguin et al. 2009).

The goal of this paper is to present a work in progress in the context of the City4Age research project (assisted ambient living for elderly people), and to describe how the MIT smartwatch-based Happimeter, by controlling the lighting environment (Philips Lamp Hue), might positively impact the mood of elderly people.

2 Research Context

2.1 The City4Age Project

City4Age—Elderly-friendly city services for active and healthy ageing, a project co-funded by the Horizon 2020 Programme of the European Commission, supports smart cities to empower social/health services for the elderly population. The City4Age (Mainetti et al. 2016b) project aims to use digital technologies (Mainetti et al. 2016a) at home and in the city to monitor behaviors of elderly people with the goal of improving their quality of life. By using a range of digital sensors, information concerning movements, locations, and activities will be recorded from participants and analyzed by a central engine to detect and predict behavioral patterns. Additionally, as a result of their behavioral pattern analysis, participants will receive interventions aimed at improving their behaviors. In the last few years, several projects funded by the European Union have dealt with the application of Information and Communication Technology (ICT) to capture personal and/or environmental data in order to derive behavioral patterns useful to prevent mental or physical diseases, like for example the Monarca project (Philips Hue n.d.) that deals with bipolar disorder. This approach is also adopted by the City4Age project that, different from other projects, proposes dynamic intervention technologies to record and observe behavioral changes.

2.2 The Measure Model of the City4Age Project

The City4Age project data model is based on the identification of indicators, currently used in geriatrics practice, that measure mild cognitive impairment (MCI) and frailty on the basis of behavior and human activities monitoring (Ricevuti et al. 2017). The project is based on two sets of measures defined in these domains, the Lawton Scale of Instrumental Activities of Daily Living (Gold 2012), and the SHARE-FI scale (Romero-Ortuno et al. 2010) that measures the "motility" domain by examining two items: (a) the capability to walk more than 100 m without difficulty and (b) the capability to climb one flight of stairs without difficulty. The geriatric team of the project selected a total of 19 geriatric factors (8 for MCI and 11 for frailty) comprising a total of 226 domains/items, from which it extracted the definition of 10 geriatric factors (GEFs), some of them further decomposed into a total of 43 geriatric sub-factors (GESs), classified in two main categories:

- Behavioral factors (6 GEFs and 28 GES, see Table 1): these are factors that can be directly related to the behavior of the person under monitoring and most of them can be measured (in principle) unobtrusively.
- Context and status factors (4 GEF and 15 GES, see Table 2): these are factors that relate to the context in which the person under monitoring lives as well as to her health status. Environment and Dependence GEFs can be normally measured "once for all", at the start of the process. The Health–Physical and Health–Cognitive GEFs can be measured more frequently, although unobtrusiveness may be an issue for some of them (Ricevuti et al. 2017).

In the context of the City4Age project, the Lecce pilot is focused on the relationship among activities performed in the home and activities performed in a "smart neighborhood", where the person lives. For more detailed information related to the adopted model see Ricevuti et al. in "Data driven MCI and frailty prevention: geriatric modelling in the City4Age project." (Ricevuti et al. 2017).

2.3 The Happimeter Project

The Happimeter is a novel device to instantaneously measure individual happiness (Gloor 2017). It uses commercially available smartwatches to build a body sensing system that can measure individual mood states and interactions between people. It consists of a Pebble smartwatch, and a smartphone app. The smartwatch is integrated with each user's smartphone to access the phone's location sensing and data transmission capacity, as well as its processing power. The smartwatches provide data on the body movement through accelerometer, lighting level and heart rate. Unlike sociometric badges, which we have used in earlier experiments (Olguin et al. 2009), the watches are designed to be worn constantly, naturally and non-intrusively, and their rechargeable batteries have robust charge length. Their

Table 1 City4Age behavioral factors

Geriatric factors	Geriatric sub-factors
Motility	Walking, climbing stairs, still/moving, moving across rooms, gait balance
Physical activity	n/a
Basic activities of daily living	Bathing and showering, dressing, self-feeding, personal grooming, toilet hygiene, going out
Instrumental activities of daily living	Ability to cook food, housekeeping, laundry, phone usage, new media communication, shopping, transportation, finance management, medication
Socialization	Paying/receiving visits, attending senior centers, attending other social places, going to restaurants
Cultural engagement	Visiting cultural or entertainment places, watching TV, reading newspapers, reading books

Table 2 City4Age context and status factor

Geriatric factors	Geriatric sub-factors
Environment	Quality of housing, quality of neighborhood
Dependence	n/a
Health—Physical	Falls, weight, weakness, exhaustion, pain, appetite, quality of sleep, visits to doctors, visit to health related places
Health—Cognitive	Abstraction, attention, memory, mood

displays also enable easy two-way communication to give status updates to wearers (Fig. 1).

The Pebble Happimeter app is extended with a smartphone Happimeter app for iPhone and Android, which provides additional information on individual and group mood state (Fig. 2).

With the "Happimeter", users are able to track how they feel and how happy they are for extended periods of time. Through machine learning algorithms, they will get regular reports with insights about their happiness as well as the factors that influenced the happiness. We use this sensing system to track work group mood/interactions. To increase accuracy of the prediction model, users can also do a standardized personality test (Neo-FFI) to learn about their personality characteristics, and further increase the precision of the Happimeter.

2.4 Philips Hue Lighting System

Philips Hue (n.d.) is a wireless home lighting system, based on LED lights, which enables users to create and control, remotely over WI-FI, the lights using their mobile smart device. Philips Hue was launched by Philips in 2012 and now is at the second

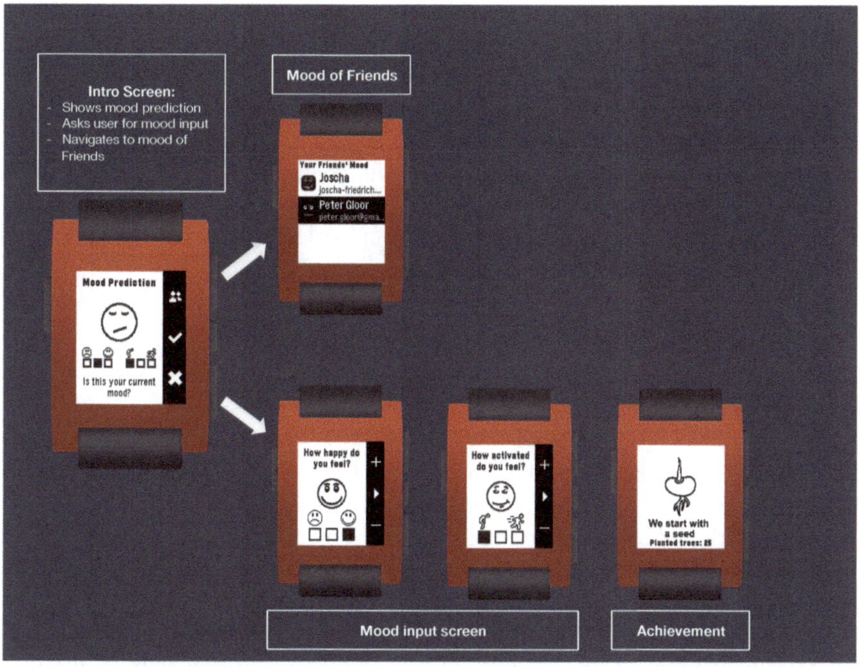

Fig. 1 Pebble Smartwatch user interface

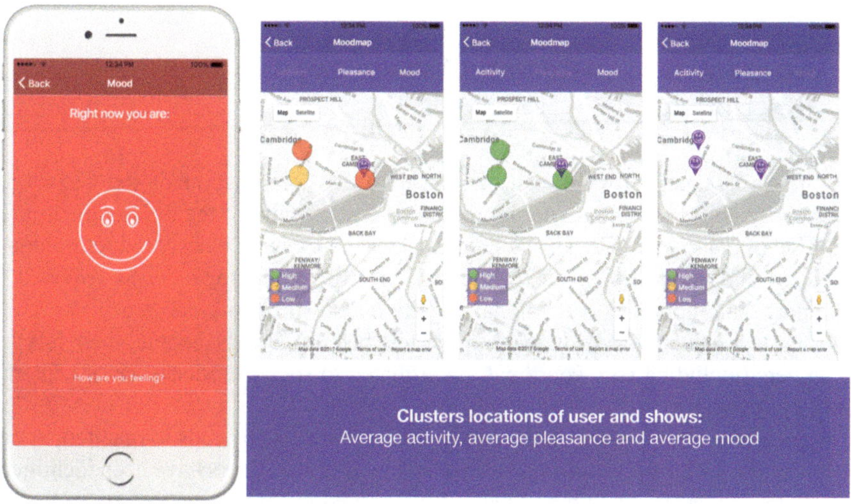

Fig. 2 Happimeter smartphone app user interface

version. The system is based on three main components: The Lights—smart bulbs containing three types of LED able to produce a wide range of colors and intensities. Lights Bulbs are connected to a bridge via an open standards protocol called ZigBee (ZigBee Alliance, n.d.). It's possible to create a mesh network, between the bulbs, extending the range and making the system more interactive. The Bridge is a device used to enable smart bulbs to communicate with controllers as well as other smart bulbs. A set of APIs is offered by the Bridge. These allow users to control all settings of the lights. These APIs are accessible only from local networks. The Portal is a web based control panel, which connects the Bridge to the Internet.

2.5 Privacy Issues

One of the key aspects of the Internet of Things is its impact on privacy (De Montjoye et al. 2013; Langheinrich 2001). In a world of smart communication and computation devices, everything we say, do, and sometimes feel, can be digitized, stored, and tracked. This calls for systems to be designed to require users to explicitly agree before taking privacy-decreasing actions (Neustaedter and Greenberg 2003). To protect the privacy of participants (Butler 2007), we designed our system to preserve anonymity, we also inform the participants of the data collected in the platform, and educate them on how the system works.

3 Adapting the Environment System and Test Bed Description

The goal of our experiment is to demonstrate the combination of the City4Age technology with the Happimeter by monitoring and adapting the environment of a small set of elderly people. This will be achieved by tracking elderly indoor/outdoor activities and mood, with the use of unobtrusive technologies, and requesting voluntary data input and professional cognitive assessing tools.

The main stakeholders involved in the test bed are elderly people, their formal caregivers (including care coordinators) affiliated to social services, senior centers, and city services.

The elderly person is the main actor in this scenario, who needs to maintain good physical self-sufficiency and an active social engagement. Users have been identified among those who frequent the social centers offered to seniors by the City of Lecce and willing to participate in our experiment. The sample is composed of 31 seniors: 11 males and 20 females, they are 70+ years old and they are in good physical condition, moving independently and frequently attending the social centers to facilitate progress monitoring. They have been selected because of their pre-medical frailty, particularly cognitive-functional, to include a segment of the population otherwise not addressed by public services. 45% of the sample is made up of pairs of husband and wife (7 couples) to analyze gender differences. In order to monitor citizens' movements, we chose people who reside in two different city districts.

During the experiment we will interact continuously with the seniors and their caregivers. They must feel the protagonists of the experiment and together we will reflect on the potential benefits that the experiment can give to them and to others close to them. Overall for seniors feeling useful can be a very important motivational lever.

The goal is to detect user behavior and mood both in indoor and outdoor environments, and to adapt their environment (mainly indoor) based on the predicted mood. Elderly users will be provided with a smartphone and a smartwatch with heart rate device. Moreover, their homes will be equipped with a complete kit of the Phips Hue Light system and beacon based indoor positioning infrastructure and some smart plugs to detect the usage of appliances (like TV and washing machine). In the city environment, beacons and smartphone GPS receivers will be used to detect elderly people's outdoor mobility.

Based on the feedback received from the Happimeter, the Philips Hue system will change the value of colors and brightness of the light. For example, if the mood is low the light bulbs might emit a soft and relaxing light.

In Fig. 3 we show the logical architecture of the system (on the left) and a photo of the prototype environment (on the right). The smartphone collects the information from the City4Age platform and other IoT devices (beacons, accelerometers, gyroscopes), such as the smartwatch with the heartrate module. The information is sent to the Happimeter platform that answers with the mood prediction. Based on mood prediction the smartphone dynamically changes the hue and intensity of the light bulbs. As we do not anticipate that the seniors will be able to train the individual happiness models, we will employ the generic preconfigured model to track their happiness. A researcher will visit each senior two times per week to check in on the system, and assist the elderly person in recharging the device. The hue system will be programmed to reflect the mood of the wearer, through adapting the warmth and intensity of the light. The color will change from cold white to yellowish warm white, based on the mood, while the intensity will change from dimmed light at low activity to very bright light at high activity.

A possible barrier to participation is related to the usability of the device. Small buttons and screens can be an insurmountable barrier for those who do not have a high degree of manual abilities and precision. For this reason, we are considering implementing a device with a speech recognition interface capable of understanding spoken language.

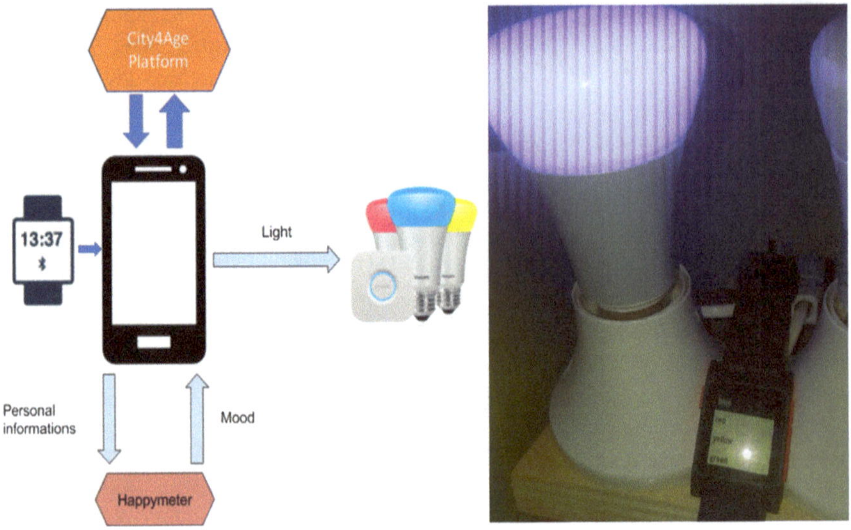

Fig. 3 Logical architecture (left)—A photo of the prototype environment (right)

4 Conclusion and Expected Results

In this paper we presented a research project in progress based on the idea of integrating two different running projects: City4Age—which utilizes data from smart cities and ad-hoc sensors for the prevention of mild cognitive impairment and frailty of aged people, detecting behavior changes and intervening on it—and the "Happimeter" project—a combined hardware and software technology to predict the individual mood based on body sensors. As first integrated prototype has been implemented, demonstrating that exploiting such technologies it is possible to dynamically adapt the living environment to a user's mood, making it more comfortable. This way we intend to improve the quality of life of elderly people with the long-term goal of unobtrusively stimulating behavior changes.

Our next research steps will be focused on defining and implementing more sophisticated intervention strategies on the user's living environment, interacting with it through sensors/actuators. We are also interested in experimenting with our prototypes and learning from actual users who participate in Lecce's City4Age test bed.

Acknowledgments This work is supported by the City4Age project funding from European Union's Horizon 2020 research and innovation programme under the grant agreement No 689731, and by Philips Lighting as part of an overall MIT research grant. Special thanks to Paolo Panarese for his contribution in developing the test prototype.

References

Butler, D. (2007). Data sharing threatens privacy. *Nature, 449*, 644–645. https://doi.org/10.1038/449644a

De Montjoye, Y. A., Hidalgo, C. A., Verleysen, M., & Blondel, V. D. (2013). Unique in the crowd: The privacy bounds of human mobility. *Scientific Reports, 3*. https://doi.org/10.1038/srep01376

Gloor, P. (2017). *Consistent excitement correlates with happiness – Predicting mood through body sensing with smartwatches*. Retrieved from http://www.ickn.org/documents/Mood_Tracking_Smartwatch.pdf

Gold, D. A. (2012). An examination of instrumental activities of daily living assessment in older adults and mild cognitive impairment. *Journal of Clinical and Experimental Neuropsychology, 34*(1), 11–34. https://doi.org/10.1080/13803395.2011.614598

Langheinrich, M. (2001). Privacy by design—principles of privacy-aware ubiquitous systems. *Ubicomp 2001: Ubiquitous Computing*, 273–291. https://doi.org/10.1007/3-540-45427-6_23

Mainetti, L., Patrono, L., & Rametta, P. (2016a). Capturing behavioral changes of elderly people through unobtruisive sensing technologies. In *2016 24th International Conference on Software, Telecommunications and Computer Networks (SoftCOM)*. https://doi.org/10.1109/SOFTCOM.2016.7772126

Mainetti, L., Manco, L., Patrono, L., Secco, A., Sergi, I., & Vergallo, R. (2016b). An ambient assisted living system for elderly assistance applications. In *2016 I.E. 27th Annual International Symposium on Personal, Indoor, and Mobile Radio Communications (PIMRC)*. https://doi.org/10.1109/PIMRC.2016.7794963

Neustaedter, C., & Greenberg, S. (2003). The design of a context-aware home media space for balancing privacy and awareness. *UbiComp 2003: Ubiquitous Computing*, 297–314. https://doi.org/10.1007/978-3-540-39653-6_24

Olguin, O., Gloor, P. A., & Pentland, A. (2009). Wearable sensors for pervasive healthcare management. *Proceedings of the IEEE, 66*, 1–4. https://doi.org/10.4108/ICST.PERVASIVEHEALTH2009.6033

Philips Hue. (n.d.). Retrieved May 20, 2017, from http://www.meethue.com

Ricevuti, G., Venturini, L., Copelli, S., Mercalli, F., & Nicolardi, G. (2017). Data driven MCI and frailty prevention: Geriatric modelling in the City4Age project. In *2017 I.E. 3rd International Forum on Research and Technologies for Society and Industry (RTSI)* (pp. 1–6). https://doi.org/10.1109/RTSI.2017.8065932

Romero-Ortuno, R., Walsh, C. D., Lawlor, B. A., & Kenny, R. A. (2010). A frailty instrument for primary care: Findings from the survey of health, ageing and retirement in Europe (SHARE). *BMC Geriatrics, 10*(1), 57. https://doi.org/10.1186/1471-2318-10-57

ZigBee Alliance. (n.d.). Retrieved May 20, 2017, from http://www.zigbee.org/

Creating Collaborative Innovation Networks (COINs) to Reduce Infant Mortality

Peter A. Gloor and Francesca Grippa

Abstract This case study illustrates the growth process of a collaborative innovation network in healthcare. It tracks e-mail communication of COIN members through a method we call "virtual mirroring", and measures the online perception of the topics of the COIN by coolhunting on social media such as Twitter and blogs. It also describes how the COIN members through "coolfarming" self-organize and identify new sub-topics for their work. In particular, the paper describes the growth process of the US Department of Health and Human Services Infant Mortality CoIIN (Collaborative Improvement and Innovation Network), applying both improvement and innovation concepts to reducing infant mortality among disadvantaged families in the US.

1 Introduction

Collaborative Innovation Networks (COINs) are self-organizing groups of intrinsically motivated people who get together to create something radically new (Gloor 2006). While they occasionally meet face-to-face, they mostly collaborate over the Internet to innovate and change the world. In this case study we illustrate the COIN creation and growth process by studying both the e-mail communication among COIN team members and the popularity of COIN-related concepts on social media. In particular, we demonstrate the use of e-mail based social network analysis and virtual mirroring to measure and support the growth of the IM-CoIIN project of the Maternal and Child Health Bureau (MCHB) of the US Health Resource Administration (HRSA). "IM-CoIIN" stands for "Infant Mortality reduction Collaborative

P. A. Gloor
MIT Sloan Center for Collective Intelligence, Cambridge, MA, USA
e-mail: pgloor@mit.edu

F. Grippa (✉)
Northeastern University, Boston, MA, USA
e-mail: f.grippa@northeastern.edu

F. Grippa et al. (eds.), *Collaborative Innovation Networks*, Studies on Entrepreneurship, Structural Change and Industrial Dynamics,
https://doi.org/10.1007/978-3-319-74295-3_7

Improvement and Innovation Network". It is defined as "a multiyear national movement engaging federal, state and local leaders, public and private agencies, professionals, and communities to employ quality improvement, innovation and collaborative learning to reduce infant mortality and improve birth outcomes". The project was started in 2012, and will be completed in 2017 and is active in all states of the US. The CoIIN as envisioned by the MCHB Associate Administrator combines both improvement and innovation concepts. For the improvement part IM-CoIIN applies the IHI breakthrough model (IHI2003), which brings together healthcare practitioners to 1–2 day learning sessions, where they share their experiences to learn from each other and improve their own healthcare processes. For innovation, IM-CoIIN is based on the COIN concept, trying to nurture breakthrough innovation in collaborative innovation networks.

As part of the IM-CoIIN, six sub-CoIINs were created: the first CoIIN has been working on improving safe sleep practices for babies. The second CoIIN is trying to get smoking mothers to stop or at least reduce smoking before, during and after pregnancy. The third CoIIN focuses on improving women's health before, after and in between pregnancies. The fourth CoIIN works to improve social determinants of health (SDOH) and equity in birth outcomes. The fifth CoIIN is trying to prevent births before 39 weeks. The sixth CoIIN works to increase the delivery of higher risk infants and mothers at appropriate level facilities.

In the remainder of this paper, we will first describe the e-mail based virtual mirroring process of the entire IM-CoIIN, then we will describe how we did coolhunting for SDOH related topics on online social media to get the innovation aspect of this sub-CoIIN started. Finally, we describe how we brought together small groups of innovators to coolfarming workshops to create new COINs around SDOH (Gloor 2011).

2 E-Mail Based Virtual Mirroring

Our first step was to apply a process of self-reflection that we call Virtual Mirroring, which has been associated with a positive impact on organizational performance (Gloor et al. 2010, 2017b). Virtual mirroring involves measuring communication patterns and mirroring the resulting social network variables back to the individual. In this study we conducted virtual mirroring sessions of seven key members of the SDOH community based on their e-mail archives from November 2014 to March 2016.

Similarly to feedback or learning sessions, which are commonly used in industrial and social psychology studies (Ramos 2007), our virtual mirroring process is a way to promote organizational awareness and change. In a recent study, (Gesell et al. 2013) presented social network analysis results to organizational leaders to support change management programs. The healthcare sector is also becoming increasingly interested in measuring information flows and team dynamics among physicians, nurses and other healthcare professionals. Grippa et al. (2012) involved three interdisciplinary care delivery teams in similar monthly learning sessions focused on social network-based results, which resulted in an increased awareness that informed decision making. Very recently, (Gloor et al. 2017a) involved leaders of 26 large accounts in monthly virtual mirroring sessions, where the communication characteristics of the teams working with clients were shared and discussed in plenary and individual sessions. In their study they measured the structure of the communication network, looking at who is interacting with whom, the average complexity of the vocabulary used, as well as the responsiveness of employees to customers' e-mails.

Another recent study (Gloor et al. 2017b) found that customer satisfaction increases after employees are involved in learning sessions to reflect on their own communication behaviors. In their study, the authors correlated employees' communication patterns with customer satisfaction and found that responsiveness, low oscillation of betweenness centrality, and complexity of communication are good predictors of customer satisfaction.

2.1 Virtual Mirroring: Dimensions and Metrics

The process of virtual mirroring relies on e-mail based social network analysis. We provided feedback to the IM-CoIIN community presenting them with results based on three dimensions: degree of connectivity, content sharing and degree of interactivity (Gloor 2006, p. 175). *Connectivity* refers to how well connected individuals are within their social network using indicators such as betweenness centrality and degree centrality (Wasserman and Faust 1994; Everett and Borgatti 2005). The second dimension, degree of *sharing*, describes the complexity of the language used based on the average difficulty of the words in each e-mail. Complexity is calculated as the likelihood distribution of words within an e-mail text, i.e. the probability of each word of a dictionary to appear in the text (Brönnimann 2014). The algorithm used to calculate complexity measures how common a word is in an individual message compared to the word's occurrence in the overall text collection; the more relatively rare words a message uses, the higher is the message's complexity. Beside complexity, we also extracted a *sentiment* indicator based on a multilingual classifier that uses a machine learning method trained on large datasets from Twitter (Brönnimann 2014). Finally, we included *emotionality* which is measured as standard deviation of sentiment: the more fluctuations in positivity and negativity an e-mail has, the more emotional it is.

The third dimension of our virtual mirroring model, *interactivity*, includes metrics such as contribution index and average response time (ART) of an actor to respond to a message. Contribution index is calculated as the frequency of sending and receiving messages: it is +1 if somebody only sends messages and does not receive any; it is −1 if somebody only receives messages; it is 0, if somebody sends and receives the same number of messages. The average response time (ART) indicates how fast an individual or a group responds to e-mails, offering some insights into the degree of "respect" and "passion" within the community. We also distinguished between "alter ART" and "ego ART". These metrics are part of the six honest signals of collaboration described in (Gloor 2016).

In other studies, we have been able to demonstrate that the faster other people respond to a person, the more they respect this person. For example, in a recent study on managerial turnover and online communication behavior (Gloor et al. 2017a), turnover is associated to e-mail responsiveness, mainly in terms of nudges shared with colleagues: the more frequently managers interact with others, the more central they and the more nudges they send and receive, the less likely they are to quit. This could be possibly explained with an increase in respect and political power that managers have acquired over time. In the same study, (Gloor et al. 2017a) found that language complexity was a good predictor of managerial turnover: managers who stay in their job tend to express themselves in a less emotional way, switching to a more emotional content over time as they approach the time they quit. These results are aligned with Pennebaker's research (Pennebaker et al. 2001; Pennebaker 2011) indicating that life-changing events influence the use of both positive and negative emotion words.

To measure collaboration among the IM-CoIIN members, we collected all IM-CoIIN related e-mails of seven key participants of the IM-CoIIN from September 2014 to March 2016 using the software tool Condor. We had shown in earlier work that having 14–18% of the mailboxes of a community was adequate to capture 90% of their e-mail traffic, thanks to community members who cc'ed each other (Zilli et al. 2006). Through this virtual mirror of seven key members of the community based on their e-mail archives we were able to give feedback to the entire community and come up with recommendations for improved collaboration.

2.2 *Virtual Mirroring Applied to the DSOH Community*

Figure 1 illustrates the overall e-mail activity of the community over the entire time period from September 2014 to March 2016. The community sent up to 3000 messages on the most active days, with an average of 500 messages per day, the weekends are clearly visible with much less traffic. The periods of intense communication and high activity are recognizable by slopes in the evolution of group betweenness centrality and high-density structure of the community. The spikes indicate the time right before a learning session, when the organization running the community (NICHQ, a Boston-based non-profit) reached out to health officials and administrators in the 52 US States inviting them to the learning sessions.

Figure 2 illustrates the average speed with which everybody within the community answers to e-mails sent by the seven owners of the mailboxes we collected. In this analysis, we found that alter ART started at an already respectable 25 hours, and has been decreasing to a quite fast 17 hours on average until an e-mail was answered. This means that mutual respect in this community has been going up clearly over the observation period of 18 months, showing a very positive sign of organizational health.

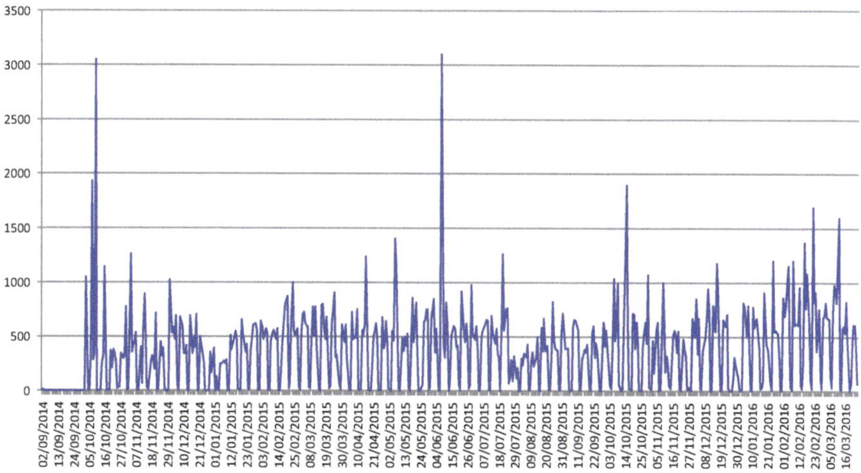

Fig. 1 Activity of e-mail from Sept 2014 to March 2016

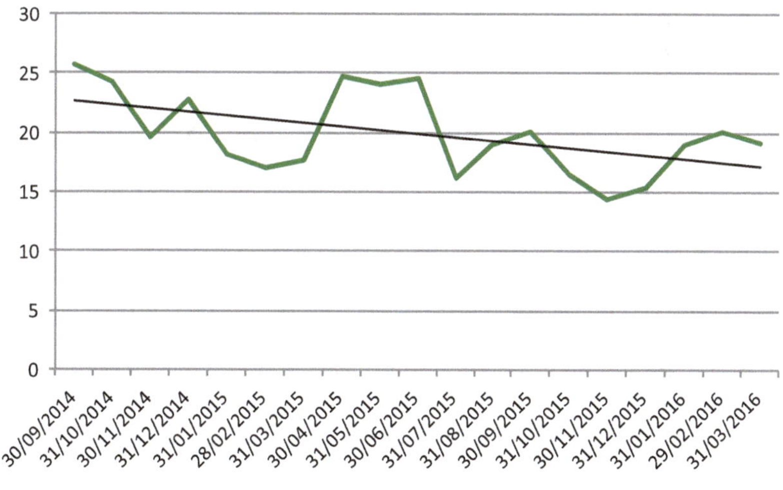

Fig. 2 Average response time of others to the mailbox owners (Alter ART)

Figure 3 illustrates the change of ego ART, which is defined as the speed with which the owner of a mailbox answers to everybody else (Gloor 2017a, b). The speed with which somebody answers to everybody else's e-mails is a proxy for the passion of the person. In this community, ego ART starts at below 20 h on average, and stays like that for the entire observation period. While we would have wished for an even stronger decrease in ego ART, what we can say is that passion is high to start with, and stays like that over the 18 months observation period.

Figure 4 illustrates the number of new contacts per person per month. A new contact is only counted if it has at least one e-mail exchange, this means that if person

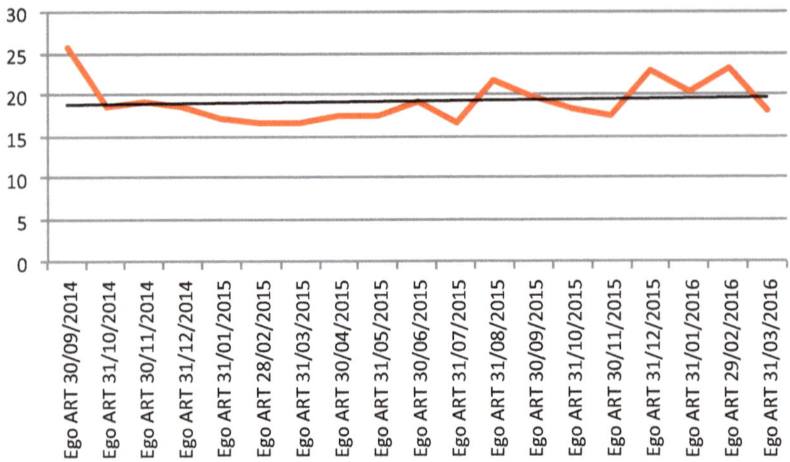

Fig. 3 Average response time of mailbox owners to all others (Ego ART)

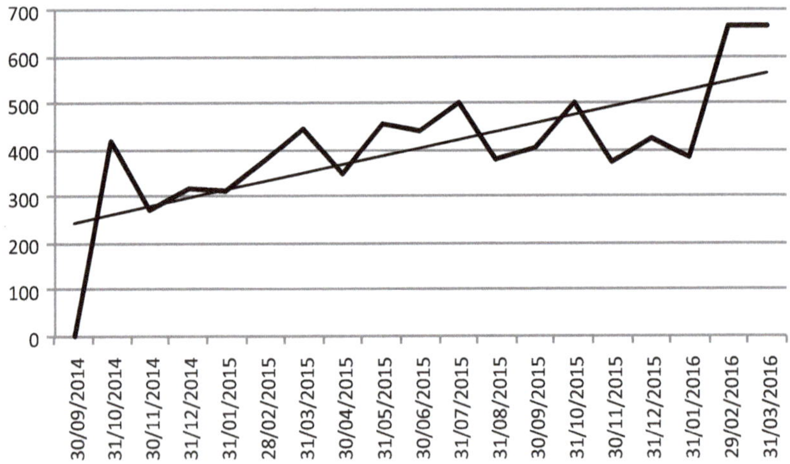

Fig. 4 Number of new e-mail contacts per month

A sends an e-mail to person B, B needs to respond to it. This exchange is included if person B appears for the first time in the analysis of the particular month. The number of new e-mail contacts is a good proxy for the growth dynamics of a community. Figure 4 tells us that growth per month more than doubled from on average 250 new community members to on average over 600 new community members per month at the end of the observation period. It illustrates the healthy growth of IM-CoIIN, which is confirmed in the real world, where participation in the learning sessions has been steadily going up.

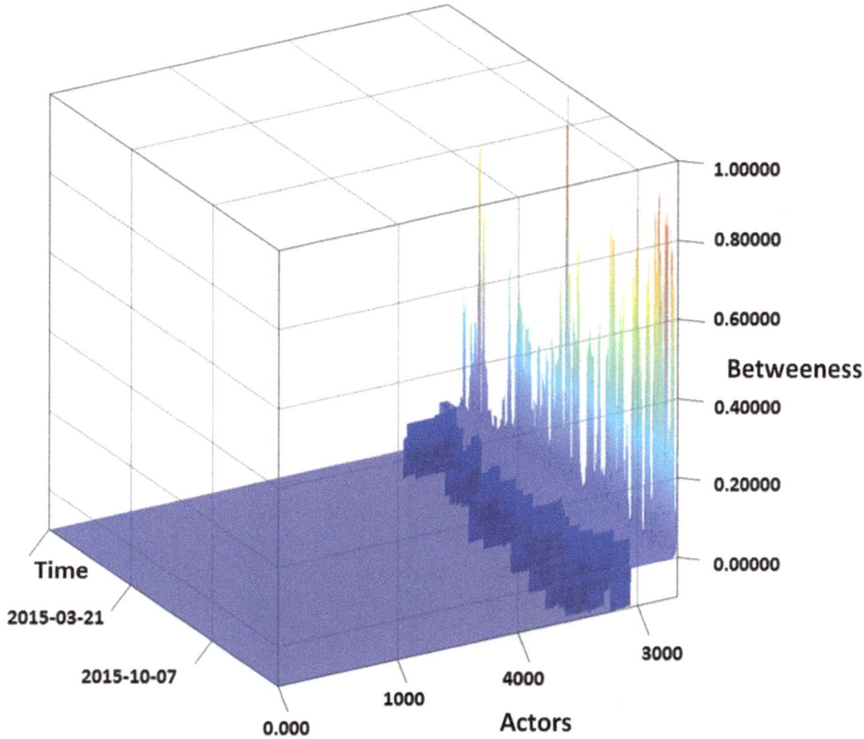

Fig. 5 Temporal social surface of combined mailboxes, a visualization of team creativity

Figure 5 shows the temporal social surface, which is a visual way to explore the creative capabilities of a community. The x-axis of Fig. 5 shows all actors involved, the y-axis shows time, from September 2014 at top left, to March 2016, at the bottom center. The z-axis shows betweenness centrality (Wasserman and Faust 1994) of each actor. The spikes at the rear of Fig. 5 display that a few people are always more central than the rest, exhibiting strong leadership. The growth pattern of Fig. 4 is again confirmed, in that the plateau, which shows the somewhat active participants, is growing over time. But we also see that the creativity of the entire community is relatively low, as the entire impression of Fig. 5 is one of a "calm sea", and not one of a "stormy ocean", which would indicate a lot of rotating leadership, which is a strong predictor of a creative community. The impression arising from this analysis is one of steady improvement, and not of radical innovation.

Figure 6 illustrates the social network structure of the entire e-mail network. Each dot is a person, each connecting line means that two people have at least exchanged one e-mail. The coloring by organization shows that the largest group of participants, not surprisingly, is from the US government from HRSA, followed by members of the non-profit organizations "March of Dimes" and NICHQ. The most central people

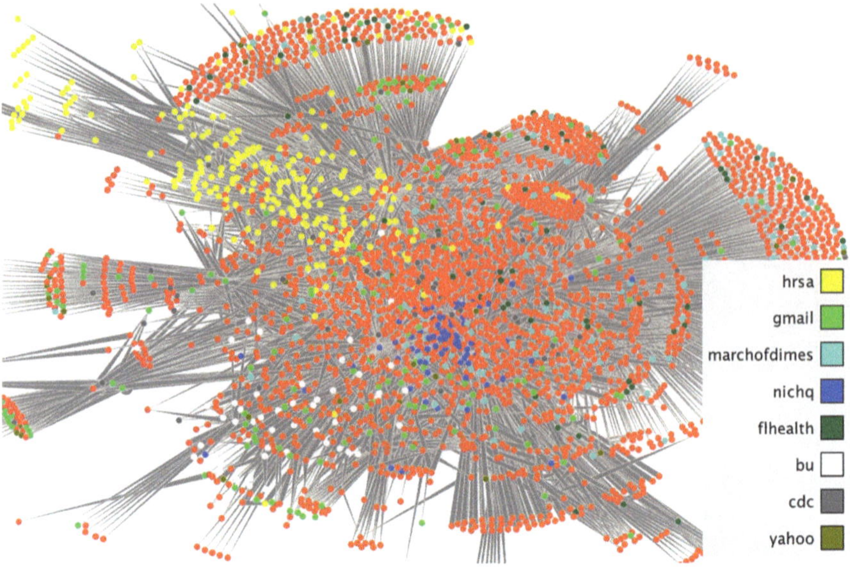

Fig. 6 E-mail social network of entire community (top 4000 users by communication frequency shown)

measured by betweenness centrality in Fig. 6 are the project coordinator from HRSA, as well as the project director from NICHQ.

Figure 7 shows the sentiment and activity over the observation period. We find that the sentiment is strongly positive, from 0.6 to 0.73. Sentiment of 0.5 is defined as neutral. This tells the observer that IM-CoIIN participants are very nice to each other, use positive language and give a lot of praise to each other. At the same time, the oscillation in sentiment also indicates that occasionally they are not shy of speaking out if something is not going as it should, which is a sign of an open and honest communication.

Figure 8 shows the word usage over time of the most frequently used words in the e-mails over the 18-month observation period. "Call" is the most popular word, used with increasing frequency over time, which tells us that setting up calls among participants is the most important activity of the IM-CoIIN. Somewhat surprising, the use of the word "infant" is going down over time. "Learning" is peaking beginning of 2015, when a face-to-face learning session was organized. The term "SDOH" (social determinants of health) is becoming somewhat more popular, as a COIN around this concept is developing. Overall, it emerges a picture of a community focused mostly on execution, indicated through usage of the term "call", surfaces, with a smaller focus on innovation, indicated through the term "SDOH".

To resume this analysis, through analyzing the e-mail communication of the IM-CoIIN community, we have been able to gain deep insights into the inner workings and knowledge flow of the community. We find that the community is

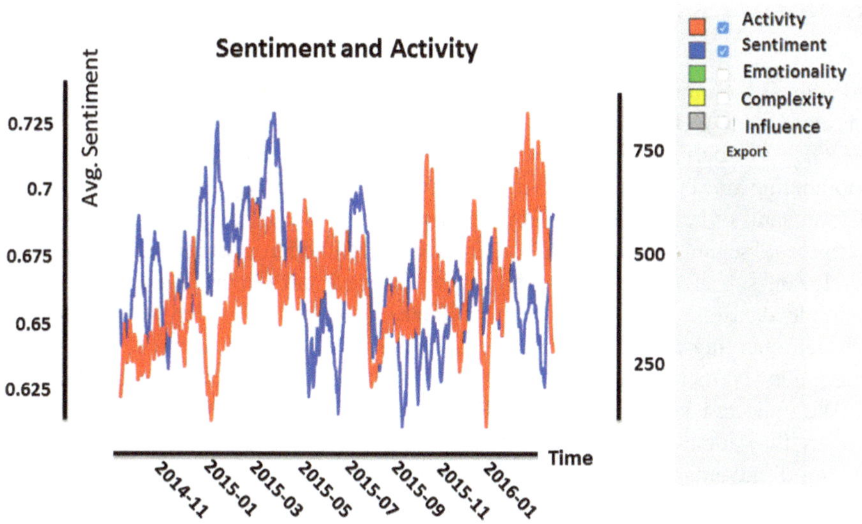

Fig. 7 Sentiment and activity of e-mail from Sept. 2014 to March 2016

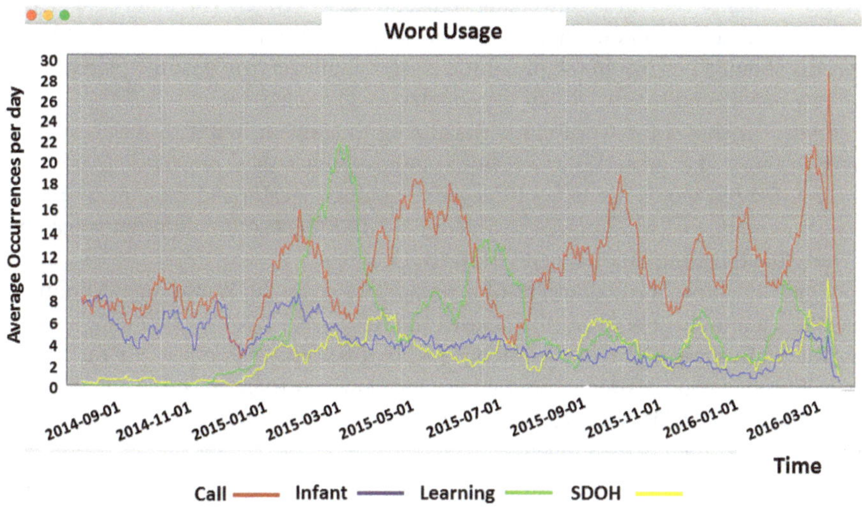

Fig. 8 Key concepts over time

showing healthy growth, and community members are treating each other with passion and respect. However, we also find that the community is focusing mostly on improvement, with the innovation component of the CoIIN somewhat lagging behind.

3 SDOH Coolhunting

To address the innovation aspect in IM-CoIIN, project leadership decided to set up an innovation COIN (with one "I") focused on social determinants of health (SDOH). As part of helping to get the SDOH COIN started, we conducted a coolhunting on Twitter and on the Web to identify the key terms around social determinants of health, and to collect innovative new ideas. Coolhunting is based on a degree-of-separation search that allows to quickly find the most influential nodes in a relevant subset of the Web (Marcos de Oliveira and Gloor 2016). Combining multiple datasets, each containing the degree of-separation Web sites collected through querying a search engine for the name of one search term (SDOH in our case), allowed us to find the most central node in a group of stars (Gloor 2006).

We collected key words from SDOH experts who are part of the IM-CoIIN. Topics they identified were to "reduce poverty", increase the "graduation rate" among disadvantaged teenagers, increase the "minimum wage", and increase general "happiness". Figure 9 shows the results of our coolhunting using Condor for these search terms on Twitter (Gloor 2017a, b). The Twitter network picture in Condor measures the importance of search terms through their betweenness centrality in the bipartite graph. Each node except the search term is a Twitter user, each connecting line means that the user is tweeting about the term, or is mentioned in a tweet by another user, or is retweeting somebody else's tweet. The main conclusion in Fig. 9 is that "minimum wage" is the most important term, while SDOH is rarely tweeted about, as shown in the pink little cluster at the very right of the picture, and the low betweenness centrality in the comparative bar chart.

Figure 10 shows the word cloud illustrating the key attributes of the four main search terms. The green color of words indicates that they are used in positive context, the red words are using in negative context. Health and happiness are the most important, and most positive words in our Twitter search, minimum wage and poverty the most important negative words.

Figure 11 shows the occurrence of the search terms on the World map. Minimum wage is a big topic in both North America and in Europe, however graduation is not an issue in Europe, where education is basically free. The Irish union SIPTU comes up in Europe, as it is talking about a raise in minimum wage in Ireland considered insufficient by SIPTU. In Asia the "harvesting happiness" talk radio show of host Lisa Cypers Kamen is mentioned.

Figure 12 illustrates an identical search done on the Web for the same search terms. Minimum wage is again the biggest topic, but social determinants of health are more popular on the Web than they are on Twitter. This is most likely because SDOH is a relatively complex topic, which is better explained in blog posts than in the 140 characters of Twitter. We can also identify the most important newsfeeds about these topics, such as PBS and NPR, and the Robert Wood Johnson Foundation.

Figure 13 shows the most important attributes related to the search terms. The context seems more positive, as more words are in green. The words are also more

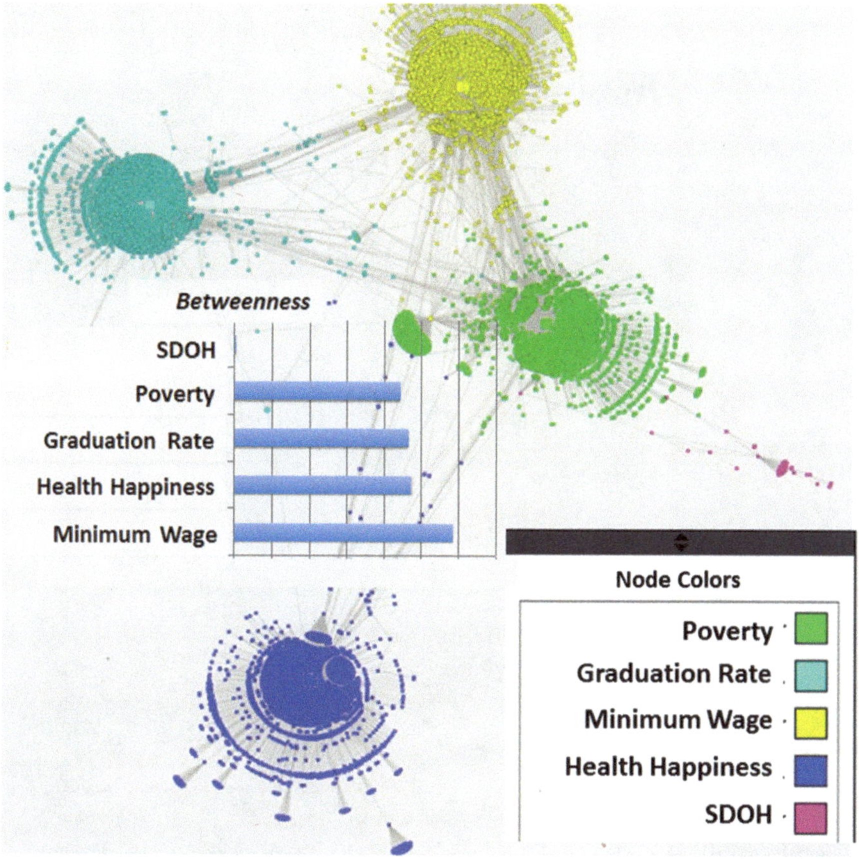

Fig. 9 Twitter coolhunting results for SDOH

factual and less emotional, such as "education", "news", "resources", and "information". What stands out is the "state of Texas".

Based on the insights from this coolhunting, it was decided to invite a small group of IM-CoIIN members passionate about SDOH to coolfarming workshops, to meet for half a day before a learning session and brainstorm innovative ideas to create new COINs.

4 Creating New COINs

We conducted two half-day workshops with the goal to create new COINs to reduce infant mortality, tackling social determinants of health as a new initiative. The goal was to reach out to innovative people with far out ideas, who were interested in

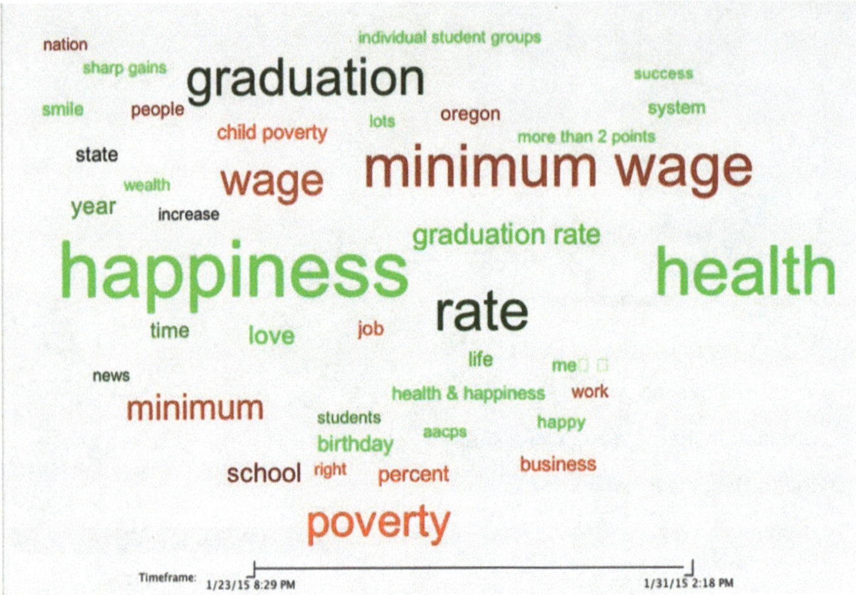

Fig. 10 Coolhunting results for all SDOH related terms on Twitter

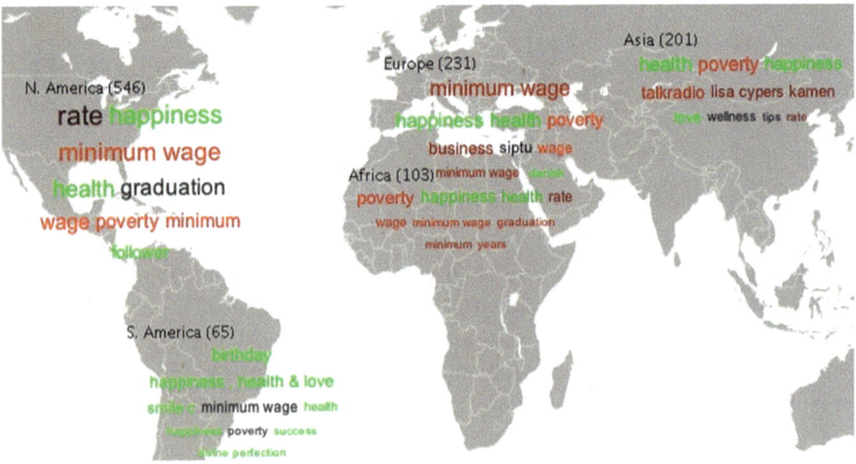

Fig. 11 Global distribution of coolhunting results for SDOH on Twitter

developing them further and recruit a team to work with turning their ideas into a first prototype. Figure 14 describes the full COIN creation process. At the beginning a small group of enthusiasts gets together for an initial brainstorming workshop, where the topics of the COIN are defined. Such an initial design workshop to create a new COIN follows a six-step process. In the first step workshop participants are

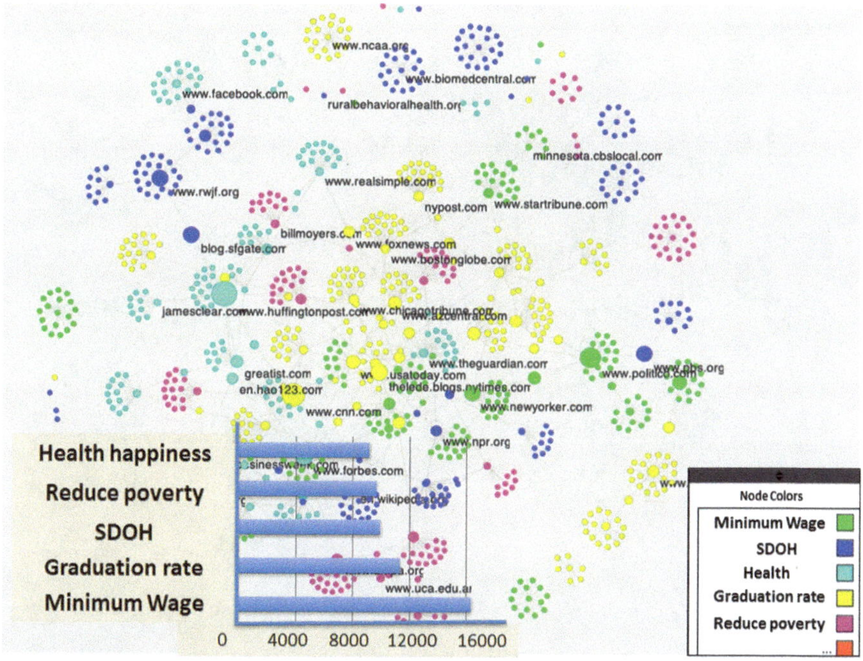

Fig. 12 Key search terms and Web sites about SDOH on the Web

familiarized with key COIN concepts such as rotating leadership and balanced contribution. In the second step, inspirational leaders—who have solved similar problems in other areas—are invited to present their approach and get the creative thinking of participants going. During step three of the COIN creation process, participants list and select the topics they would like to turn into products of COINs. Step four consists of the creation of small groups around each topic for a COIN, working on developing a vision for their COIN. Once they have defined the vision, step five requires participants to map out an action plan. In the final, sixth step COIN members do a "waggle dance", developing a marketing plan to recruit additional outside COIN members.

Not all topics at the workshop will become successful COINs. COINs with passionate leaders will recruit more members for their COIN, and do an in-depth coolhunting to learn what's already out there and available. They will set up regular meetings, do more coolhunting, set up a Website, advertise their COIN, and grow the community. As the community grows, other communities get created as a product of the COINs members' "waggle dance". Gloor (2006) found that through the application of social analysis, it is possible to recognize two types of these networks: Collaborative Interest Network (CIN) and Collaborative Learning Networks (CLN). Members of a CLN share a common interest, knowledge and a practice, being motivated to join the network by a desire to learn from each other. Members of

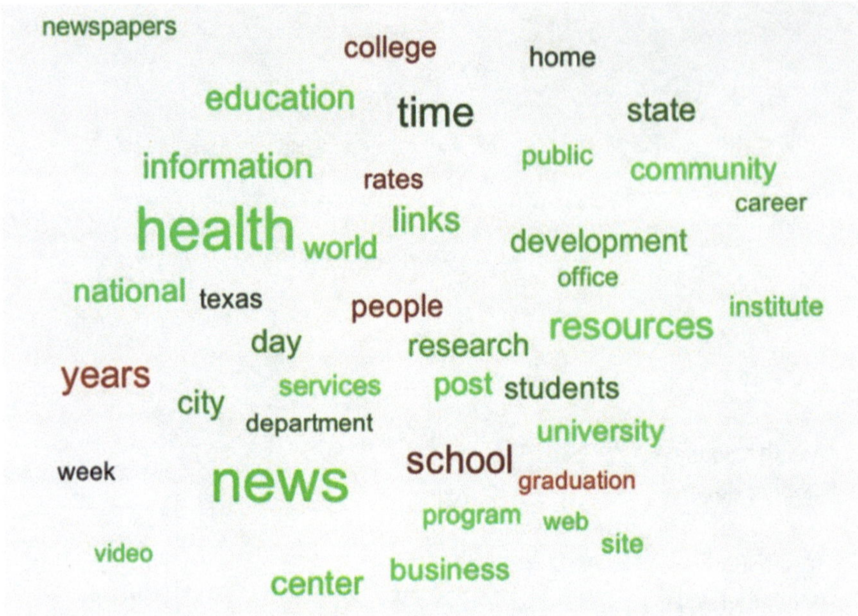

Fig. 13 Coolhunting results for all SDOH related terms on the Web

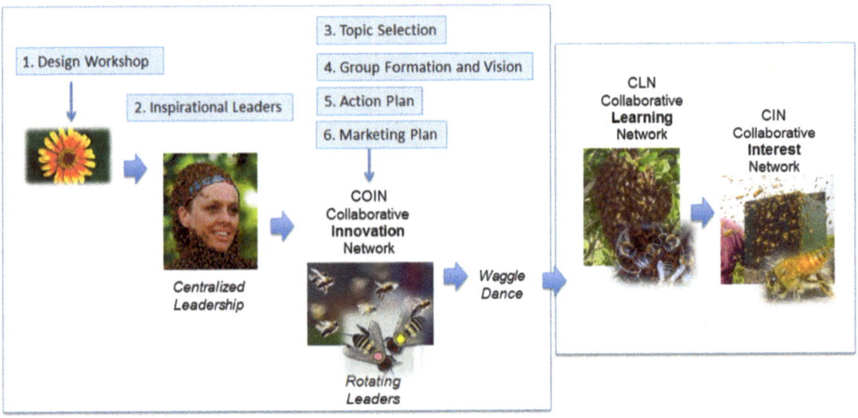

Fig. 14 Coolfarming and COIN creation process

CIN have similar interests, without necessarily working together. Both CLN and CIN tend to be characterized by specific network properties, such as lower density and high group centrality, since external members are mainly connected to core members, but not among themselves.

Collaborative Interest Networks and Collaborative Learning Networks are created through the same waggle dance and spreading of "attraction pheromones" that is at the basis of the creation of COINs. To continue with the metaphor, "*Coolhunter bees mark the location of the new hive by spraying it with attraction pheromone, such that the flying swarm of bees will find their goal irresistible as soon as they get close. At the same time, the coolhunting bees will direct the flying swarm by rapidly flying back and forth in the midst of the flying cloud of bees*" (Gloor et al. 2014, p. 12).

5 Discussion and Conclusion

In this paper we have illustrated the use of virtual mirroring, coolhunting, and coolfarming to create COINs. While our case study focused on the HRSA IM-CoIIN to reduce infant mortality in the US, this process is widely applicable. It has been applied in other healthcare environments, for instance for patients of chronic diseases as described in Grippa et al. (2012), but it has much wider applicability. COINs offer huge potential for any organization not afraid of creating an environment supportive of disruptive innovation.

The two workshops conducted at IM-CoIIN learning sessions led to the creation of a vibrant COIN on the impact of early childhood trauma inspired by the ACES (Adverse Childhood Experiences) study. Three more COINs, on Babybox for safe sleep (giving poor mothers a cushioned cardboard box as a baby bed), doulas (women trained to assist mothers at childbirth), and "Care Bundles" (groups of services provided to mothers on welfare) are in the process of being formed.

Through the application of a virtual mirroring process, we offered community members the opportunity to reflect on their communication styles. A longitudinal analysis of the e-mail communication patterns of the community "Social Determinants of Health" indicated an exponential growth in only a few months (150% more members). Over 16 months, there was an increase in both the degree of respect (reduced average response time) and passion (average response time of 20 h). By measuring sentiment, emotionality and complexity of the content exchanged via e-mail, we noticed that the community exchanged a creative, emotional, though positive response.

The application of the virtual mirroring to the SDOH community is based on extensive previous studies demonstrating how promoting self-awareness of people's communication style has the potential to induce behavior change and increase organizational effectiveness (Gloor et al. 2017b). This is aligned with the results of several studies on the effect of feedback sessions on individual, team and organizational performance (Ivancevich and McMahon 1982; Barr and Conlon 1994; Kluger and DeNisi 1996), which indicated that providing employees with the opportunity to reflect on their performance could enable positive behavioral change. Virtual mirroring sessions take this approach to a deeper level, by providing monthly description of individuals' communication patterns. This continuous mirroring process lets individuals receive timely and practical information about their communication patterns that can be used to improve their individual and community performance.

Besides reflecting on their own online communication, participants were offered the opportunity to visualize topics that were attracting the interest of the swarm. Through the Coolhunting process, community leaders were able to recognize the importance of themes that impacted infant mortality, such as reducing poverty, increasing the graduation rate among teenagers, increasing the minimum wage, and promoting general happiness. The process helped community leaders to identify important terms used by online users in various parts of the world, such as minimum wage and poverty. Creating new COINs and coolhunting for trends on the Web represent important methods to help design quality improvement initiatives. Similarly, virtual mirroring gave participants the ability to recognize the impact of their communication behavior, and to observe how their connections grew across and beyond the community boundaries.

References

Barr, S. H., & Conlon, E. J. (1994). Effects of distribution of feedback in work groups. *Academy of Management Journal, 37*, 641–655.

Brönnimann, L. (2014). *Analyse der Verbreitung von Innovationen in sozialen Netzwerken*. M.Sc. Thesis, University of Applied Sciences Northwestern Switzerland. See also http://swarmcreativity.blogspot.com/2014/03/how-to-measure-influence-in-social.html

Everett, M., & Borgatti, S. P. (2005). Ego network betweenness. *Social Networks, 27*(1), 31–38.

Gesell, S. B., Barkin, S. L., & Valente, T. W. (2013). Social network diagnostics: A tool for monitoring group interventions. *Implementation Science, 8*, 116.

Gloor, P. A. (2006). *Swarm creativity. Competitive advantage through collaborative innovation networks*. New York: Oxford University Press.

Gloor, P. A. (2011). *Coolfarming: Turn your great idea into the next big thing*. New York: AMACOM.

Gloor, P. A., Margolis, P., Seid, M., & Dellal, G. (2014). *Coolfarming – Lessons from the beehive to increase organizational creativity*. MIT Sloan School Working Paper No. 5123-14.

Gloor, P. (2016). What e-mail reveals about your organization. *MIT Sloan Management Review, 57* (2), 8.

Gloor, P. A. (2017a). *Sociometrics and human relationships: Analyzing social networks to manage brands, predict trends, and improve organizational performance*. Bingley: Emerald.

Gloor, P. A. (2017b). *Swarm leadership and the collective mind: Using collaborative innovation networks to build a better business*. Bingley: Emerald.

Gloor, P. A., Oster, D., Raz, O., Pentland, A., & Schoder, D. (2010). The virtual mirror: Reflecting on the social and psychological self to increase organizational creativity. *International Studies of Management & Organization, 40*(2), 74–94.

Gloor, P. A., Colladon, A. F., Grippa, F., & Giacomelli, G. (2017a). Forecasting managerial turnover through e-mail based social network analysis. *Computers in Human Behavior, 71*, 343–352.

Gloor, P., Colladon, A. F., Giacomelli, G., Saran, T., & Grippa, F. (2017b). The impact of virtual mirroring on customer satisfaction. *Journal of Business Research, 75*, 67–76. https://doi.org/10.1016/j.jbusres.2017.02.010

Grippa, F., Gloor, P. A., Bucuvalas, J. C., & Palazzolo, M. (2012). Supporting development efforts of clinical care teams. *International Journal of Organisational Design and Engineering, 2*(2), 149–166.

Ivancevich, J. M., & McMahon, J. T. (1982). The effects of goal setting, external feedback, self-generated feedback on outcome variables: A field experiment. *Academy of Management Journal, 25*(2), 359–372.

Kluger, A. N., & DeNisi, A. (1996). The effects of feedback interventions on performance. A historical review, a meta-analysis, and a preliminary feedback intervention theory. *Psychological Bulletin, 119*, 254–284.

Marcos de Oliveira, J., & Gloor, P. (2016). The citizen is the journalist: Automatically extracting news from the Swarm. In *Proceedings of the 6th International COINs Conference on Designing Networks for Innovation and Improvisation*, June 9–11, 2016, Rome, Italy (Springer Proceedings in Complexity).

Pennebaker, J. W. (2011). The secret life of pronouns. *New Scientist, 211*(2828), 42–45.

Pennebaker, J. W., Francis, M. E., & Booth, R. J. (2001). *Linguistic inquiry and word count: LIWC 2001* (p. 71). Mahway: Lawrence Erlbaum Associates.

Ramos, C. M. (2007). Organizational change in a human service agency. *Consulting Psychology Journal: Practice and Research, 59*(1), 41.

Wasserman, S., & Faust, K. (1994). *Social network analysis: Methods and applications* (Vol. 8). New York: Cambridge University Press.

Zilli, A., Grippa, F., Gloor, P., & Laubacher, R. (2006). One in four is enough–strategies for selecting ego mailboxes for a group network view. In *Proceedings of the European Conference on Complex Systems ECCS* (Vol. 6, pp. 25–29).

Muse Headband: Measuring Tool or a Collaborative Gadget?

Aleksandra Przegalinska, Leon Ciechanowski, Mikolaj Magnuski, and Peter Gloor

Abstract We have conducted an observational study on persons participating passively in public lectures. During a lecture we were measuring the level of focus of listeners using the Muse EEG-headband as well as conducting an observational study of the usage of the device by experiment participants. The purpose was twofold: to understand to what extent commercially available portable EEG-devices can record synchronicity of experience among the audience and to check what kind of usage participants make of this multi-purpose device. While we got some preliminary insights, we found that the usefulness in measuring EEG signal of consumer-grade devices such as Muse is extremely limited in non-laboratory conditions.

1 Introduction and Theoretical Background

Simultaneously to self-tracking community formation the users were able to experience the evolution of tracking hardware and software. Responding to the need for "ambient intelligence" (Calvo and Peters 2014) in which intelligent devices can be integrated into the everyday surroundings and provide diverse services to everyone, trackers became sophisticated technologies that uncovered users' activity that would otherwise be inaccessible. We observe the change from simple assisting devices to the rise of more and more sophisticated trackers, including those that measure brain

A. Przegalinska (✉)
Kozminski University, Warsaw, Poland
e-mail: aprzegalinska@kozminski.edu.pl

L. Ciechanowski · M. Magnuski
University of Social Sciences and Humanities, Warsaw, Poland
e-mail: lciechanowski@swps.edu.pl; mmagnuski@swps.edu.pl

P. Gloor
MIT Center for Collective Intelligence, Cambridge, MA, USA
e-mail: pgloor@mit.edu

F. Grippa et al. (eds.), *Collaborative Innovation Networks*, Studies on Entrepreneurship, Structural Change and Industrial Dynamics,
https://doi.org/10.1007/978-3-319-74295-3_8

activity (such as Muse[1]—the brain sensing headband for training relaxation and meditation, as well as similar brain-trackers such as Melon, Emotiv and several others). These trackers enter a different level of interaction with users and bring about profound changes in how the role of a tracker is understood. They are more personalized, unobtrusive, and usable anytime and anywhere. Despite the fact that they measure very complex activities (such as affects or emotions) and provide feedback on them, they have a high degree of portability. Thus, people can use them in various spaces, for instance at group meetings or workplaces (such collaborative relaxation sessions is what Muse users are encouraged to do). Moreover, the rise of big data analytics is enabling more insightful analyses of all users digital footprints.

Increasing numbers of mind-related wearable devices becomes commercially available. Some of these devices fulfill purely passive functions, whereas others actively support alterations of cognitive states (Mazurek and Tkaczyk 2016; Kopeć et al. 2015; Calvo and Peters 2014). In our series of experiments the intention was to investigate brain activity tracking of commercially available wearable devices' effects on attention building. Among currently available devices, most popular are those that introduce motivation building programs, allowing users to foster increased creativity or work productivity and/or reduce stress. These technologies aspire to foster human well-being and potential and can be classified as "positive computing" devices. In our case, the wearable technology under investigation was Muse—the brain-waves sensing headband.

2 Motivation

We have conducted an observational study on persons participating passively in events where knowledge is shared. For the experiment we were measuring the level of focus of listeners during a lecture using the Muse headband. Researchers provided strong evidence (Abujelala et al. 2016; Wiechert et al. 2016; Alrige and Chatterjee 2015) that Muse might be used outside its prior functionality (meditation training device) and become an effective portable tool for attention measurement while performing various assigned tasks. For instance, in a recent study, Muse has been already used for experiments in which users' focus was measured while they were playing video games (Abujelala et al. 2016) or while listening to recorded lectures (Kasperiuniene et al. 2016), whereas live lectures were not examined so far.

Via EEG studies, mindfulness meditation has been associated with measurable changes to brain waves including major changes in alpha waves and certain increases in theta and gamma rhythms (Lutz et al. 2008). Other authors (Chiesa and Serretti 2009) report that, in addition to significant increases in alpha and theta activity, the states of mindfulness and meditation are associated with activation of the prefrontal cortex and anterior cingulate cortex, areas related to attention. Thus,

[1]http://www.choosemuse.com/

Muse can also serve as "attention recorder" capturing alpha waves while performing some (usually passive) tasks. Muse was initially designed as a personal meditation assistant. It is portable, and can be paired with any tablet or smartphone and operate with the Muse application, which also trains the user in meditation exercises and records EEG data. Muse uses two frontal channels on the left and two on the right of forehead, and thus can explore hemispheric asymmetries. Muse is also equipped with two micro-USB ports on the back of the ear pods where two auxiliary electrodes can be attached. These electrodes can be used to measure EMG, ECG, or EEG on other areas of the head or body.

In our experiment, the main goal was to understand what kind of role the device fulfils, both scientifically and socially, in real life situations. We wanted to see to what extent it accurately records the signal and how is it going to be used by the experiment participants as it is consumer-friendly and open to individual exploration.

3 Methodology

The study included participants participating in a public event (lecture). Through social media channels we selected five participants to use Muse headbands while attending a public academic event.

In the experiment, after giving consent to participate in the study, participants answered relevant demographic questions. Then, participants were fitted with the Muse headset. Conductivity for all four channels was checked before proceeding to the experimental phases. After proper connection with the Muse was ensured, the baseline phase ("Relax") was established. During this time, participants were asked to close their eyes and listen to calming white noise for 120 s, while their EEG data was recorded. Subsequently, the active phase ("lecture listening") was established. During each of these phases, the participants were asked to listen to the lecture for 30 min, while their EEG data is recorded on the Muse Monitor application. The main goal of the study was to check the Muse behavior during an outdoor study, and—if successful—assess the level of attentiveness, active engagement, distraction, and concentration during the lectures and compare them between persons.

For the first part of the experiment the researchers have used Muse Monitor to collect raw data. Simultaneously, Muse App designed to collect and visualize data in a simplified and gamified manner was turned on to display the users the results of their session with Muse. Data collected by the Muse App is non-exportable and the algorithm used for computing them is patent-protected. Muse App shows general results of each Muse session compared with previous results and thus the results may vary according to general experience with the device and the amount of overall time spent with it on.

4 Results

The conducted study has shown that the data collected by Muse headband with a Muse Monitor application, are of poor quality in noisy conditions, such as a public lecture. There were a couple of problems with the data, which we present below.

First of all, the EEG signal looks very noisy just on the face of it. Figure 1 presents the signal for one participant.

Second, and it is the most crucial problem—time difference between subsequent samples is unstable. This means that the stream of samples can't be treated as a signal with specified sampling frequency—difference between time stamps reported by Muse for adjacent samples ranges from −10 to 150 ms (see Fig. 2).

Third, there is a lot of missing values. The reason for it is unknown; probably Muse is already cleaning the data on the raw-level, or some of the packets sent via Bluetooth to the Muse Monitor application are lost. Figure 3 illustrates the person number one and the missing values.

In the end we are presenting a power spectrum derived from the data, since it is often used to assess spontaneous brain activity. The average spectrum seems to contain theta-like peaks, but closer inspection demonstrates that this peak does not reflect brain oscillations but is powered by rare, but strong, events like eye blinks (Fig. 4).

This conclusion is further supported by performing median power spectrum where all the peak-like structure evaporates (Fig. 5). Taking the median instead of the mean removes influence of eye blinks, and other artifacts, that originally caused the signal to look as if it contained spectral peaks similar to those present in actual

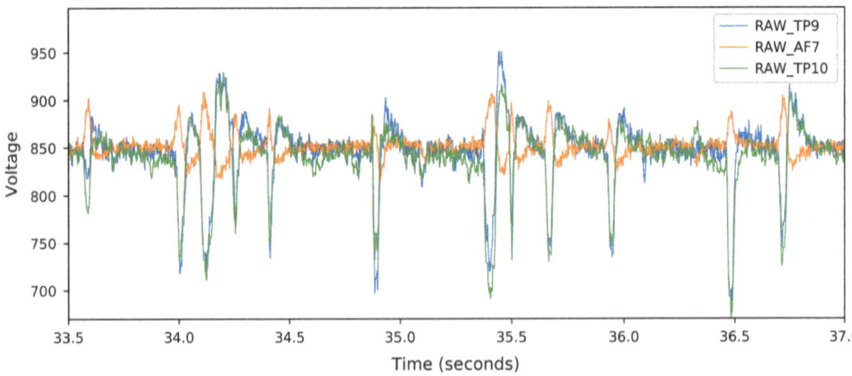

Fig. 1 The figure presents raw EEG signal for one person. It is clearly visible that the three electrodes do not provide a proper signal. Most of it consists of eye blinks and no oscillations of brain origin are present. We removed one electrode from the data for this person, since it was not properly attached, and the signal for it spanned randomly across the whole figure

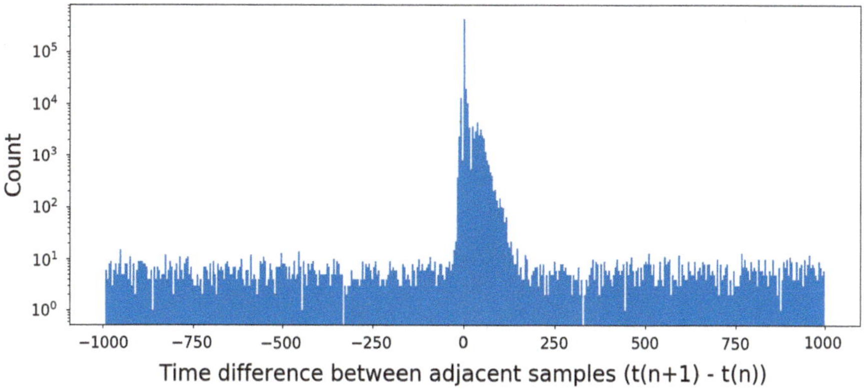

Fig. 2 The figure shows the histogram of time differences for subsequent samples. Most differences are within −10 to 150 ms. This variability shows that the gathered raw signal did not have a proper temporal resolution. At most times the consecutive samples properly differ by one millisecond, while at other times there can be a difference of 100, or occasionally even more than 250 ms. What is worse, the time difference span is non-systematic, therefore making it more difficult to deal with the problem. Such variability is unacceptable for research purposes. Note that the y axis is in logarithmic units

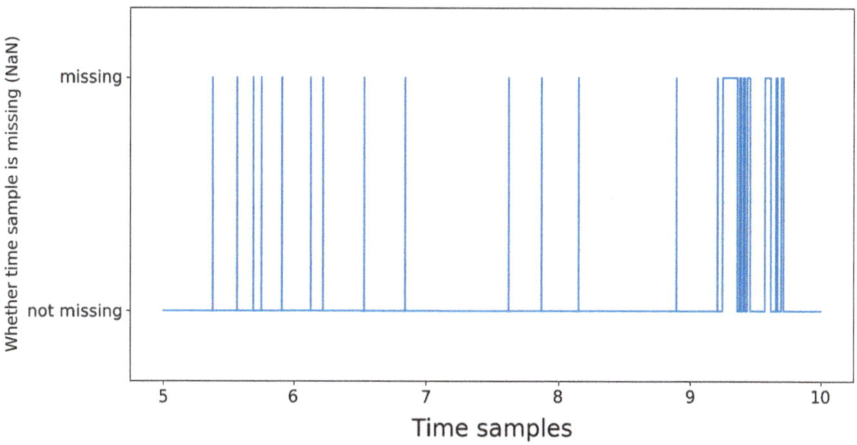

Fig. 3 Missing time samples for a selected time range of one participant. We observed around 0.01–0.05% missing samples across all participants. While it comprised all in all 1000 samples per subject, it is not that significant—the missing data can be interpolated. Most of the missing samples were marked by muse as eye blinks or similar artifacts—while actual eye blinks were left untouched in the signal. This raises the possibility that artifact detection algorithms used by Muse fail to detect standard artifacts

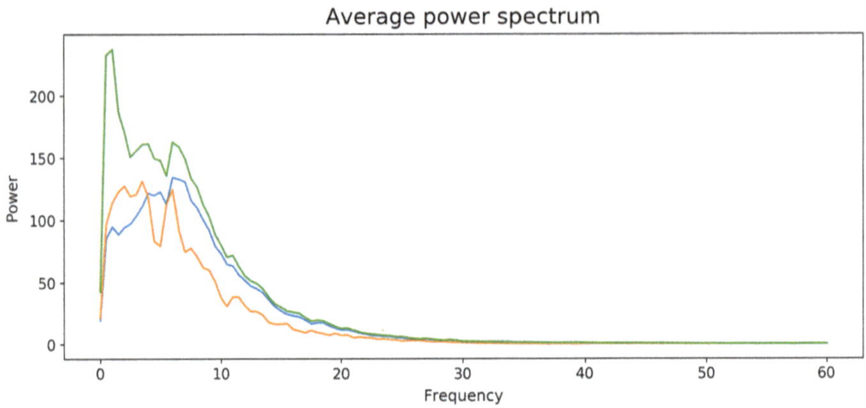

Fig. 4 The average power spectrum for the subject number 1

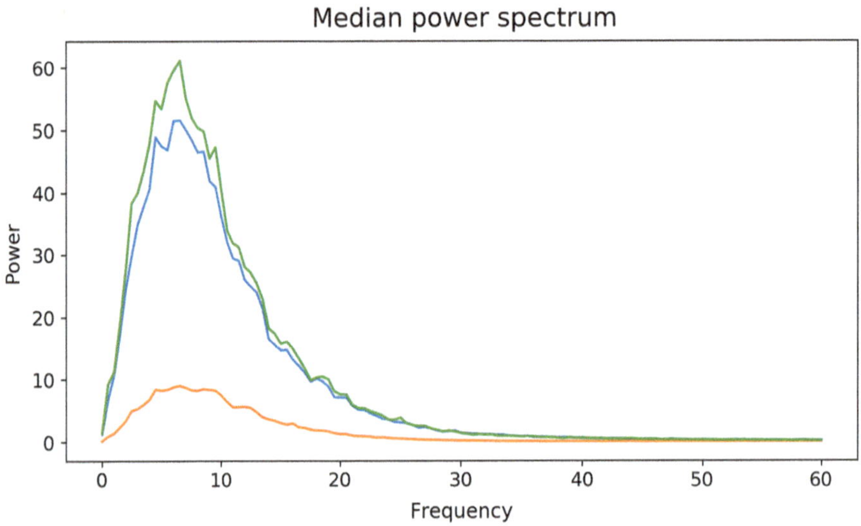

Fig. 5 The median power spectrum for the subject number 1

brain recordings. Therefore the spectrum does not provide any evidence of oscillatory signal originating from the brain.

5 Discussion

Reliability of Muse and similar devices may be questioned. The number of electrodes on these devices is limited compared to the clinical grade devices. Also, their resolution is lower, and the electrodes are usually focused on a specific area of the brain. Eye movement, muscular activity, and other electronic devices in the vicinity introduce artifacts to the signal and disrupt the measurement of actual brain waves. The inability of Muse and similar trackers to cancel out such "noise" generates less reliable signal that does not seem to contain much brain activity. This reliability could, however, be improved by including more sensors and using blind source separation algorithms like Independent Component Analysis (ICA)—to separate artifacts and noise from brain activity. However, that increases costs, weight and design of the product making it less attractive for consumers to purchase (Rettner 2016). What is more, the devices currently present on the market are still struggling with devising proper and individualized algorithms that would be able to produce reasonable and truthful output based on psychophysiological data.

It is important to note that frequency spectrum of any signal can be computed and divided into pre-defined frequency ranges like theta and alpha. The sole fact of decomposing the signal into frequency ranges known to be abundant in brain electrical recordings (as muse does) does not constitute measuring actual brain oscillations. In all Muse recordings that we investigated, we found no evidence of brain oscillations. Moreover, it is very possible that eye movements and eye blinks contribute to theta and alpha frequency ranges reported by Muse. Therefore, it is possible that theta and alpha measurements reported by Muse are actually mostly noise-driven.

On the other hand, Muse and several other portable EEG devices are way more simple to set up than typical EEG. They connect well via Bluetooth to a smartphone, a computer, or a microcontroller, where data can be analyzed directly. Dry electrodes used in most of these devices do not require intensive preparation or clean-up, and these electrodes connect to the skin without the need for any liquid. These changes have helped evolve EEG applications in both novel and established fields and allowed consumers to use without any particular expertise or preparations devices previously reserved for medical and scientific purposes only.

Whereas their accuracy for research purposes is problematic, the devices generate interesting social effects. Most users, while returning Muse, reported they have made attempts to stay focused all the time and listen to the lecture very carefully. The researchers also noticed that subjects equipped with Muse formed a collective that one could carefully dub a micro-tribe (Gulati 2007; Weller 2012). Without any prior suggestions from the researcher supervising the experiment, each time subjects wearing Muse decided to sit together without knowing each other previously. Most of them asked questions after the lecture and then engaged in conversation about the topic of the lecture with others who were using Muse. They were also comparing compiled results of their Muse sessions collected by the Muse App and exchanging information about how to enhance their results in the future. One could assert that subjects equipped with Muse presented certain degree of spontaneous tribalism, possibly based on a strong shared experience of a selected group whose brain activity was accessed and sensitive data were collected. This is how one could explain visible emerging relations of proximity between Muse-wearing experiment participants.

6 Conclusion

As mentioned before, nowadays, many portable EEG devices are consumer-grade, low-cost devices that are targeted for lifestyle applications. These products also often rebrand EEG data with a simpler, easily-understood term neurofeedback, understood as a type of biofeedback that uses real-time displays of brain activity—most commonly EEG—to teach self-regulation of brain function. It is clear that from self-tracking of simple and easily quantifiable activities we are moving to more collaborative and sophisticated, even though scientifically unsatisfactory forms of tracking.

Trackers such as Muse enter a different level of interaction with users and bring about profound changes in how the role of a tracker is understood. They are more personalized (as data collected by the Muse app adjust to previous Muse sessions) and usable anytime and anywhere. Despite the fact that they provide feedback on very complex activities, they have a high degree of portability.

The very nature of our relation with tracking devices is also one of the crucial reasons of why the self-tracking industry is developing so rapidly. From our research, and also from other authors who addressed this problem (Nafus and Tracey 2002; Nafus and Sherman 2014; Lupton 2016) we know that on the individual level self-tracking (if not becoming addictive) frequently becomes either boring or frustrating over time. When, however, it becomes elevated to a level of smaller or bigger group or community is when the collaborative aspect steps in. Most probably, the future of tracking lies in collaborative endeavours, because the individual uses become easily boring. Being part of something larger than themselves can, however, have an empowering and motivating effect. The producers know it, too and this is why their efforts are to bring trackers into wellness programs of organizations and corporations and make them become transparent companions of everyone's routines.

References

Abujelala, M., Abellanoza, C., Sharma, A., & Makedon, F. (2016). Brain-EE: Brain enjoyment evaluation using commercial EEG headband. In *Proceedings of the 9th ACM International Conference on PErvasive Technologies Related to Assistive Environments* (pp. 33:1–33:5). New York, NY: ACM.

Alrige, M., & Chatterjee, S. (2015). Toward a taxonomy of wearable technologies in healthcare. In *New horizons in design science: Broadening the research agenda* (pp. 496–504). Cham: Springer.

Calvo, R. A., & Peters, D. (2014). *Positive computing: Technology for wellbeing and human potential*. Cambridge, MA: MIT Press.

Chiesa, A., & Serretti, A. (2009). Mindfulness-based stress reduction for stress management in healthy people: A review and meta-analysis. *Journal of Alternative and Complementary Medicine, 15*, 593–600.

Gulati, R. (2007). Tent poles, tribalism, and boundary spanning: The rigor-relevance debate in management research. *Academy of Management Journal, 50*, 775–782.

Kasperiuniene, J., Jariwala, M., Vaskevicius, E., & Satkauskas, S. (2016). Affective engagement to virtual and live lectures. In G. Dregvaite & R. Damasevicius (Eds.), *Information and software technologies* (pp. 499–508). Cham: Springer.

Kopeć, J., Pacewicz, K., Przegalińska, A., et al. (2015). *Gamification. Critical Approaches.* Warsaw: University of Warsaw.

Lupton, D. (2016). *The quantified self.* Cambridge: Wiley.

Lutz, A., Slagter, H. A., Dunne, J. D., & Davidson, R. J. (2008). Attention regulation and monitoring in meditation. *Trends in Cognitive Sciences, 12*, 163–169.

Mazurek, G., & Tkaczyk, J. (2016). *The impact of the digital world on management and marketing.* Warsaw: Poltext.

Nafus, D., & Sherman, J. (2014). Big data, big questionsl This one does not go up to 11: The quantified self movement as an alternative big data practice. *International Journal of Communication Systems, 8*, 11.

Nafus, D., & Tracey, K. (2002). Mobile phone consumption and concepts of personhood. In J. E. Katz & M. A. Aakhus (Eds.), *Perpetual contact* (pp. 206–221). Cambridge: Cambridge University Press.

Rettner, R. (2016). Wearable devices move toward disease treatment. Retrieved January 24, 2018, from https://www.livescience.com/53344-wearables-disease-treatment.html

Weller, J. (2012). Shedding new light on tribalism in health care. *Medical Education, 46*, 134–136.

Wiechert, G., Triff, M., Liu, Z., et al. (2016). Identifying users and activities with cognitive signal processing from a wearable headband. In *2016 I.E. 15th International Conference on Cognitive Informatics Cognitive Computing (ICCI*CC)* (pp. 129–136).

Creative Systems Analysis of Design Thinking Process

Namino Sakama, Haruka Mori, and Takashi Iba

Abstract In this paper, we study design thinking using concepts of Creative Systems Theory. Design thinking is a methodology of solving problems and is aimed at achieving innovation based on the idea of human centred design. The five stages of the design thinking process, as defined by Stanford d.school, are widely known: Empathise, Define, Ideate, Prototype and Test. Since each stage has different functions that should occur in the whole process, we consider each of the functionalities with the use of the concepts of Creative Systems Theory, which looks at creativity based on the autopoietic systems theory where the creative process is described as a chain of discoveries. Our consideration implies that design thinking could be grasped as a meaning process, where each stage facilitates different types of chains of discoveries in the creative system. This paper makes a first step towards understanding the design thinking process via the application of the Creative Systems Theory.

1 Introduction

In recent years, the importance of innovation, as a means of solving the problems of an increasingly complex society, is growing, and design thinking is used in various fields as one of the approaches to imaginative thought. Design thinking is a method used to realise innovation in the technology as well as business domains using a human-centred approach with the designer's sensibility and cognition.

N. Sakama (✉)
Graduate School of Media and Governance, Keio University, Tokyo, Japan

H. Mori
Faculty of Policy and Management, Keio University, Tokyo, Japan

T. Iba
Graduate School of Media and Governance, Keio University, Tokyo, Japan

Faculty of Policy and Management, Keio University, Tokyo, Japan

F. Grippa et al. (eds.), *Collaborative Innovation Networks*, Studies on Entrepreneurship, Structural Change and Industrial Dynamics,
https://doi.org/10.1007/978-3-319-74295-3_9

Design thinking is a process constructed on several stages, and there is a hypothesis that a deeper recognition of the functions of each process of design thinking can make for its more effective application. The Creative System Theory, developed by Takashi Iba, recognises the creative process as autopoietic reproduction networks of *discoveries*, based on the system theory of autopoiesis (Iba 2011). If the process of design thinking is to be a 'creative process', it may also be possible to capture the mechanism and essential function of each stage by grasping it as one autopoietic creative system, reproducing networks of *discoveries*.

In what follows, we will overview design thinking, introduce the Creative Systems Theory, and then demonstrate the analysis of design thinking with the use of this theory.

2 Design Thinking and Its Process

Design thinking is a methodology that is constructed to apply and nurture creativity. It was originally described as a method for architects and city planners in 'Design thinking' (Rowe 1987). Subsequently, it was introduced into the business domain by David Kelly, a founder of IDEO, a design firm in the USA. In current times, methodology and values that have been regarded as general knowledge can no longer be applied to the development of new businesses and services due to the rapid changes in the social environment resulting from the progress in technology. Richard Buchanan defined these issues as 'wicked problems', and design thinking is an approach meant to solve them through the power of design (Buchanan 1992).

Human-CENTRED design is one of the concepts necessary for the resolution of complicated problems, and design thinking can be conducted in compliance with the approach of human-centred design. Tim Brown depicts design thinking as follows: 'Design thinking can be described as a discipline that uses the designer's sensibility and methods to match people's needs with what is technologically feasible and what a viable business strategy can convert into customer value and market opportunity' (Brown 2009).

Currently, the application of design thinking takes various forms, but for the purposes of this paper we will analyse the 5-stage process proposed by Stanford d. school, the Hasso Plattner Institute of Design at Stanford University, which David Kelly, one of the IDEO founders, established as an educational institution (Plattner 2010). Figure 1 represents the five stages of the design thinking process: **Empathise**, **Define**, **Ideate**, **Prototype** and **Test**.

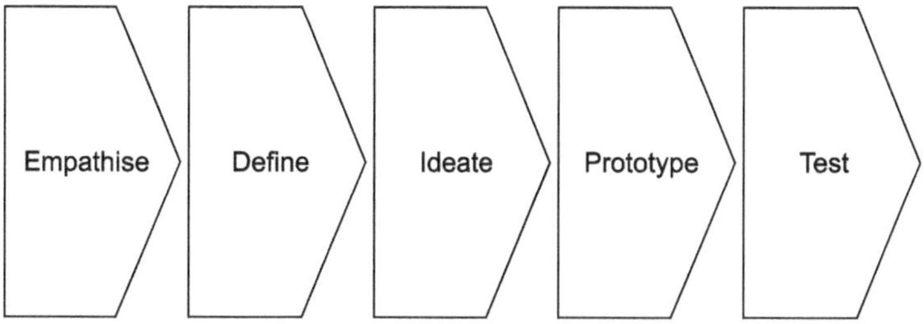

Fig. 1 Five stages of design thinking as promoted by Stanford d.school

3 Creative Systems Theory

In this paper, the process of design thinking will be considered as a method of conception from the viewpoint of Creative Systems Theory (Iba 2011). The theory captures the process in which the element of *discovery* is continuously generated in the creative system. The creative system is formulated as an autopoietic system, where the unity of the organisation is defined by the process of a reproduction network of elements. Autopoiesis, as a concept and theory, was originally proposed by Humberto Maturana and Francisco Varela in biology (Maturana and Varela 1972; Maturana and Varela 1980) and was later applied to sociology by Niklas Luhmann (Luhmann 1995).

Based on these theories, Iba (2011) proposed the application of autopoiesis to the understanding of the creative process, and named the theory Creative Systems Theory. Creative systems are defined as autopoietic system consisting of a chain of *discoveries*. Note that, it is quite important that the creative system is defined as a construct different from that of the psychic and social systems (Fig. 2). Psychic and social systems are defined by Niklas Luhmann in his Social Systems Theory to describe the human mind and society. A psychic system is an autopoietic system whose element is *consciousness*; and a social system is an autopoietic assembly whose element is *communication.*

Although creativity has been studied in psychology, Creative Systems Theory claims that the creative process should be studied as itself, and not as it is related to the psychic process. Therefore, the theory describes the creative process as an autopoietic system that is autonomous and operationally closed as a system, where the input and the output of the element is impossible in terms of operation.

Of course, this does not imply that the creative process can happen without human beings or society. The theory focuses on the creative process itself and postulates that the human and the societal are located on the environment side of the creative process. In the next section, we will understand the creation aspect of design thinking as a creative system that continuously keeps reproducing *discoveries* as it aims to create a final product. Note that in this paper, the technical terms used in Creative Systems Theory are italicised.

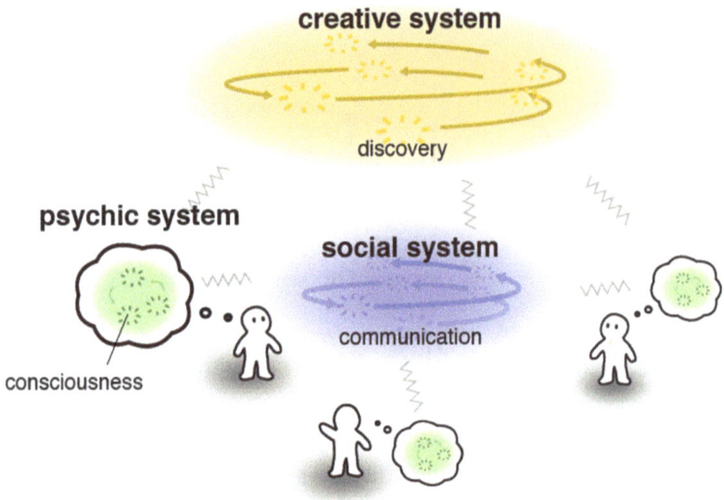

Fig. 2 Creative systems are defined as different from psychic and social systems

4 Chain of Discoveries in the Design Thinking Process

In the following section, we will see what happens in each stage of the design thinking process—**Empathise**, **Define**, **Ideate**, **Prototype** and **Test**—when we use the perspective of a chain of *discoveries* based on Creative Systems Theory. As mentioned above, according to Creative Systems Theory, 'Elements of a creative system are *discoveries*, where each *discovery* is produced based on previous *discovery*, associating the on-going creation' (Iba 2011), and the chain of *discoveries* cannot happen without *contingency* (Iba 2016).

Since design thinking is an approach to creating solutions for problems, it could be described as the reproduction of *discoveries*, where each of the five stages has different types of *discoveries* (Fig. 3).

4.1 Empathise

Empathise is the stage of finding emotional understanding by observing pain points in the living context around the stakeholder's problem. To use the process of human-centred design, it is necessary to set up certain users and to empathise with them. There are three major modes of this stage: *observe*, *involve* and *immerse*. The mode of observation monitors behaviour in the user's living environment. Users are interactively interviewed in the involvement mode and in the immerse mode, what users are living through is experienced.

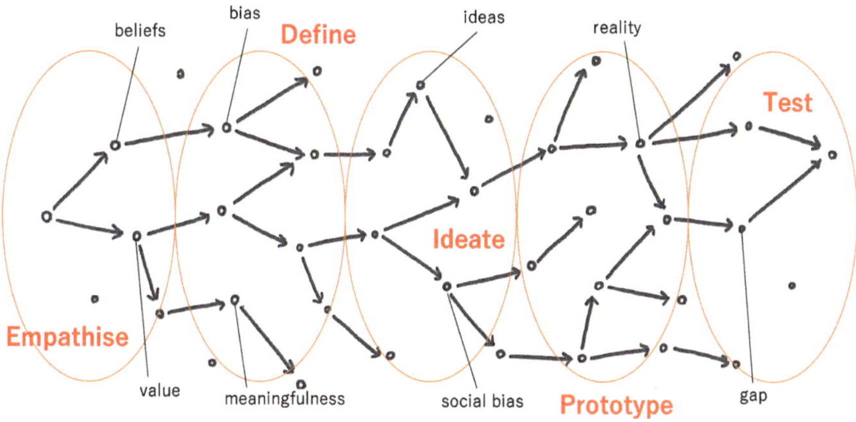

Fig. 3 Several types of discoveries happen in each stage of the design thinking process

In the **Empathise** stage, the observer will acquire *discoveries* about the user's living context with regard to their problem to find the user's insight. If the reproduction of *discoveries* is to occur in this stage, they will be *discoveries* of 'beliefs' and 'value' obtained by observing and engaging with the user's living context. These help to learn the story of the person for whom one is designing. The design developer must focus not only on the user's actions but also should observe the living environment of the user, and thus gain an insight into and speculate on the potential needs. In-depth interviews serve to access the feelings accompanying the facts and the values hidden behind the feelings are gained through empathy with the target, aiming to generate *discoveries* about the desire in depth. This is called the 'insight' (Fig. 4).

Through this stage, information concerning beliefs and values lead to unexpected *discoveries* of insight that are made more remarkable because they are not noticed by the users themselves. These clear nuggets of the potential movement of the mind could not be understood superficially without this stage of the process. As *discoveries* in this stage, the needs and insights are decomposed and integrated, and then the user's characteristics and image are defined. Insights obtained in this stage are reflected in the form of Point of View (POV) syntax, which is '<User's name> needs a way to <Needs (verb)> because due <Surprising Insight>', and the ideal is visualised in the form of a persona.

Soup Stock Tokyo is a Japanese food chain, and the business concept was created from user needs derived through interviews, which called for a lot of empathy. The company created a persona called 'Tsuyu Akino' who had a specific need. It is said that the enterprise constructed its marketing strategy by thoroughly 'empathising' with her. This became a major factor in the company's success and helped the organisation achieve sales of 4.2 billion yen from 52 stores (as of 2016) in 10 years (Toyama 2006). The detailed taste and personality profile created through this process made it easier for the developers to perform actions such as, empathise with the persona create menus, set shop locations, brainstorm. Soup Stock Tokyo

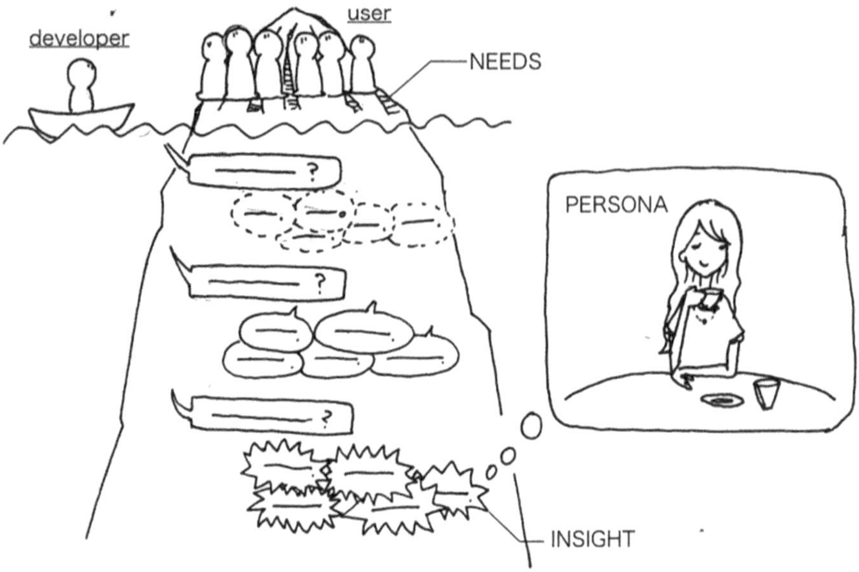

Fig. 4 Making a persona by empathising with users to generate discoveries about user personalities

was finally the result of empathising with all that is familiar and important to the everyday life of 'Tsuyu Akino'.

4.2 Define

The next stage is **Define** and it identifies and delineates the problem to solve. A point of view that is based on user needs and insights is constructed in this stage, and it sets the scope for the situation to shift into a better position. Establishing an approach helps create the focus for the next stage of ideation, and to create a challenge, team members need to be aware of themselves and their characteristics.

In the creative systems method of cognition, *discoveries* about 'meaningfulness' and 'bias' around specified issues help to identify the insight of the users. This stage has the important task of generating *discoveries* about the problems users are eager to solve.

By way of example Wii, released by Nintendo, a Japanese game company in 2008, is one of the examples of innovation that took advantage of prototypes. By applying new technologies such as acceleration and vibration measuring meters to game machines, Wii became a game everyone could enjoy by moving their bodies (Nintendo 2006a, b). The major obstacle to improving the sales of game machines was the mother of a child who was a conventional primary user. The developer thought to dispel the negative idea of gaming in the mind of the mother and sought to involve her to play the game. This involved considering every kind of user's 'meaningfulness' that could be achieved through the game so that everyone could enjoy it and find it satisfying as an experience.

4.3 Ideate

Ideate, the next stage, aims to define the approach and the design goal to the solution. In this stage, the intention is to embody the approach which broke the bias with concrete ideas to resolve the problem. In this stage, methods are also devised for the creation of alternative designs to replace those already conceived.

Generally, the method of idea generation is divided into two steps: divergence and convergence. Divergence is the phase that conducts approaches to break the mental block and bias that a person unconsciously sees as common sense. It emphasises the quantity rather than the quality to promote the conception of a large variety of ideas. In the phase of convergence, the created ideas are integrated and evaluated. Problem solving decisions are then made based on axes such as appropriateness and originality. This is supported by the reproduction of discoveries about the ideal but concrete solution.

When divergence and convergence are executed, it is necessary to recognise the characteristics required to use them appropriately. This is because there is a concern that high quality output cannot be obtained due to inability of the mind to switch between divergence and convergence. The divergence process encourages the *discovery* of 'ideas' based on the other ideas that were brainstormed because quantity is more necessary than quality in this phase. However, the convergence phase is more focused on quality rather than quantity so that 'social bias', which we do not always recognise about our design goal will be the *discovery*. The ideation begins with brainstorming (Osborn 1957) and brain writing, and then a co-creation session such as the KJ method (Kawakita 1967) and dynamic framing (Hamaguchi 2013) is held to share and integrate the ideas that are thus issued.

In the co-creation session, the visualization of ideas into words and diagrams can break the bias and create a shift of the viewpoint to lead to new ideas. For example, when Hamaguchi, the CEO of Ziba Tokyo, created the concept of the USB Flash, he found a new idea area in data storage by destroying the existing bias. At that time, with the development of digital cameras and PowerPoint, the data became larger and there was a background that it was necessary to think of a new means of data sharing to follow the floppy disk (Hamaguchi 2013).

Figure 5 is a frame of the USB Flash visualised by dynamic framing: the vertical axis shows the user experience in data handling and the horizontal axis shows the size of the data handling capacity. The idea created from brainstorming is plotted into the axes. Then, the idea is settled in the quadrant of 'network'. Because of the background of the development of the internet and wireless communication, it was a bias that the experience of transferring data becomes intangible and the data size becomes large. That is why the idea of attaching USB to flash memory emerged by paying attention to the quadrant 'data is tangible and large in size' contrary to the

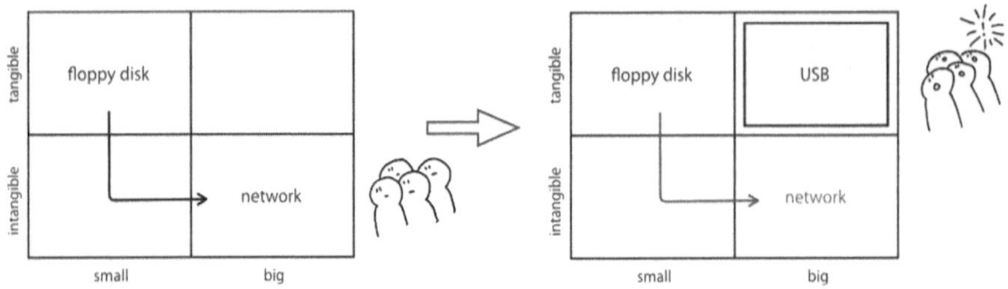

Fig. 5 Creating the concept of the USB flash memory by breaking the bias as visualised by dynamic framing

bias. This viewpoint shift encourages the ideation process of developers because the direction setting gives them an efficient mindset to ideate not only in the range of direction but also beyond the given scope.

In the phase of convergence, developers categorise and evaluate ideas by finding common points and differences in order to narrow them down. The main ideas are refined by focusing on evaluation axes that developers provide based on the project's terms as they have been handled so far. Because of the axes, developers can cause continuous discoveries directing the creation to the embodiment that optimises the ideal.

In the **Ideate** stage, the thinking process is vague and pros or cons are unclear and confusing for developers. However, when all factors, divergence, convergence and the essence of the problem are united and one suitable answer comes out, developers find the way to promote the idea to embody over others in order to solve the user's problem in reality. The method for divergent and convergent thinking, as mentioned above, can be considered as a *media* for chain of *discoveries*.

4.4 Prototype

The fourth stage, **Prototype,** builds representations of the solution to test it. By quickly making a model, one can find the deviation of recognition and improvement points of detail. Prototypes should be made quickly and changed as often as necessary, using simple materials such as sticky notes, toy blocks, and role playing which cost less money than building a normal prototype.

Being iterative makes one learn rapidly and this enables a person to investigate many different possibilities so that many *discoveries* can be generated. Prototypes are most effective when others, including teams and users, get experiences from them and give feedback. At the same time, developers can move their hands to reconsider the ideas for themselves, and gain instant feedback. Moreover, they can more realistically comprehend and infer how the user behaves, thinks and feels through the actual interaction with the output. This is important because all of them are generating *discoveries*. In the **Prototype** stage, the *discovery* of 'reality' in the

Fig. 6 Improvement of the remote controller of the Nintendo Wii through prototyping

physical experience advances learning by recognizing the gap between the object and the concept.

In the development process of the Wii, released by Nintendo, countless prototypes were generated (Fig. 6). The ideas that the developers thought of were prototyped using styrene foam and clay, aiming at 'a design not to be disliked by anyone'. While creating various things such as super lightweight materials and single-button design, the developers tried to create a controller that could be used with one hand like a remote control when a controller for both hands was in common use at the time (Nintendo 2006a, b). The design of the present controller emerged as the result of repeated prototyping for the number, the position and the shape of the buttons with the aim of triggering a 'reality' of physical experience.

In this stage, the *discoveries* are based on thinking and communication mediated by the substance, the prototype, and the rapid assembly of the model to the next *discovery* like a chain. Meinel and Leifer, who provided the four rules of design thinking, mention 'The Tangibility Rule: Making Ideas Tangible Always Facilitates Communication' (Plattner et al. 2013) as one of tenets of design thinking.

4.5 *Test*

Finally, **Test** is the iterative process that provides evaluation and feedback for the improvement of the solution. This process can be said to be the most critical in design thinking in terms of human-centred design, because the developers cannot see whether their ideas and designs or targets are appropriate without feedback on the idea from the end users. In this stage, the 'gap' between the user's feedback and the developer's idea continuously promotes the improvable *discovery* (Fig. 7).

In the user test of Spotify and SoundCloud, the music streaming service, the usability of each function was compared and verified from the viewpoint of seven

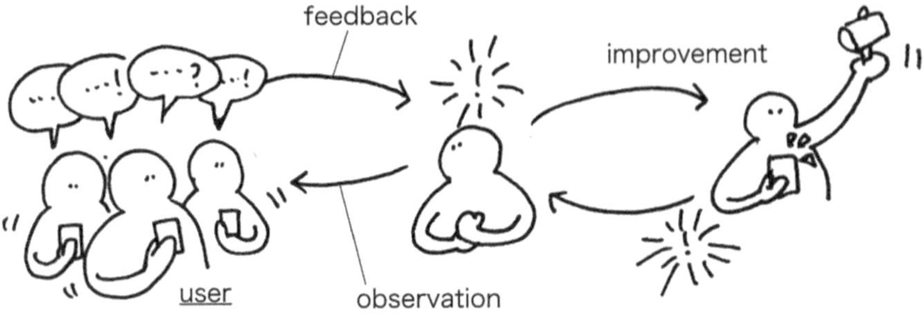

Fig. 7 Reflection and improvement of ideas through user test with discoveries

items regarding an operation to 'create a playlist' (Taylor et al. 2014). While it is true that developers design their services with confidence, it is also true that there is a 'gap' between how users employ the services and how they feel about them. That is why users can test them in their living environment and make a relative evaluation with the products and services offered by other companies to refine the output. The makers may not have the bird's-eye view of the communication that happens in the system that they are configuring, but by putting in a third person who gives a comprehensive and objective outlook and can evaluate the innovation, developers can pay attention to their blind spot.

Through this **Test** stage, discoveries are generated based on user feedback about what is effective and what is not valid for their needs and wants. Based on the learning, developers can go back to any of the previous stages and make modifications to the idea. Therefore, testing plays the vital role of generating the reproduction of *discoveries* to refine ideas by conducting the process of design thinking again after a reflecting practice based on user feedback.

5 Conclusion

Design thinking is a method of creating ideas by making use of the sensibility of designers. It cultivates creativity based on the idea of human-centred design. In this research, we primarily considered five processes in design thinking by relating them to the concept of *discoveries* in Creative System Theory. Future research projects may be undertaken to gain a more thorough understanding of how the reproduction of *discoveries* may be realised with methods, rules and tips in each stage.

References

Brown, T. (2009). *Change by design*. New York: Harper Business.
Buchanan, R. (1992). Wicked problems in design thinking. *Design Issues, 8*(2), 5–21.

Hamaguchi, S. (2013). *USB memory wo umidashita dynamic flame-working〜The Dynamic Frame-working which created USB flash memory〜*. http://diamond.jp/articles/-/44157

Iba, T. (2011). Autopoietic systems diagram for describing creative processes. *Procedia – Social and Behavioral Sciences, 26*, 30–37.

Iba, T. (2016). Sociological perspective of the creative society. In *International Conference on Collaborative Innovation Networks (COINs2016), Rome*.

Kawakita, J. (1967). *Hassouho: Sozosei Kaihatsu notameni* [*Abuduction method: For development of creativity*], Chuokoronsha.

Luhmann, N. (1995). *Social systems*. California: Stanford University Press.

Maturana, H., & Varela, F. (1972). *Autopoiesis and cognition: The realization of the living*. Holland: Reidel.

Maturana, R., & Varela, J. (1980). *Autopoiesis and cognition: The realization of the living*. Boulder: Westview Press.

Nintendo. (2006a). The President talks about Wii project. *Reasons for creation of Wii*, Vol. 1. Wii Hard ver. https://www.nintendo.co.jp/wii/topics/interview/vol1/02.html

Nintendo. (2006b). The President talks about Wii project. *Reasons for creation of Wii*, Vol. 2. Wii Remote Controller ver. https://www.nintendo.co.jp/wii/topics/interview/vol2/index.html

Osborn, A. (1957). *Applied imagination: Principles and procedures of creative thinking*. New York: Charles Scribner's Son.

Plattner, H. (2010). *An introduction to design thinking PROCESS GUIDE*. https://dschool-old.stanford.edu/sandbox/groups/designresources/wiki/36873/attachments/74b3d/ModeGuideBOOTCAMP2010L.pdf?sessionID=1b6a96f1e2a50a3b1b7c3f09e58c40a062d7d553

Plattner, H., Meinel, C., & Leifer, L. (2013). *Design thinking understand – Improve – Apply*. Berlin: Springer.

Rowe, P. (1987). *Design thinking*. Cambridge: The MIT Press.

Taylor, K., Candace, Q., Megan, O., Alec, D., & Nicole, L. (2014) *Usability study: SoundCloud vs. spotify*. http://www.indiana.edu/~iucdp/FinalProject3.pdf

Toyama, M. (2006). *Soup de ikimasu Shousha-man ga Soup Stock Tokyo wo tsukuru (I am going with soup ~ An employee of a trading company creates soup stock Tokyo)*. Tokyo: Shichosha (in Japanese)

Part III
Society and Culture

Indigenous Siberian Food Sharing Networks: Social Innovation in a Transforming Economy

John P. Ziker and Karen S. Fulk

Abstract The sustainability of indigenous communities in the Arctic, and the vulnerable households within, is in large part dependent on their continuing food security. A social food-sharing network within the Ust'-Avam community on the Taimyr Peninsula in northern Siberia is analyzed for underlying patterns of resilience and key evolutionarily stable strategies supporting cooperative behavior. Factors influencing the network include interhousehold relatedness, reciprocal sharing, and interaction effects. Social association also influences sharing. Evidence for multiple determinants of food sharing in this sample is discussed in reference to major evolutionary hypotheses and comparable studies. In sum, the findings illustrate the robustness of self-organizing distribution networks in an economic context of uncertainty.

1 Introduction

Anthropologists have documented traditions encouraging generous transfers of essential foodstuffs among a wide variety of indigenous groups as diverse as the Hadza of Tanzania (Wood and Marlowe 2013), Ache of Paraguay (Kaplan and Hill 1985) and Apache of southwestern United States (Basso 1996). These traditions of sharing are conventions that prioritize social relationships, and such customs still are observed by many indigenous householders in Siberia. The present article identifies the mechanisms by which sharing networks developed to provide food security during the economic crisis that ensued following the collapse of the Soviet Union. Here, we present results from a social network analysis of food sharing events documented among ten women in the community of Ust'-Avam in 2001, and discuss these results in light of comparable network analysis studies.

J. P. Ziker (✉) · K. S. Fulk
Department of Anthropology, Boise State University, Boise, ID, USA
e-mail: jziker@boisestate.edu

F. Grippa et al. (eds.), *Collaborative Innovation Networks*, Studies on Entrepreneurship, Structural Change and Industrial Dynamics,
https://doi.org/10.1007/978-3-319-74295-3_10

Ust'-Avam is situated near the confluence of the Avam and Dudypta Rivers on the Taimyr Peninsula in north central Siberia. Two indigenous peoples are represented in the community—the Dolgan and the Nganasan—along with a small minority of ethnic Russians and other former Soviet nationalities. The community is approximately 250 km by air from the regional center, Dudinka, and 400 km by water from the large industrial city of Noril'sk (Ziker 2002). Transportation to and from the cities is expensive and time-constrained, and the community depends primarily on the production from hunting, fishing, and trapping activities for nutrient dense foods. Approximately 60% of caloric intake (and almost all the protein) is derived from local hunting and fishing (Ziker 2014).

Ichikawa (2004) describes three common phases of food sharing for hunter-gatherers: (1) obligatory sharing after the kill; (2) voluntary sharing of raw meat (large, first-butchering portions) to those not participating in the kill; and (3) sharing portions prepared for consumption. Individual decisions and structural constraints vary across the distribution cycles of large-game kills. Making these distinctions is important because each phase of distribution is the potential outcome of varying socio-ecological pressures, and may be dependent on the resources being procured and residence patterns.

In the Ust'-Avam context, obligatory sharing amongst individuals taking part in the hunt immediately follows the kill. A second wave of sharing is done after hunters return to their homes. Normally, the wife or mother of the hunter will manage the distributions at this phase. Women often share portions with their friends, and they, in turn, share to their friends. Interhousehold sharing in the third phase of distribution is also a common occurrence in Ust'-Avam (Ziker and Schnegg 2005). In the present article, we focus on the second wave of sharing in Ust'-Avam, particularly the women's sharing network, whereby food portions are redistributed to households without a resident hunter. We consider the cross-cultural work on food sharing and evolutionary hypotheses for cooperation to examine this sharing network. The research questions can be summarized thus: (1) What is the relative importance of kinship, reciprocity, indirect reciprocity, demand sharing, and costly signaling in women's sharing networks? and (2) How does the evidence for food sharing in Ust'-Avam compare with other kinds of social networks?

2 Explanatory Hypotheses and Comparative Studies

Studies of food sharing among other hunter-gatherer groups demonstrate a variety of correlations relevant to explanatory hypotheses for helping behavior, namely: kin selection, reciprocal altruism, indirect reciprocity, signaling, and demand sharing (Gurven 2004). Indicators of kinship are linked to food sharing behaviors in numerous studies. For example, among the Indonesian Lamalera whale hunters, Nolin (2011) finds that biological kinship is a better predictor of food-sharing relationships than social kinship (i.e., patrilineage membership). Consanguineal (blood) relatedness predicts food sharing on Ifaluk Atoll (Betzig and Turke 1986), Ache farmer-foragers in Paraguay (Gurven et al. 2001), Hadza hunter-gatherers in Tanzania (Wood and Marlowe 2013), and Mayangna and Miskito horticulturalists in Nicaragua (Koster and Leckie 2014). Favoring relatives in food sharing follows the psychology of nepotism and the predictions of inclusive fitness theory for the evolution of altruistic behaviors via improved outcomes for descendants and collateral relatives (Hamilton 1964).

According to theory of reciprocal altruism (Trivers 1971), rewards accrue directly to cooperative individuals, benefits can be delayed and favoring kin is not necessary. In their work with the reservation Ache, Gurven et al. (2000) find significant positive correlations between the amounts of food transferred among pairs of families—demonstrating the contingency component required of reciprocal altruism models. Reciprocal food sharing has been postulated to be a mechanism that reduces the variance in daily food intake among regularly cooperating members of a community through delayed returns (Cashdan 1985; Kaplan and Hill 1985). Nolin (2010) also finds that reciprocity was the strongest predictor of Lamalera (Indonesia) food sharing patterns. Similarly, reciprocal altruism is the strongest predictor of the intensity and balance of interhousehold meal sharing among the Ye'kwana of Venezuela (Hames and McCabe 2007).

In indirect reciprocity based on image scoring (reputation), individuals invest only in partners that have sufficiently helped others in the past and who are, therefore, interested in how others view them (Alexander 1987). Among Ache, Gurven et al. (2000) find that consistently high food producers give more than they receive. However, these hunters gain the least on a daily basis because on any given day they are more likely to have their own supplies. The explanation Gurven et al. provide for this apparent generosity is that high producers receive additional food during hard times. Generosity signaling is hypothesized to provide long-term risk-buffering benefits to the signaler by maintaining social norms of sharing and may represent indirect reciprocity via image scoring. A recent study of men and women Martu hunters in the western desert of Australia (Bliege Bird and Power 2015) also finds support for prosocial signaling. "Those who consistently pay higher costs to share, [were]...not necessarily...better hunters," but they were "preferred...for cooperative hunting" activities (Bliege Bird and Power 2015, 389). Another form of hypothesized indirect reciprocity is generalized reciprocity (Bshary and Bergmüller 2008). Rather than purposefully investing to receive benefits in the future via a good image score, individuals who receive help simply are willing to invest into third parties to create a more generous environment. This is synonymous with the concept of *pay it forward*, so wonderfully represented in the film by the same name (Abrams et al. 2000).

The costly signaling model proposes that big-game hunting evolved as part of competitive displays, rather than as part of provisioning relatives, risk buffering, signaling, or avoidance of defense costs (Zahavi 1975). Marcel Mauss (1954 [1925]) discusses the obligatory, public, and sometimes antagonistic nature of gifts, particularly amongst hunter gatherers on the northwest coast of North America, and notes that this type of gifting is likely a form of costly signaling. Hawkes and Bliege Bird (2002), using data from Torres Strait Meriam and Tanzanian Hadza, argue that the distribution of meat can best be seen in light of the evolution of men's subsistence work, where "honesty is at a premium" and political alliances contribute to status acquisition. Similarly, Smith et al. (2003) find that Meriam turtle hunters gain social and reproductive benefits via meat distribution, which is consistent with the idea that hunting is a form of costly signaling. Nolin's (2012) most recent analysis of sharing by Lamalera men with leadership positions finds excessive giving by leaders is consistent with the sharing-as-signaling hypothesis. Among Lamalerans, however, status did not explain much of the variation in sharing patterns because the exchanges observed in high-status households were best explained by the same factors that defined the activities of other households. This pattern suggests that while multiple mechanisms may operate simultaneously to promote sharing in Lamalera status acquisition is not driving that system.

When the consumption of food stores exhibits declining marginal value to the producer, then marginal portions are worth more to other individuals who have no food. As a result, there may be a cost associated with defending these food reserves and a producer should relinquish marginal portions to other individuals if the price of defense is greater than the additional value gained by others. Blurton Jones (1984) refers to this as tolerated scrounging. An additional prediction of this model is that the disparity in amounts should be low, since portions are given out until the marginal consumption value or utility is equal for all potential recipients (Winterhalder 1996). For example, Bliege Bird et al. (2002) find that the marginal valuation of the food to the acquirer conditioned Meriam sharing, but is only weakly affected by harvest variance—leading the authors to conclude that sharing on Mer does not function to reduce foraging risk. Similarly, Peterson's (1993) concept of demand sharing emphasizes the social and symbolic significance of requests for food and other resources. While acknowledging its correspondence to the tolerated-scrounging model, Peterson views demand sharing as part of a wider *testing behavior* that is used to establish relationships by incurring *debt*. Both tolerated scrounging and costly signaling models are more egocentric in their hypothesized benefits than are the kinship, reciprocal altruism, indirect reciprocity, and generosity signaling models. However, economic need can intersect with kinship to drive sharing without the presence of tolerated theft or demand sharing, as Koster (2011) demonstrates for the Mayangna and Miskito horticulturalists in Nicaragua.

Most empirical research on indigenous food sharing networks indicates a multiplicity of mechanisms at play (Nolin 2012). The particular combination of sharing strategies in any given society is likely to make the most sense when viewed in light of the local socio-ecology of food production and embeddedness in surrounding economies and societies. A case in point is Elspeth Ready's (2016) consideration of the multiplicity of mechanisms in food sharing as demonstrated in the northern Canadian community of Kangiqsujuaq. Ready finds that food sharing did not serve a single function, such as reciprocity. Instead, she argues that food sharing "emerge [d] as a complex of social, political and economic phenomen[a] that accomplishe [d] different [objectives] for actors based on their social position[s]" (Ready 2016, 155). The network approach adopted in Ready's research highlights the conjugate role of individual decisions and structural constraints on the economic strategies available to households. Her detailed analysis demonstrates that the benefits of food sharing are concentrated among high income/high harvest households—those who are able to give the most. Likewise, a basic premise of the Ust'-Avam research is that a multiplicity of factors informs decisions to share food beyond the household. What these factors are and how they change during each phase of sharing, is of interest to the comparative studies of network organization.

3 Methods

John Ziker's (JPZ) research in the Ust'-Avam community comprised a sum of 36 months from 1994 through 2007. During field trips in 2001 and 2003, Ziker investigated the primary distributions of hunters and their respective households (Ziker et al. 2015), as well as women's sharing patterns discussed here. Women residing in a household without a hunter ($n = 10$) were asked to complete a *diary* (a survey developed specifically for this investigation) by making entries for 7 days, every 3 weeks. Diary responses and the results of interviews and observations JPZ conducted over a 12-week period (August–October 2001) were combined with community census and genealogical data for our analyses. These data included 162 distributions among 69 household dyads. One report from August 2002 and the remainder of the 2003 data were not included in this analysis.

To analyze the independent variables influencing the Ust'-Avam sharing patterns we used matrix regression, specifically the MRQAP (double-Dekker semi-partialling) process in UCINET (Borgatti Everett and Freeman 2002). Genealogies were analyzed in the Descent program (Hagen 2007). The independent variables used in the matrix regressions included: kinship, calculated as the maximum genealogical relatedness between households (r_{max}), the transpose of the dependent variable matrix representing reciprocal food transfers (*reciprocity*), ego-to-sharer returned gifts in non-food goods and services (*returned gifts*), sharer-to-ego visitation frequency (*social association*), the differences in the number of active individual sharers in sharing households (*active sharers differences*), and the differences in the number of total household occupants (*occupant differences*). These variables were used to represent the predictions derived from explanatory hypotheses (Gurven 2004; Ziker and Schnegg 2005). Interhousehold kinship and reciprocal food sharing were relevant to kin selection (Hamilton 1964) and reciprocal altruism (Trivers 1971), respectively. The returned gifts variable was relevant to the costly signaling hypothesis (Zahavi 1975).

We also included the differences in the number of active sharers in each household as a control variable. Obviously, if more than one individual in each household was sharing, the frequency of food shared could be greater than in households with only one sharer. The differences in the total number of household members for each household represented in the sample were used to provide indices of relative need (Blurton Jones 1984). The sharer-to-ego visitation frequency provided an independent measure of social association (following Koster and Leckie 2014). Finally, we checked an additional attribute matrix: the sum of active individual sharers in sharing households. This variable was relevant to the hypothesized risk-buffering function of

Table 1 Variance explained for interhousehold food transfers (main effects)

Independent variables	Model R^2
Kinship (r_{max})	0.072***
Reciprocity	0.052***
Returned gifts	0.014**
Social Association	0.013**
Active sharers differences	0.012**
Occupant differences	0.001[a]

** $p < 0.01$, *** $p < 0.001$, [a] not significant $p > 0.05$

reciprocal altruism, but it was an insignificant predictor of the food sharing in this sample.

4 Results

The following independent variable matrices were found to individually predict the overall food sharing pattern (see Table 1): maximum genealogical relatedness between households (r_{max}), reciprocal food transfers (*reciprocity*), ego-to-sharer returned gifts in non-food goods and services (*returned gifts*), sharer-to-ego visitation frequency (*social association*), and the differences in the number of active individual sharers in sharing households (*active sharers differences*). The variables in Table 1 were arranged by the strength of each individual model's R^2, and provided an indication of the relative magnitude of the variance explained in the frequency of sharing.

Taken alone, each of the main independent variable's effects tells a limited story. To explore underlying patterns in more detail, we introduced interaction terms using the product of each pair of independent variable matrices. The new set of matrix regressions included the paired main effects along with their interaction to reveal more about the structural features underlying the pattern. Finally, a series of combined models were generated to arrive at a model that explained the most variation in the derivative sharing network with the least number of variables. Our best, combined model (see Table 2) included the following main effects and one interaction: interhousehold genealogical relatedness (r_{max}), reciprocal food transfers (*reciprocity*), the dissimilarity in number of active household members (*active sharers differences*), an interaction term (r_{max} × *reciprocity*), and sharer-to-ego visitation frequency (*social association*). The model $R^2 = 0.117$ ($p < 0.001$) indicated that this set of independent variables explained 12% of the variance in the total food sharing pattern.

Two things were noted about this combined model when it was compared to the main effects presented in Table 1. First, the variable representing the frequency of returned gifts, which appeared to be strong in the individual results, dropped out of significance (also found in Ziker et al. 2015). When we included the frequency of returned gifts in the model, the overall model coefficient was unchanged and the standardized variable

Table 2 Best combined model for frequency of interhousehold food transfers

Independent variables	Unstandardized coefficient	Standardized coefficient
Kinship (r_{max})	0.720	0.210***
Active sharers differences	0.024	0.122**
Reciprocal food transfers	0.126	0.126**
r_{max} × reciprocity	0.161	0.053*
Social Association	0.085	0.053*

* $p < 0.05$ ** $p < 0.01$ *** $p < 0.001$

coefficient ($p = 0.135$) was not statistically significant. The fact that this variable dropped out of significance in the multiple regression model indicates that the variation in food sharing explained by returned gifts was better understood by other variables. This had obvious implications for the hypotheses under consideration. Second, the interaction between kinship and reciprocity was statistically significant, and it remained in the combined model along with the main effects of kinship and reciprocity. Ziker and Schnegg (2005) and Ziker et al. (2015) found a similar interaction in food shared at meals and in the primary distributions in Ust'-Avam. In both studies, this effect represented something more than generous giving to kin—likely childcare and meat pooling among extended households, respectively. Correspondingly, Axelrod and Hamilton (1981) theorized that kinship could help initiate systems of reciprocity in small groups.

The combined model in Table 2 shows that interhousehold relatedness (as measured by the strongest genealogical link between households) was statistically the most significant variables to explain the food sharing pattern. The number of active sharers in each household pair, a control variable, was also significant. In addition, reciprocal food sharing, the interaction of kinship and reciprocity, and the social association indicator were relevant variables in this network. Uncooked portions of meat and fish provided to egos by other households were shared to additional households by the pathways of kinship and social association (friendship). Unlike many ethnographically documented food-sharing networks, status striving (as measured by gifts returned) did not appear to be a factor in conditioning resource flows in this network. While reciprocal exchange could have indeed have functioned to serve risk buffering in the network, it appeared that kinship and friendship ties manifest as the predominant criteria by which partner choice operated for resource redistribution in this data set.

5 Discussion

A few words from the sharing diaries of the women in Ust'-Avam would help to contextualize these findings. Regarding the question, "Why did you share? What do you get out of sharing?" answers include: "Pleasure, joy"; "Nina also shared"; "I simply gave it when I was outside"; "You need meat, just take it"; and "She's a neighbor, I simply gifted it." Regarding the question "What did you or do you do for the person who shared?" answers include: "I thanked them"; "I give to her too—if she has it she gives it to me and if I have it I give it to her"; and "Together we drank tea, ate breakfast, and went to gather berries." As can be seen here, there are a combination of factors that lead to sharing, but the desire to attain status or leverage over other households is not among them. This finding is consistent with traditional knowledge about sharing patterns in the community (Ziker et al. 2015).

Comparing the results of three food sharing studies in Ust'-Avam, we find that the women's food sharing network is influenced by some of the same variables that condition the network of primary distributions as reported by hunters (Ziker et al. 2015) and the consumption events observed by JPZ in 1994 through 1997 (Ziker 2002; Ziker and Schnegg 2005). There are important distinctions that illustrate the relevance of sharing phase. One difference relates to the inclusion of the r_{max} × *reciprocity interaction*. Ziker et al. (2015) report that when the r_{max} × *reciprocity interaction* is added into a combined model for primary distributions with the main effects, the coefficient on the main effect of reciprocity changes signs from positive to negative, indicating that the frequency of food sharing by hunters increases as reciprocal sharing by recipient households decreases. This result provides evidence for three hypothesized kinds of sharing: (1) nepotistic food sharing; (2) food sharing increasing with reciprocal relationships between related households; and (3) food sharing as indirect reciprocity, as either generosity signaling (Gurven et al. 2000; Bliege Bird and Power 2015) or indirect reciprocity (i.e., paying it forward) (Bshary and Bergmüller 2008).

We find the analogous effects for the first two types of sharing in this women's sharing network, but the opposite effect for the third type. There is a positive correlation between interhousehold relatedness and food sharing, as well as a positive correlation between food sharing and the interaction of interhousehold relatedness and reciprocal sharing. However, when controlling for kinship and the interaction effect in our final model, the sign on reciprocal sharing remains positive. This indicates that reciprocal sharing (i.e., giving back) with relatedness held constant is the predominant pathway, rather than indirect reciprocity. Furthermore, since we are controlling for differences in the number of household members participating in the network sample, social association, and gifts returned, it is likely that such reciprocal sharing is related to a risk-buffering function, rather than from incurring *debt* for prestige (Hawkes and Bliege Bird 2002; Nolin 2012; Smith Bliege Bird and Bird 2003).

Overall, household economic need appears to be prompting the later phases of food sharing (i.e., meal sharing), rather than the earlier phases. Although providing goods or services back to givers is individually predictive in the primary distribution and women's sharing networks, it drops out of significance in the combined models, thereby suggesting that this effect is part of the reciprocal relationships households have as kin or friends, rather than payback for food transfers or status-seeking activities as predicted by the costly signaling hypothesis. All in all, in Ust'-Avam sharing is more prosocial and less influenced by egocentric pathways.

One limitation of this study is that it is based on a partial snowball sample of the community. Although our analysis finds several independent variables that are highly significant predictors of flows, the use of social network variables (as in Ready 2016) is not justified without a complete network of the community. This may be why the amount of total variation explained is low. Future studies should integrate network statistics from a complete network sample to test the relative importance of network position of households versus other kinds of independent variables (such as the interhousehold relatedness) as analyzed here.

A second limitation of our study is in comparing the novel sharing patterns developed in this economically challenged community with that of other remote groups. While our study relies heavily on the foundational research of traditional hunter-gatherer groups, comparisons with more industrialized populations need further exploration. For example, there are similarities in some of the patterns of sharing behaviors identified in online communities and those found in our study. Virtual networks enable people to overcome distance constraints and garner access to a broader range of resources, making them a conduit for social innovation. While status striving is often an attribute of members in online groups (Hanson and Jiang 2016; Utz and Jankowski 2016), it is not the only reason for group participation. Porter et al. (2011) report that status striving is but one of the common needs fulfilled—others being information seeking, desire to help others, relationship building, belonging, enjoyment, and social identity. In short, participation in virtual networks permits individuals to fulfill psychological needs, whether utilitarian or hedonic (Hanson and Jiang 2016; Porter et al. 2011; Utz and Jankowski 2016). Using this terminology, when looking at the women's sharing network in Ust'--Avam, partner selection through kinship and social association likely fulfills hedonic needs, while reciprocity fulfills more utilitarian functions.

Regardless of an individual's motivation, successful virtual networks, like those of face-to-face systems, require membership participation and contribution. Porter et al. (2011) note that successful virtual networks demonstrate reciprocity through member contributions—allowing individual fulfillment of needs—and when member needs are supported, group trust increases. Once trust is established an environment exists to foster cooperation and continued sharing within the group. Further work should look at the relationship between online sharing and the sharing of material resources. When considering multiplex networks, communication and material flows are likely candidates for theoretically relevant interactions.

6 Conclusion

Following Ichikawa's (2004) typology, we find that the second phase of food distribution operating through women's networks in Ust'-Avam is a kind of social innovation facilitating household resilience in the face of change. In the Ust'-Avam women's network, kinship, reciprocity, and social association are the predominant pathways by which food is shared beyond the household. These food sharing events appear to be driven by social relationships and cooperation, rather than status striving in the Ust'-Avam community.

Importantly, this research illustrates how traditional sharing strategies structure community resilience. Since the demise of its planned economy following the 1991 collapse of the USSR, cooperation among community members has been essential for survival in this remote Siberian Arctic location. We hypothesized that successive waves of food sharing serve complementary economic and social functions. Food sharing helps to establish and maintain these important social ties, providing a buffer against the unpredictable economic conditions. This social innovation of food sharing provides a safety net for vulnerable households and is founded in multiple evolutionarily stable strategies promoting cooperation.

Acknowledgments JPZ is grateful to friends in Taimyr who participated in the research and hosted repeated visits. JPZ wrote the article. KSF conducted data manipulation and commented on earlier drafts. JPZ's field research was supported by grants from the National Science Foundation OPP 0631970, the L.B.S. Leakey Foundation, and the Max Planck Institute for Social Anthropology, Halle (Saale), Germany. We thank Amanda M. Fulk for comments on previous drafts of the paper.

References

Abrams, P., Feuther, S., Levy, R. L. (Producers), & Leder, M. (Director). (2000). *Pay it forward* [Motion picture]. Burbank, CA: Warner Bros.

Alexander, R. D. (1987). *The biology of moral systems*. New York: Aldine de Gruyter.

Axelrod, R., & Hamilton, W. D. (1981). The evolution of cooperation. *Science, 211*(4489), 1390–1396.

Basso, K. (1996). *Wisdom sits in places*. Albuquerque, NM: University of New Mexico Press.

Betzig, L. L., & Turke, P. W. (1986). Food sharing on Ifaluk. *Current Anthropology, 27*(4), 397–400.

Bliege Bird, R., & Power, E. A. (2015). Prosocial signaling and cooperation among Martu hunters. *Evolution and Human Behavior, 36*(5), 389–397.

Bliege Bird, R., Bird, D. W., Smith, E. A., & Kushnick, G. C. (2002). Risk and reciprocity in Meriam food sharing. *Evolution and Human Behavior, 23*(4), 297–321.

Blurton Jones, N. G. (1984). A selfish origin of human food sharing: Tolerated theft. *Ethology and Sociobiology, 5*(1), 1–3.

Borgatti, S. P., Everett, M. G., & Freeman, L. C. (2002). *Ucinet 6 for Windows: Software for social network analysis*. Lexington, KY: Analytic Technologies.

Bshary, R., & Bergmüller, R. (2008). Distinguishing four fundamental approaches to the evolution of helping. *Journal of Evolutionary Biology, 21*, 405–442.

Cashdan, E. (1985). Coping with risk: Reciprocity among the Basarwa of northern Botswana. *Man, 20*(3), 454–474.

Gurven, M. (2004). To give or not to give: The behavioral ecology of human food transfers. *Behavioral and Brain Sciences, 2*(4), 543–583.

Gurven, M., Allen-Arave, W., Hill, K., & Hurtado, A. M. (2000). It's a wonderful life: Signaling generosity among the Ache of Paraguay. *Evolution and Human Behavior, 21*(4), 263–282.

Gurven, M., Allen-Arave, W., Hill, K., & Hurtado, A. M. (2001). Reservation food sharing among the Ache of Paraguay. *Human Nature, 12*(4), 273–297.

Hagen, E. (2007). *Descent 02.02*. Retrieved September 6, 2016, from https://code.google.com/archive/p/descent/
Hames, R., & McCabe, C. (2007). Meal sharing among the Ye'kwana. *Human Nature, 18*(1), 1–21.
Hamilton, W. D. (1964). The genetical evolution of social behavior I. *Journal of Theoretical Biology, 7*(1), 1–16.
Hanson, S., & Jiang, L. (2016). The low status advantage: The effect of status structure on participation in an online community. *Electronic Markets, 26*(3), 233–244.
Hawkes, K., & Bliege Bird, R. (2002). Showing off, handicap signaling, and the evolution of men's work. *Evolutionary Anthropology, 11*(2), 58–67.
Ichikawa, M. (2004). Food sharing and ownership among Central African hunter-gatherers: An evolutionary perspective. In T. Widlok & W. Tadesse (Eds.), *Property and equality* (Vol. 1, pp. 151–164). New York: Berghahn Books.
Kaplan, H., & Hill, K. (1985). Food sharing among Ache foragers: Tests of explanatory hypotheses. *Current Anthropology, 26*(2), 223–246.
Koster, J. M. (2011). Inter-household meat sharing among Mayangna and Miskito horticulturalists in Nicaragua. *Human Nature, 22*(4), 394–415.
Koster, J. M., & Leckie, G. (2014). Food sharing networks in lowland Nicaragua: An application of the social relations model to count data. *Social Networks, 38*, 100–110.
Mauss, M. (1954 [1925]) *The gift: The forms and functions of exchange in archaic societies*. London: Cohen & West.
Nolin, D. A. (2010). Food-sharing networks in Lamalera, Indonesia. *Human Nature, 21*(3), 243–268.
Nolin, D. A. (2011). Kin preference and partner choice. *Human Nature, 22*(1-2), 156–176.
Nolin, D. A. (2012). Food-sharing networks in Lamalera, Indonesia: Status, sharing, and signaling. *Evolution and Human Behavior, 33*(4), 334–345.
Peterson, N. (1993). Demand sharing: Reciprocity and the pressure for generosity among foragers. *American Anthropologist, 95*(4), 860–874.
Porter, C. E., Donthu, N., MacElroy, W. H., & Wydra, D. (2011). How to foster and sustain engagement in virtual communities. *California Management Review, 53*(4), 80–110.
Ready, E. (2016). *Food, sharing, and social structure in an arctic mixed economy*. Dissertation, Stanford University.
Smith, E. A., Bliege Bird, R., & Bird, D. W. (2003). The benefits of costly signaling: Meriam turtle hunters. *Behavioral Ecology, 14*(1), 116–126.
Trivers, R. L. (1971). The evolution of reciprocal altruism. *The Quarterly Review of Biology, 46*(1), 35–57.
Utz, S., & Jankowski, J. (2016). Making "Friends" in a virtual world: The role of preferential attachment, homophily, and status. *Social Science Computer Review, 34*(5), 546–566.
Winterhalder, B. (1996). Social foraging and the behavioral ecology of intra-group resource transfers. *Evolutionary Anthropology, 5*(2), 46–57.
Wood, B. M., & Marlowe, F. W. (2013). Household and kin provisioning by Hadza men. *Human Nature, 24*(3), 280–317.
Zahavi, A. (1975). Mate selection: Selection for a handicap. *Journal of Theoretical Biology, 53*(1), 205–214.
Ziker, J. P. (2002). *Peoples of the tundra: Northern Siberians in the post-communist transition*. Prospect Heights, IL: Waveland Press.
Ziker, J. P. (2014). Subsistence and sharing in Northern Siberia: Experimental economics with the Dolgan and the Nganasan. In J. Ensminger & J. P. Henrich (Eds.), *Experimenting with social norms: Fairness and punishment in cross-cultural perspective* (pp. 337–356). New York: Russell Sage Foundation.
Ziker, J., & Schnegg, M. (2005). Food sharing at meals: Kinship, reciprocity, and clustering in the Taimyr Autonomous Okrug, northern Russia. *Human Nature, 16*(2), 178–210.
Ziker, J. P., Nolin, D. A., & Rasmussen, J. (2015). Indigenous Siberians solve collective action problems through sharing and traditional knowledge. *Sustainability Science, 11*(1), 45–55.

Protecting New Zealand Native Birds: An Investigation of Founder Motivations in the Squawk Squad Collaborative Innovation Network

Stephen J. Thorpe and Leanne Bint

Abstract Student social enterprise is an ideal breeding ground for Collaborative Innovation Networks (COINs) to thrive. Students and graduates are fresh with learning, are tech savvy, have uncolonised minds, and they default to working in non-hierarchical cooperative ways when working with their peers. This paper identifies the motivations of the founders still involved in the Squawk Squad initiative in New Zealand. Squawk Squad is a new social enterprise using smart sensors, modern trapping technologies, and a wider social network to tackle the problem of pests decimating the populations of endangered native birds. The ideas behind this social enterprise were developed by a team at a local start up week-end, and within 6 months, the team had launched a successful Kickstarter Campaign that brought in three and a half times its target. Interviews were conducted with two of the founding members to identify what motivated them to work on and grow the initiative without clear tangible rewards. Themes were identified using open coding, and seven motivational concepts were identified. Many of the themes identified will not be new to those involved in COINs research and its applications. However, this investigation does provide an interesting case study and may provide a new contribution regarding the role of technology and social networks in the democratization of conservation in New Zealand. This may have further relevance to academics and practitioners seeking to foster and grow student social enterprise and seeking to harness the power of the swarm and collaborative innovation networks.

S. J. Thorpe (✉)
Department of IT and Software Engineering, School of Engineering, Computer and Mathematical Sciences, Auckland University of Technology, Auckland, New Zealand
e-mail: sthorpe@aut.ac.nz

L. Bint
Department of External Relations and Development, School of Engineering, Computer and Mathematical Sciences, Auckland University of Technology, Auckland, New Zealand
e-mail: lbint@aut.ac.nz

F. Grippa et al. (eds.), *Collaborative Innovation Networks*, Studies on Entrepreneurship, Structural Change and Industrial Dynamics,
https://doi.org/10.1007/978-3-319-74295-3_11

1 Introduction

One of the joys of creating student enterprise activities outside of the classroom, such as the AUT Kickstart Weekend at the Auckland University of Technology in New Zealand, is that the amazing can occur. The Kickstart Weekend is an event part of a suite of student enterprise and innovation activities on campus that is all about creating a safe container where many things can come together—learning, fun, randomness, fear of the unknown, serendipity, ideas, knowledge, diversity, passion—and they mix together under the pressure of a facilitated process as essential ingredients in network building and transformation. Bringing together students with different skills, smart brains, great vision, and lots of goodwill creates an opening for the possible and the new to be created.

Innovation weekends, like the one at our university, are happening the world over, and they bring people together who wouldn't otherwise meet. They create fresh networking and learning opportunities. People swarm around an idea during these events. Often after the event is over, the effort to maintain and drive the initiative further dissipates. Some, however, take a on a life of their own, grow and develop, and quickly generate a following. One such weekend ignited something special for Fraser McConnell, Alex Hannon, Racheal Herlihy and five others in their team as they transformed the beginnings of an idea into a viable solution at the Startup Weekend Auckland in November 2016. The formula that took the team to the winning podium brought together the three worlds of conservation, technology, and social media to tackle the threat of introduced pests decimating New Zealand's native birds. The Squawk Squad solution involved a combination of modern trap technology, smart sensors, solar powered base stations, satellite connectivity, and a mobile social platform that allows people to buy a trap, or take a part-share in one, and to receive updates when their trap has successfully eradicated a pest.

1.1 The Uniqueness of New Zealand's Native Birds

The land mass of New Zealand broke away from Gondwana around 65 million years ago. Ever since it broke from what is today's Antarctica, it has been an isolated island free from large mammals. It has developed a rich and unique range of plants, fungi, and animals. The level of distinctive biodiversity is as high as such world-renowned ecosystems as the Galapagos Islands; the ecosystem that fascinated the naturalist Charles Darwin and inspired his contributions to the science and theory of evolution.

For reasons that are not yet apparent, New Zealand was not inhabited by many mammals (only two species of bats). Instead, our fauna became dominated by birds and insects. Birds became the predators, the scavengers, the herbivores, and the insectivores. They lived everywhere from the highest mountains to the seashore. With few predators, many lost the ability to fly and became ground dwellers. Insects evolved to extremes of the big and small, and occupied a range of habitats.

Since the arrival of humans, introduced pests have thrived in the rich and predator-free environment. The combination of opossums, stoats, ferrets and rats now sees an estimated 25 million native birds killed each year in the country's wildlife reserves and forests. Of the 196 native species (Taylor and Smith 1997) 56 bird species have been lost forever, and 77 are now on the endangered list, including the kiwi, the nation's national symbol (Hitchmough et al. 2007).

The default approach of the Department of Conservation to tackling this problem is the controversial dropping of 1080 poison, initiated in the 1970s. 1080 is a poison that mammals are particularly susceptible to. However, ethical issues aside, the cost and distribution of the poison across 30% of the country's land mass, much of it in remote inaccessible areas, produces challenges of its own. Despite a range of community and grass-roots conservation efforts over the years, the pests are still winning. The Squawk Squad initiative brings a new innovation, a digital mind-set, and fresh thinking to the task, and seeks to place conservation directly into the hands of the population through their mobile devices.

1.2 Collaborative Innovation Networks

Collaborative Innovation Networks (COINs) are self-organizing groups of intrinsically motivated people who get together to create something radically new (Gloor 2006). While they may occasionally meet face-to-face, they mostly collaborate over the Internet to innovate and change the world. Defined by Peter Gloor (2006) as "a cyberteam of self-motivated people with a collective vision, enabled by the Web to collaborate in achieving a common goal by sharing ideas, information, and work" (p. 4). Typical traits of COINs include internal transparency, sharing, and direct communication. COINs are ideal in social innovation as they see the initiators come together around a shared vision, they are altruistically motivated to tackle a problem, and they aim to bring about significant change.

Gloor (2006) identifies the five essential elements of collaborative innovation networks: evolve from learning networks; feature sound ethical principles; are based on trust and self-organization; make knowledge accessible to everyone; and operate in internal honesty and transparency.

1.3 Student Enterprise and Founder Resilience

Uncovering the factors that contribute to founder resilience, especially following a collaborative innovation network-generating event such as a kickstart weekend, is important to identifying what influences ongoing success. A range of factors come into play after the energy and excitement of the event fades. Study, work, family, sport, church, and a raft of other commitments can take precedence. Such is the case with the Squawk Squad winning team of eight members dwindling to a core of three founders. Many questions surface, such as, what does this team do differently? What is keeping them going? What is driving them internally that sees the initiative continue? What were the barriers for others that were in the winning team that didn't see them continue in the core team? How do the remaining founders see their role moving forward?

These questions have led to the creation of the study in this paper, along with a desire to identify the important learning opportunities that do sustain a social initiative once the excitement, energy and container of an event conclude. Understanding founder resilience may contribute to developing more effective processes and thus better facilitate social innovation. If articulated and known, then perhaps they can be identified and replicated in future social enterprise endeavors and contribute to the knowledge of known success factors in social enterprise startups (Katre and Salipante 2012).

2 Method

Open coding was used to identify concepts within the transcripts of interviews undertaken with two of the founders of Squawk Squad. The development of the motivational concepts were intended to be both exploratory and explanatory. There was a desire to explore what the founders themselves might describe as guiding their own experience. Our aim was to integrate aspects of what was already known about how collaborative innovation networks form and evolve with what might be unique from the lens of this particular student social enterprise.

2.1 Research Question

The research question was: what motivations have driven the growth and development of the Squawk Squad initiative?

2.2 Research Design

Social entrepreneurs are reflective practitioners (Schön 1993). They "think in action; that is, they practice while reflecting mindfully on their actions, in order to continuously improve both their theories and their practices" (Martin and Osberg 2015, p. 6). They are interested in improving their own practice and the ongoing sustainability and functioning of the team they work within.

As the initiators and hub of Squawk Squad, the founders were central to the study and were considered as experts who would be able to reflectively articulate their own experiences, and common synthesized themes would surface through interviews.

The intent of the research design was to explore the founders' motivations and ways of looking at things; their experiences would be at the heart of the data generated. As the nature of personal motivation can be highly contextual and subjective, the investigation needed to be exploratory to identify any underlying attitudes, beliefs, and traits that were shaping the initiative's success. There was a need to identify the shared concepts by looking for patterns within and across the interviews, and to identify how they linked to each other as shared constructs that supported the ongoing resilience of the core team.

2.3 *Open Coding Technique*

The transcripts were brought together and coded using open coding techniques (Lincoln and Guba 1985; Strauss and Corbin 1990). Open coding involves "the naming and categorization of phenomena through close examination of data" (Strauss and Corbin 1990, p. 62). The aim of the coding of each criterion was to develop clusters, and ultimately category titles, that would capture the meaning of the motivations provided. A strength of this approach is that open coding is key to keeping the contribution and voice of the participants at the forefront of the synthesis. Open coding is an accepted approach in Grounded Theory (Glaser and Strauss 1967), combining a pragmatic and interpretivist philosophy.

3 Results and Discussion

From the synthesis of the coding, merging, and categorization, a set of seven motivation concepts were identified.

Table 1 presents a concise set of motivational concepts identified within the interviews with the Squawk Squad founders. These are not intended to be exhaustive, but to represent a synthesis of those identified by the founders involved in the study. Each of the categories and criteria are articulated further with the following descriptions.

Table 1 Motivational concepts of founders

Concept	Description
Learning	Both from others and the needs of the initiative
Educating	A desire to take learnings to others
Problem orientation	Focusing on the problem rather than attachment to a solution
Sharing of knowledge	A non-hierarchical and open approach
Driven with a goal	Driven members with a significant stretch goal calling them forward
Shared values	It's not about the money
Energy	Underpinned by freedom and creativity

3.1 Motivators

Learning Learning was considered an important motivational concept for the founders. Being together with different people and the needs of the new initiative led to opportunities for learning exchange and the need for just-in-time learning. These were opportunities that wouldn't otherwise have been experienced.

> I've been doing a lot of our website and things like that, which is a lot of fun and lots of learning. So I've been learning different languages to get on that and part of the [learning] process. P1

> I get to learn in the process as well, good to learn lots of different skills, learn about our birds, it's all win-win for me. P1

> I've learnt so much. . .everything you learn needs to be used right then and there. It's not just learning just in case, it's learning just in time. Everything sticks with you so much more. P2

More than just skills and knowledge, team learning was also seen as an important:

> I've learnt a lot around probably team management has been really interesting. And people management in general. P1

Educating A deep motivation within the conception of the initiative was seeing a gap in the knowledge of young New Zealanders.

> So we want to start doing an educational piece and go out and educate about predator-free New Zealand, about our birds, about pests and about the Squawk Squad initiative. P1

> We're going out to engage school's through Squawk Squad so we want to, for example, get two year twelves in each school in the region that we install the project. They can come with us to install the project and see what conservation looks like in the field and on the ground. We can educate them throughout the day. . .they can take that back to the schools and speak at assemblies. P2

> . . .we actually educate a younger generation on what conservation means and how to protect our wildlife. P2

> I was in a school in Wanaka today educating them on Squawk Squad and conservation and what predator-free New Zealand means. It's awesome to see how enthusiastic these young awesome kiwis are. P2

A Problem Focus One of the founders said that defining and focusing on the problem, not the solution, was a guiding motivator for him and he wanted to instill it in the team as a way of working together. For him it meant that addressing the problem was of primary importance, and there was less attachment to the solutions developed or how to get there. This meant they didn't get stuck on particular things or became demotivated.

> For me the biggest thing was really what is the problem we are trying to solve?... I was solely around what is the problem we are trying to solve. Which was saving as many birds as possible and engaging as many New Zealanders as possible. The more we can work on achieving or better solving that problem is what kept us moving. P2

> That's what made it really easy for us is focusing on the problem not the solution and it wasn't about the money. P2

Sharing of Knowledge Although there is a clear, passionate creator of the initial idea within the team, they take a non-hierarchical approach to their knowledge-sharing among the team members.

> We've got a really cool team and everyone shares knowledge really well I find, so we've set up a group Facebook [page] and the team members will share different books they're reading or 'you should check out this Ted Talk'. We're always chat-ting about that and it's always a really interesting conversation between the team... P1

> We've got a collaborative and very open team which is cool. P2

Driven with a Goal Being driven internally and seeing others in the same light came through in the interviews.

> We're all quite driven, and yeah, I find sometimes I struggle to work on different things but Squawk Squad I could work on all night. I just don't know, I'm just passionate about it. P1

A contributor motivation and also providing team alignment is the articulation of their stretch goal.

> So we have got quite big goals. We want to in—I want to say 3 years, but it could be five, three maybe—we want to have engaged 100,000 people and yeah, we just want to get it running nationwide. P1

> The attractor was definitely the bigger picture in how can we help New Zealand in a bigger and forward-thinking way?. . .that was the attractor. P2

Shared Values Several values resonated for the founding members. One of those values strongly evident was the altruistic and selfless virtue of not being in it for the money.

> What we are doing is a benefit for New Zealand and it's not a money-driven project so people are a lot more willing to listen to us... they seem to be more willing to share what we're up to as well. P1

> We set a bunch of criteria to run off and it was really quickly that we decided that this wasn't going to be about the money. This wasn't about zeros at the end of our wage. This wasn't about the success we were going to achieve for ourselves. We wanted to do something bigger than ourselves. P2

> For me, I think actually for the team in general, the ones that have stayed, especially, that we were attracted to an idea that was actually making a difference rather than money—we're purpose over profit, that's what we kind of go by. P1

> For me I think that [the values] is the main driver for sure as there's no money in it at the moment so that's the only driver. P1

> I truly believe in trying to make a difference than making a dollar. P2

> I will continue to work on it just without money, or hopefully with money, but I'll just do it because I love it. P1

Involving Community The other aspect identified and described as a value was in the way they worked together on involving the community. While it was seen as an important aspect to value and to include in their working approach, it was also linked to achieving the initiative's purpose.

> You know, you could have run the risk of assuming it's a good idea and spent hours building it but instead with kickstarter we've built a community there and validated it. P1

> We have plans for when we do our installing, we want to invite those backers to come along on the day and be a part of that because that's very much what Squawk Squad is. The community. Without our community we are nothing, so we need those people. The more they can be involved, I'm sure the more they will share it as well and get more people involved, and hopefully everyone's out there helping rid the pests. P1

> They are also out there spreading the word because they want it to be successful so that they get their reward, they get their trap and their t-shirt and whatever, so you kind of create these little brand ambassadors and they're out there doing the work for you, which is amazing. P1

> We only look to make the data that we provide the feedback that we provide more and more engaging. P2

Energy Energy was identified as a motivator.

> Whenever I have a phone call with any of them, I have this burst of energy and I just start working on Squawk Squad. P1

> And I think as well our team, there is an energy and I think it just comes down to us being passionate about being passionate New Zealanders as well. P1

For one of the founders, the energy motivator also saw its roots embedded in freedom and creativity. Having the opportunity to follow through on an idea, to see it supported by others, and to put it into action and see it contribute to the initiative generated vitality.

> I really loved the startup energy and the freedom that I actually can be creative. I'll come up with an idea and I'll send that through to the team and they're like, 'cool let's try that, why not?' whereas I don't think you'd have as much freedom if you were working under a big corporate. P1

> And again, it's that energy. You know, everyone's excited and passionate about what they are working on and it's too early for dreams to be crushed. P1

The role of external validation wasn't considered a strong motivator by the founders. However, given their success in exceeding their $20,000 kickstarter goal by bringing in $70,000, along with TV and radio coverage, and an invitation to TEDx Youth, it would be hard to see the external validation not playing a contributing role in the ongoing motivation of the team. External validation has certainly provided momentum to the initiative, if not the founders themselves.

> We had a target of twenty thousand and we hit that in 10 days...so I contacted Forest and Bird and said 'hey look, we've still got 20 days left of our campaign, we could potentially fund enough for another project. Do you have any sanctuaries in mind? P1

This led to the kickstarter campaign funding three more projects, taking the initiative beyond a sanctuary in the Auckland region to becoming a national campaign.

> So we went from thirty thousand to raising just over seventy thousand by the end of our campaign, so we were pretty stoked by that. P1

> It's been pretty quick but everyone says they're quite impressed with how fast we've moved, and actually we did have team members that struggled with the fast pace; they just weren't used to that so they've dropped out from that. P1

> The Department of Conservation ended [up] writing about us on their website saying we were the most inspiring and innovative group there, and I think they are quite excited by a young group that are coming through in a space that's predominantly an older sort of person. P1

The next steps for Squawk Squad involve the public launch of their mobile platform in November and the efforts to grow their collaborative learning network and expand the network of interest. As these expand, it will be worthwhile seeing how the motivations of the founders change over time, as well as the impact from the concretization of an organizational structure.

4 Conclusion

For those involved in student social enterprise, Collaborative Innovation Networks (COINs) provide a useful framework for considering long-term success. The study in this paper identified seven motivational concepts that can be encouraged as student social enterprises form and evolve. It provides some validation that following a collaborative innovation framework provides a useful roadmap for the next steps in the journey following a startup or hackathon style event designed to bring innovative new ideas, fresh thinking, and people together to tackle problems.

Emerging technologies and the rise of a digitized and connected world will continue to offer new and innovative ways of tackling some of our shared challenges in our environment and wider society. At the intersections of technology, data, and mobile connectivity, new opportunities arise, and we seek effective ways to assist people through processes and knowledge to effectively work together.

Orientating to shared values, having an open and shared approach to learning, focusing on the problem, energizing one another, and involving the community have all been motivators for the founders of the Squawk Squad initiative. These are likely to be common to many successful social enterprise initiatives and are worth making explicit within the process of an initiative's development moving forward.

For practitioners seeking to foster and grow student social enterprise, consider harnessing the power of the swarm and collaborative innovation networks. Like the bees, let's see them take an innovative idea to reality through their swarm and learning network, and go out and make the world anew.

References

Glaser, B. G., & Strauss, A. L. (1967). *The discovery of grounded theory: Strategies for qualitative research*. Chicago, IL: Aldine.

Gloor, P. (2006). *Swarm creativity, competitive advantage through collaborative innovation networks*. Oxford: Oxford University Press.

Hitchmough, R. A., Bull, L., & Cromarty, P. (2007). *New Zealand threat classification system lists, 2005*. Wellington: Department of Conservation, Science & Technical Publication.

Katre, A., & Salipante, P., Jr. (2012). Start-up social ventures: Blending fine-grained behaviors from two institutions for entrepreneurial success. *Entrepreneurship Theory and Practice, 36*, 967–994.

Lincoln, Y. S., & Guba, E. G. (1985). *Naturalistic inquiry*. Beverly Hills, CA: Sage.

Martin, R., & Osberg, S. (2015). *Getting beyond better: How social entrepreneurship works*. Boston, MA: Harvard Business Review Press.

Schön, D. (1993). *The reflective practitioner: How professionals think in action*. New York: Basic Books.

Strauss, A., & Corbin, J. (1990). *Basics of qualitative research: Grounded theory procedures and techniques*. Newbury Park, CA: Sage.

Taylor, R., & Smith, I. (1997). *The state of New Zealand's environment 1997*. Wellington: Ministry for the Environment.

Analyzing the Evolution of World Cultures Through Epic Stories: From Gilgamesh to Games of Thrones

Peter Praeder, Gloria Volkmann, and Peter A. Gloor

Abstract We study humanity's attitude towards violence by looking at the plots of 110 epics in Wikipedia. Starting with Gilgamesh dated 2100 BC, and ending with Games of Thrones firmly anchored in the twenty-first century we analyze the plot section of each epic described in Wikipedia, using different automatic sentiment analysis tools such as LIWC and IBM Watson ToneAnalyzer and AlchemyLanguage to calculate average sentiment. We find an increase in positive sentiment over the centuries, confirming Steven Pinker's theory of a reduction in overall violence despite a still high potential for conflicts in today's globalized interconnected fast changing world; indicating growing societal resilience towards violence. We also find more positive emotion in Asian and African epics.

1 Introduction and Related Work

The goal of this project is to investigate if humankind's attitude towards violence has changed over the last 4000 years. According to the arguments made by psychologist Steve Pinker in his seminal book "The Better Angels of Our Nature" (Pinker 2011), humanity is becoming less and less violent. Pinker shows that tribal warfare was nine times as deadly, and the murder rate in medieval Europe thirty times higher than it is today. This decrease in violence is still on-going, with today's wars killing a fraction of the people killed by wars in the past. In a 2015 update to his book Pinker shows that this trend of decreasing violence is continuing, with homicide rates further dropping, as are rape and violence against children.In earlier work (Gloor et al. 2015) we used Wikipedia as a "socioscope" to study different aspects of intercultural

P. Praeder (✉) · G. Volkmann
University of Cologne, Cologne, Germany
e-mail: praederp@outlook.de; volkmann@wim.uni-koeln.de

P. A. Gloor
MIT Center for Collective Intelligence, Cambridge, MA, USA
e-mail: plgoor@mit.edu

F. Grippa et al. (eds.), *Collaborative Innovation Networks*, Studies on Entrepreneurship, Structural Change and Industrial Dynamics,
https://doi.org/10.1007/978-3-319-74295-3_12

human evolution. We drew on different-language Wikipedias to provide a mirror of today's historical understanding of World history by different cultures (Kleeb et al. 2012), to measure differences in gender equality (Marcos de Oliveira and Gloor 2016), and track emotionality and positivity in sentiment in different-language news, and assess whether war and conquest or science and art are considered more important in different cultures and identify the most influential thought leaders (Frick et al. 2013).

In this project we apply our Wikipedia-based approach to the longitudinal study of violence, as expressed in World literature with the goal of analyzing the evolution of humankind's attitude towards violence by using literature as a mirror of human society and its values. Art and literature, specifically, produces subjectively modulated images of the real world and experiences made in the world. However, as those subjective images and experiences are shaped not only by internal conflicts, concerns and wishes of the producing artist, but also by relations of the artist to other people, relations to nature, traditions of ancestors passed on, spiritual forces imagined and believed in, and whatever the artist and society anticipates might happen in the future, those images are shaped by society and thus mirror our societies and culture (Carrol 2017). To investigate humankind's attitude towards violence expressed in world literature over time we analyzed the plots of 110 epics through their representation in Wikipedia.

Epics are poetic narratives of length and complexity that center around deeds of grandeur or heroism of significance to the community (Beissinger et al. 1999). Thus epic poems are a literature genre that most likely reflects the tensions, conflicts, and moral codes of society (Carrol 2017). They thus also mirror the evolution of human societies and their attitude towards violence.

The epics in Wikipedia start with "Gilgamesh" which was written in ancient Syria sometime between 2100 and 1500 BC, and end with Games of Throne.[1] Our hypothesis is that if Pinker is right, a change in humankind's attitude to violence should also be reflected in world literature. Thus either epics and in accordance the language used to describe the plots of epics, might get less violent—which is hard to believe considering all the violence used in the most modern epos "Games of Thrones"—or the opposite is to be observed, namely that violence moved from the real world into the fantasy world of epics and might be going up. In addition to the main focus of this study, the evolution of humankind's attitude towards violence, this study also seeks to answer the question whether the description of the plot of an epic in Wikipedia is suitable for automatic sentiment analysis. Wikipedians strive to write in a style they call "NPOV" (Neutral Point of View), trying to be as factual as possible. We hypothesize that this might work to our advantage, as the plot is described in more general language through the neutral eyes of the Wikipedia editors, one step removed from the artistic prose of the original author.

[1] https://en.wikipedia.org/wiki/Game_of_Thrones

2 Method

We analyzed the plots of the world's major epics available in Wikipedia by collecting all articles categorized in the English Wikipedia as "Epic_poems". The English Wikipedia contains 178 articles in this category. Each of the Wikipedia entries for an epic contains a "plot" section where the storyline of the epic is described. We analyzed the language used within these sections by means of natural language processing methods with regard to the tendency towards violence of an epic.

For natural language processing, only the articles with more than 300 words of text in the plot were included, leading in the end to 110 articles with a "plot" descriptive enough to provide a basis for our content analysis. The limit of 300 words was derived from the recommendation of the LIWC manual (Pennebaker et al. 2001), indicating that meaningful sentiment analysis needs at least that many words.

The plots were extracted and linguistically analyzed with regard to violence tendencies by means of three different types of "tone information" that can be derived from text: emotional tone (i.e. anger, fear, joy, sadness, and disgust), author social tendencies (i.e. big five psychological author personally traits: Agreeableness, Conscientiousness, Extraversion, Emotional range, Openness) and language style (i.e. analytical tone, tentative tone, confident tone). For this purpose three automatic sentiment analysis tools, namely LIWC and IBM Watson ToneAnalyzer and IBM Watson AlchemyLanguage were used.

To calculate emotional tone LIWC, IBM Watson ToneAnalyzer as well as IBM Watson AlchemyLanguage were used.

LIWC (Pennebaker et al. 2001; Pennebaker 2011) calculates the basic negative and positive emotion of a text based on an extensive dictionary. We put particular emphasis on the basic emotional tone, and on fear, anger, and sadness. Besides LIWC, IBM AlchemyLanguage (IBM 2016a) was used to compute the polarity of a text ranging from -1 to $+1$ as well as key terms used in the text. IBM AlchemyLanguage components to compute the polarity of a text as well as IBM ToneAnalyzer (IBM 2016b, c) are based on Pennebaker's research and compute emotional tendency, in particular anger, disgust, fear, joy, and sadness.

To Analyze Wikipedia plot author social tendencies IBM AlchemyLanguage was used. AlchemyLanguage uses the big five personality model (Costa and McCrae 1992) to categorize the personality of the author in the five dimensions openness to experience, agreeableness, conscientiousness, extraversion, and neuroticism.

Agreeableness is a person's tendency to be compassionate and cooperative toward others. Persons that show high agreeableness are rather altruistic and find that helping others is genuinely rewarding. They tend to dislike confrontation and are perfectly willing to compromise or to deny their own needs to get along with others. They are often modest, self-effacing, and humble even though they do not necessarily lack self-confidence or self-esteem. They are generally sincere and thus see no need for pretense or manipulation when dealing with others and are therefore candid, frank, and genuine. They are often empathetic, tender-hearted, compassionate and trusting and often assume that most people are fundamentally fair, honest, and have good intentions.

Conscientiousness is a person's tendency to act in an organized or thoughtful way. Highly conscientious person often try hard to achieve excellence. They are very deliberate and thus generally are disposed to think through possibilities carefully before acting. They have a high sense of responsibility, duty and obligation and are well-organized, tidy, and neat. They are rather Self-assured and confident in their ability to accomplish things and are rather persistent with the self-discipline, or "will-power," to persist at difficult or unpleasant tasks until they are completed.

Extraversion is a person's tendency to seek stimulation in the company of others. Highly extroverted persons are very quick, energetically and are involved in many activities. They are assertive and like to take charge and direct the activities of others and thus tend often to be leaders in groups. They are mostly positive, cheerful, and also excitement- seeking. They are friendly and outgoing and genuinely like other people and are very sociable and find the company of others pleasantly stimulating and rewarding.

Emotional range, also referred to as neuroticism, is the extent to which a person's emotions are sensitive to the individual's environment. Increasing values of emotional range indicate that a person is quicker to anger, prone to worry, more easily depressed and moody, less self-consciousness and more stress sensitive than a persons with lower values of emotional range.

Openness to experience, is the extent to which a person is open to experiencing a variety of activities. Persons with a high openness to experience are eager to try new activities, show high artistic interests and love beauty, both in art and in nature. They have good access to and awareness of their own feelings, are very imaginative and have a high readiness to challenge authority, convention, and traditional values, They are intellectually curious and tend to think in symbols and abstractions.

To analyze the language style also, IBM AlchemyLanguage was used.

IBM AlchemyLanguage distinguishes the style of language between "analytic", "confident", and "tentative". The parameters range from 0 to 1, with 1 corresponding to a 100% likelihood that the particular emotional tone is present in the text

Besides the sentiment analysis, the social network of all actors in an epic was calculated and visualized on a Web site (see http://master.it-praeder.de), and their indegree, outdegrees as well as network size and density was calculated (Wasserman and Faust 1994). This additional analysis allows to better understand and explain possible changes in humankind's attitude towards violence, as conflicts (Dziubinski et al. 2015) and thus violence are affected by the underlying social network of humans. Because conflicts between two or more entities affect not only the conflicting parties but often lead to spillovers through the network of relations on other neighboring third parties (Dziubinski et al. 2015). Thus comparing the development of epics social networks size and structure over time to the development of language and its violence tendencies in epics plots over time can support and help explain the observed changes in language.

3 Results

Figure 1 shows the results of the sentiment analysis of the 110 epics from 2100 BC to 2010AD, aggregated by averages per century, and calculated with ToneAnalyzer and LIWC. As we can see, the overall emotionality tents to be more negative, with particularly high levels of sadness and fear. However this is to be expected, considering that epics center around deeds of grandeur or heroism of significance to the community (Beissinger et al. 1999) and that such heroic deeds are most often performed by raising and solving mostly violent conflicts.

In addition, particularly in the first millennium AD, we observe high fluctuation in emotionality.

Figure 2 illustrates the development of sentiment (i.e. overall emotional tone of the plots of the epics) calculated with AlchemyLanguage. While the sentiment trend line is slightly positive indicating a positively increasing emotional tone, it is in the negative range reflecting the generally more negative emotionality observed in Fig. 1 and is not statistically significant. Informally, we nevertheless can say that the sentiment of the epics has been increasing slightly over the last 4000 years, in spite of all the violence in the most recent epic we analyzed, Games of Thrones. For the analysis in Fig. 2 only the 49 epics with a sentiment deviation of 0.3 on the positive or negative side were included.

Figure 3 shows the sadness of all 110 epics distributed over time, calculated with IBM ToneAnalyzer. We find that sadness is decreasing over time, although again not statistically significant. Nevertheless, this further supports our hypothesis that positivity in epics is going up, and sadness going down.

From Figs. 1, 2, and 3 emerges a differentiated picture, where the subcomponents of sentiment show different trajectories. It appears that most epics have overall strong negative sentiment.

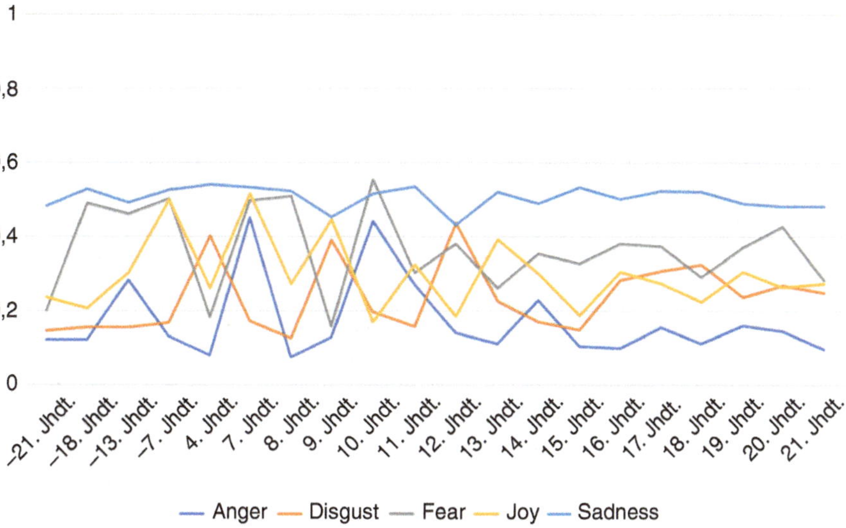

Fig. 1 Different emotions over the centuries from 2100 BC to 2010 AD

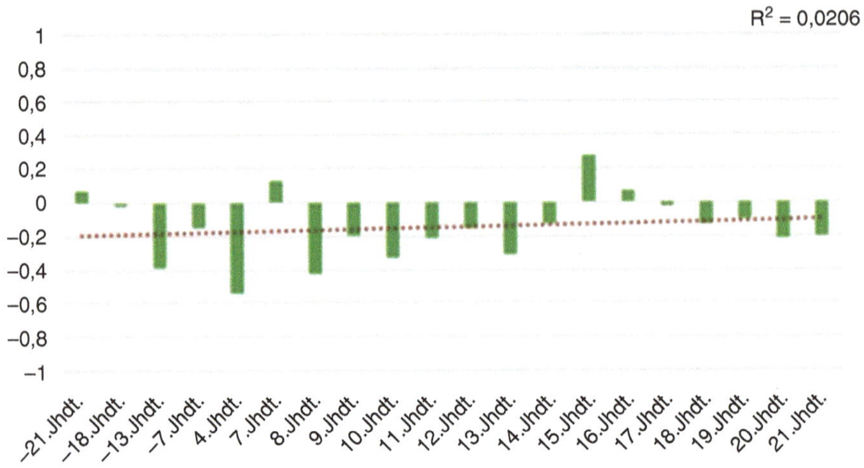

Fig. 2 Sentiment average over the centuries from 2100 BC to 2010 AD using AlchemyLanguage

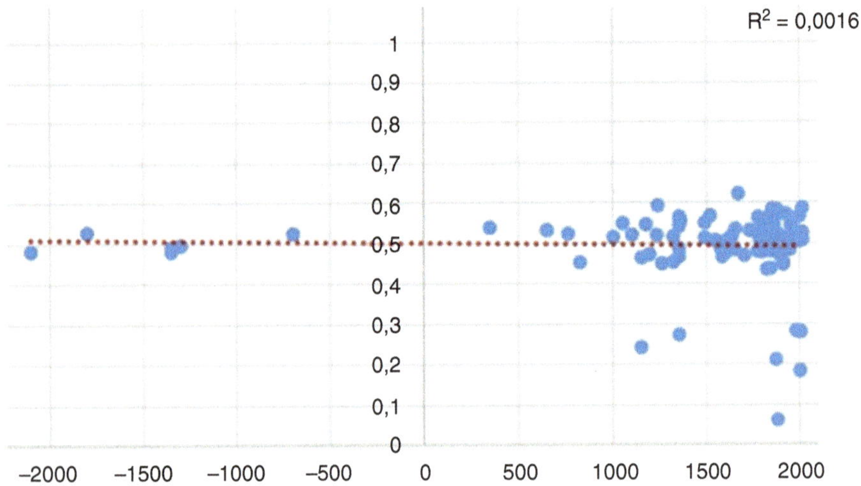

Fig. 3 Sadness (y-axis) for all epics, calculated with IBM ToneAnalyzer (x-axis is time)

Further condensing sentiment into four major phases, we observe a u-shaped curve as shown in Fig. 4, with negative sentiment (i.e. more negative emotions) until 1350, more positive sentiment (i.e. more positive emotions) from 1350 to 1800, and negative sentiment for the period from 1800 until today.

Sadness is quite dominant for all epics, in all epochs, however it is decreasing for the immediate past. Fear however is growing over time, measured and aggregated into 4 data points. Happiness has a spike in 1500, and is slowly increasing overall.

In a final analysis we categorized the epics by region of origin, into five regions: MiddleEast, Asia, Africa, America, and Europe. When simply comparing the average values of the epics from the different regions, we found that the ancient Middle

Fig. 4 Overall sentiment development (y-axis) over time for four major time phases (x-axis), calculated with IBM AlchemyLanguage

East epics such as Gilgamesh are more "tentative". Asian epics have more "joy", and African epics have more "positive emotions". On the other hand, European and American Epics show more "analytical thinking" and are less "tentative". We suspect that these last two properties might be influenced by the more recent modern epics such as "Games of Thrones".

When applying a varying intercept multilevel regression model to the 110 epics of the five different regions with "age" as dependent variable (Table 1), we found that the age of an epic is explained partially through the language style of the epic. The variables "emotional range" (the authors' level of neuroticism) and "tentative language" are significant. The less tentative the language is, and the less emotional range (less neuroticism) the language has, the more modern is the epic.

The negative effects of "tentative language" as well as "emotional range" we observe, might be due to a shift in the purpose and knowledge of the epics over time. Modern epics like "Games of Thrones" are fictional, written particularly for entertainment purposes. Therefore the universe, i.e., the time, environment and interdependencies of an epos are fully known, which might be reflected in the language. The main purpose of ancient epics is the preservation of historical events and teaching of moral concepts. Due to lack of knowledge of the actual historical event and changing environment circumstances in human history in the long timespan the epos was passed down, there is much more uncertainty that might be reflected in the language. Therefore we see a decline in "tentative language" and "emotional range" over time. In addition a the negative effect of emotional range, i.e. a decline in neuroticism might also be a reflection of the observed although not significant positive increase in emotional tone even if the overall sentiment (i.e. emotional tone) is on the negative side.

Table 1 Varying intercept multilevel regression results, regressing the 110 Epics in the 6 different Regions against their age. Predictors are group (region) mean centered

Depended variable: age	Model 1	Model 2	Model 3	Model 4
Regression coefficients (fixed effects)				
Intercept	1023.974	1023.935	1023.537	1022.843
	(0.080)	(0.080)	(0.080)	(0.081)
Emotional tendency				
Anger		51.95902	154.9731	276.4459
		(0.893)	(0.693)	(0.462)
Disgust		55.71526	173.0391	384.4662
		(0.862)	(0.589)	(0.216)
Sadness		−413.9309	−123.5488	281.1427
		(0.469)	(0.835)	(0.625)
Author personality traits				
Openness			−20.65198	532.5112
			(0.964)	(0.271)
Agreeableness			156.3928	327.548
			(0.535)	(0.249)
Conscientiousness			497.2998	354.0083
			(0.140)	(0.271)
Extraversion			192.9523	267.3015
			(0.537)	(0.386)
Emotional range			−895.5592	−1190.146
			(0.039)**	(0.005)***
Language style				
Confident				−23.11262
				(0.951)
Tentative (LIWC)				−23917.62
				(0.003)***
Analytical thinking (LIWC)				16.06683
				(0.098)
Variance components (Random effects)				
Intercept (variance among epics between regions)	1297.246	1297.37	1298.641	1300.862
Residual (variance among epics within regions)	485.6962	484.4044	470.9669	446.4617
Interclass correlation	0.8770547	0.8776485	0.8837644	0.894623
Log likelihood	−848.03549	−847.75614	−844.80511	−839.19953
LR chi2	0	0.56 (3)	6.46 (8)	17.67(11)
Prob. > chi2	0	0.9058	0.5958	0.0895*

*p < 0.1, **p < 0.05 ***p < 0.01

In line with this observation the high interclass correlation as well as the substantial variation of mean age in the five regions with a standard deviation of 1300 years reflect human evolution over time and mirror the rise and fall of advanced civilizations and with it the evolution of cultural heydays of different regions over

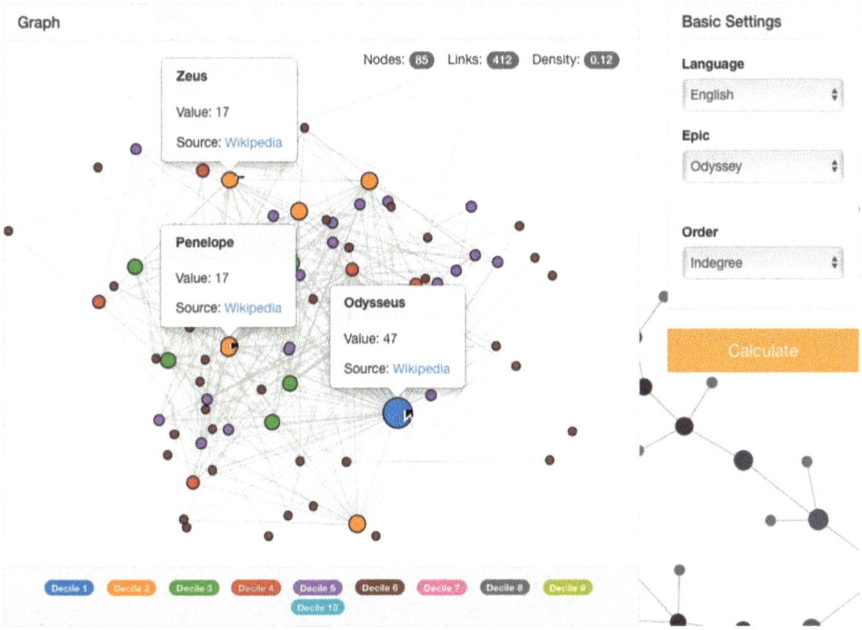

Fig. 5 Actor network of Ulysses (see http://master.it-praeder.de/graph/ for live online version)

time. Putting it in other words, regions subsume the change of language over time and a large part of the difference in language can be explained by the different regions where the epics are originating.

Besides the sentiment, also the social network of actors in the different epics was calculated and visualized because conflicts and violence affect not only the conflicting parties but through the network of relations also other neighboring third parties (Dziubinski et al. 2015). A change in networks of actors in epics over time reflects a change in networks in societies of time and thus gives further insight to changes of humanity's attitudes towards violence over time.

The network of actors of each epic was constructed based on links between actors on Wikipedia. A link is drawn if the Wikipedia page of an actor in an epic links to the Wikipedia page of another actor in the same epic (Fig. 5).

Figure 6 illustrates the actor network of "Games of Thrones", with Tyron Lannister, Jon Snow, and Joffrey Baratheon being the most central characters. This corresponds to the plot of "Games of Thrones" where these three actors are key figures.

While the number of actors is growing over time (Fig. 7) with the older epics having fewer actors (Gilgamesh has 14), the density of the social network is going down over time (Fig. 8), which means that in the ancient epics almost every actor was interacting with most other actors, while in the more recent epics there are subplots, where only a subgroup of actors is interacting with each other.

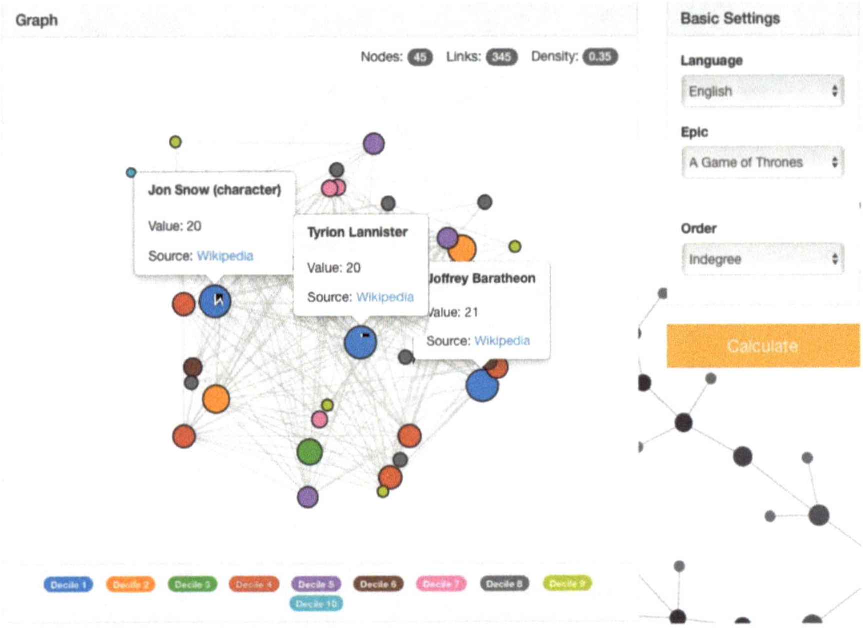

Fig. 6 Actor network of "Games of Thrones" (see http://master.it-praeder.de/graph/ for live online version)

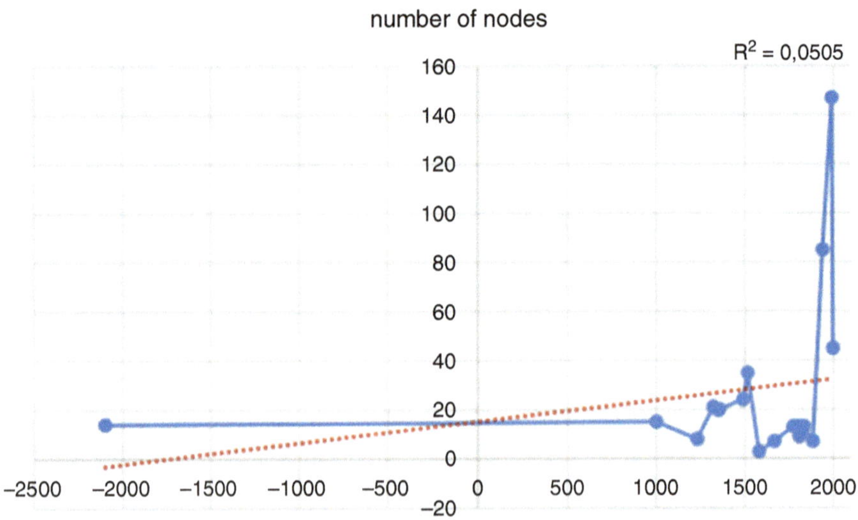

Fig. 7 Development of epic actor network size (y-axis) over time (x-axis)

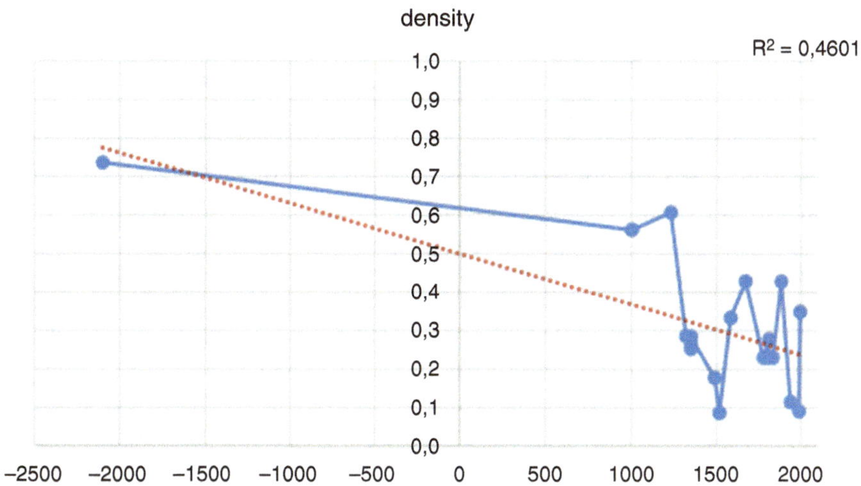

Fig. 8 Development of epic actor network density (y-axis) over time (x-axis)

Assuming that dense networks lead to an increased and faster diffusion of conflict and violence (Dziubinski et al. 2015), the increase of actors in epics and decline in density of epic actor networks over time help to explain and support the decline in violence expressed in world literature.

The observed albeit not significant positive increase in emotional tone as well as the significant observed decline in neuroticism and tentativeness indicate a decline in violence expressed in world literature. A decline in actor network density which theoretically should reduce or at least slow the spread of conflict and violence thus further explains and support the in world literature observed violence decline over time.

4 Discussion and Conclusion

We have introduced a novel way of looking at the evolution of cultures and their attitudes towards violence through the style of language in epics over time. We find that in spite of the neutral writing style of Wikipedia, the synopsis of the plot differs enough to demonstrate key differences in the use of words over time and regions. As a long-ranging trend we find indeed more positive and less sad language as time progresses, older epics are sadder and more negative than newer ones. We also find that older epics tend to have fewer actors, who are all connected, while more modern epics tend to split into subplots of isolated groups of actors. We also found that African and Chinese epics show more positive emotions than epics from the Western world.

While the number of our analyzed epics is comparatively small, the analysis still has led us to interesting results. If we wanted to verify our findings on a larger scale, we would have to build a system on the scale of Google ngrams, analyzing the full text of a representative sample of epics over 4000 years. Such a project unfortunately is right now far above the resources of our team. In the meantime, it would be more feasible to increase the scope and the number of works of World literature, which are available as a synopsis in Wikipedia, to include in our analysis additional categories besides epics such as for example plays and novels.

To conclude, we have indeed been able to show that epics in modern times show more positive sentiment—in spite of all the violence in Games of Thrones—and consequently support Steven Pinker's argument that humanity is getting less and less violent and thus that societal resilience seems to be increasing.

References

Beissinger, M., Tylus, J., & Wofford, S. (1999). *Epic traditions in the contemporary world: The poetics of community*. Berkeley: University of California Press.

Carrol, J. (2017). Evolutionary studies. In M. Ryan, G. Castle, & R. Eaglestone (Eds.), *The encyclopedia of literary and cultural theory*. Chichester: Wiley-Blackwell.

Costa, P. T., & McCrae, R. R. (1992). Four ways five factors are basic. *Personality and Individual Differences, 13*(6), 653–665.

Dziubinski, M., Goyal, S., & Vigier, A. (2015). *Conflict and networks*. Working Paper. Last retrieved July, 2017, from http://www.econ.cam.ac.uk/people/faculty/sg472/wp15/conflict&networks.pdf

Frick, K., Guertler, D., & Gloor, P. (2013). Coolhunting for the world's thought leaders. In *Proceedings of the 4th International Conference on Collaborative Innovation Networks COINs 2013*, August 11–13, Santiago de Chile.

Gloor, P., De Boer, P., Lo, W., Wagner, S., Nemoto, K., & Fuehres, H. (2015) Cultural anthropology through the lens of Wikipedia – A comparison of historical leadership networks in the English, Chinese, and Japanese Wikipedia. In *Proceedings of the 5th International Conference on Collaborative Innovation Networks COINs15*, Tokyo, Japan, March 12–14.

IBM (Hrsg.) (2016a). AlchemyLanguage documentation. Accessed January 03, 2017, from http://www.ibm.com/watson/developercloud/doc/alchemylanguage/

IBM (Hrsg.) (2016b). The science behind the tone analyzer service. Accessed December 19, 2016, from http://www.ibm.com/watson/developercloud/doc/tone-analyzer/science.shtml

IBM. (2016c). Tone analyzer service release notes. Accessed December 19, 2016, from http://www.ibm.com/watson/developercloud/doc/tone-analyzer/updates.shtml

Kleeb, R., Gloor, P., Nemoto, K., & Henninger, M. (2012). Wikimaps: Dynamic maps of knowledge. *International Journal of Organisational Design and Engineering, 2*(2), 204–224.

Marcos de Oliveira, J., & Gloor, P. (2016). The citizen is the journalist – Automatically extracting news from the Swarm. In *Proceedings of the 6th International COINs Conference on Designing Networks for Innovation and Improvisation*, Rome, Italy June 9–11 (Springer Proceedings in Complexity).

Pennebaker, J. W. (2011). The secret life of pronouns. *New Scientist, 211*(2828), 42–45.

Pennebaker, J. W., Francis, M. E., & Booth, R. J. (2001). *Linguistic inquiry and word count: LIWC 2001* (p. 71). Mahway: Lawrence Erlbaum Associates.
Pinker, S. (2011). *The better angels of our nature: Why violence has declined* (Vol. 75). New York: Viking.
Wasserman, S., & Faust, K. (1994). *Social network analysis: Methods and applications* (Vol. 8). New York: Cambridge University Press.

GalaxyScope: Finding the "Truth of Tribes" on Social Media

Joao Marcos De Oliveira and Peter A. Gloor

Abstract This paper introduces GalaxyScope, a novel system to distinguish different interpretations of "truth" for different virtual tribes. It extracts the tribes from Wikipedia through analyzing its categories "Ideologies", "Lifestyles", and "Culture", leading to tribes such as "capitalism", "socialism", and "liberalism". It then calculates the most influential "tribe leaders" through their association on Wikipedia with these concepts. To score their influence in Wikipedia, we use a novel metric we call "reach2" which measures how many people somebody can reach within two degrees of separation on Wikipedia living people pages. It subsequently calculates the vocabulary on Twitter of the tribe leaders, and uses these words to automatically assign individuals to tribes, as well as calculating the relevance of text documents such as tweets or news items for each tribe.

1 Introduction

Quantum physics suggests that there are many different universes, with our current world being embedded into just one out of infinitely many other universes. Currently it seems humans are breaking up locally in many different multiverses. Each of these universes has its own reality, defining fact or fiction for the inhabitants of the universe. Each universe is inhabited by its own tribe, with its own belief system. Based on most recent history, we can for instance group these different multiverses into three main universes, each inhabited by a different tribe. The three tribes are the

J. M. De Oliveira (✉)
Galaxyadvisors AG, Aarau, Switzerland
e-mail: jmarcos@galaxyadvisors.com

P. A. Gloor
MIT Center for Collective Intelligence, Cambridge, MA, USA
e-mail: pgloor@mit.edu

F. Grippa et al. (eds.), *Collaborative Innovation Networks*, Studies on Entrepreneurship, Structural Change and Industrial Dynamics,
https://doi.org/10.1007/978-3-319-74295-3_13

ultra-patriots, which we term the "fatherlanders", the technocrats, which we call the "nerds", and the environmentalist, here called the "treehuggers". We use these three simple tribes to explain the basic idea, later in the paper we will describe how we develop a more fine-grained tribal hierarchy. While members of these three tribes are spread out around the world, living side by side, they are living in different worlds. Members of these three tribes live in all countries, although usually members of one tribe dominate a particular region or country. The fatherlander tribe wants to recreate the national states of the early twentieth century with strong borders protected by fences and walls. The members of the nerd tribe are believers in a global world ruled by capital and technology. Together with the members of the third tribe, the treehuggers, who want to conserve nature and the environment, they are currently on the defense against the fatherlanders.

Each of the three virtual tribes is living in their own reality, and is defining their own truth. Law and order, family values, and God and fatherland are the undisputed foundation of the fatherlanders, as is unquestioning belief in progress through science and technology for the progressives, and the quest to conserve the environment while restricting economic growth at any price for the treehuggers. Note that while we have split humanity in three main tribes for this introductory analysis, reality is much more complex, and all of us are members of many smaller and larger tribes. In the remainder of this paper we describe a system to automatically categorize anybody into their different tribal affiliations, and also check for the "truth content" of particular statements in the context of each tribe.

2 Building a Tribe Detection System

Through Coolhunting in social media, on newsfeeds, Twitter, Wikipedia, and online forums we can try to shed some light on these alternate realities. When looking at news, key topics, and social networks among the key people in each of these universes, we can make these different echo chambers transparent, and try to increase awareness among the different tribes for alternate realities. What is fake news for one universe is fact for another!

With the cacophony of new information appearing daily on social media and the Web, a tool to separate fact from fiction is sorely needed (Gloor et al. 2017). The continuous stream of tweets from Donald Trump and other influencers in the alt-right sphere creates a confusing mix of real and fake news (Allcott et al, 2017). The goal of the proposed system GalaxyScope, is to categorize and visualize News information on social media and the Internet. GalaxyScope will extract the most relevant information about

- key people
- key brands and topics
- fake and real news

on any search topic, such as for example "Steve Bannon", "Pizzagate" or "Nike". GalaxyScope is motivated by the three "T"'s: "Trust", "Transparency", and "Tribes". Through making the influencers behind fake and real news transparent, it will increase trust by identifying the tribes, whose members are living in their own separate alternate realities.

2.1 Analyzing Fake News

What is truth for one tribe, is fake news for the other tribes (Gloor et al. 2016). For example, at the end of the 2016 US Presidential elections, in early November an absurd claim was made, accusing Hillary Clinton to run a pedophile ring out of a pizza restaurant in Washington. Called "pizzagate", it became a favorite call to arms among right-wing extremists and Donald Trump supporters, leading one incensed fanatic to drive a few hundred miles from Salisbury, North Carolina to Washington DC, and firing his automatic gun in the pizza restaurant. Most of this rumor spreading was happening on social media (Petrovic et al. 2013).

The next picture shows the word cloud generated from the 18,000 tweets, most of the words are dark red, indicating that they are used in negative context. The word "Clinton" is in dark red, as the tweeters are mostly accusing Hillary Clinton to molest little children. The word "Trump" stands out in green, as they see him as the savior (Fig. 1).

Figure 2 below shows the Twitter network, each node is a person tweeting, a link between two people means either that one person is retweeting a tweet sent by the other person, or is mentioning the other person in a tweet.

There is a large cluster in the center of the network, made up of believers in the fake news. They are reinforcing each other, and increasing the traffic in their echo chamber. The few supporters of Hillary, trying to debunk the fake news, are pushed aside, their tweets are ignored by the large echo chamber of conspiracy theory believers. The people in the periphery (the "asteroid belt") are tweeting into the void, as their tweets are ignored from friends and foes alike.

Figure 2 illustrates the challenges that an automatic fake news detection system faces. While the fatherlanders discussions pizzagate form a large connected component on Twitter, the nerds defending Hillary Clinton, and debunking the fake news, are quite isolated, and are not spreading each other's news. In order to identify the pizzagate discussion leaders (which we call the tribe's leaders), we need to calculate their network position using metrics such as betweenness centrality. At the same time, as the Word Cloud in Fig. 1 illustrates, the consistent word usage and sentiment will also identify the context of the fake news, with the fatherlander's tribe's leader (Trump) shown in positive context, and the rest of the words shown in consistently negative context. The discussion about the same news item by another tribe, the nerds, would show the same descriptive words, with the same sentiment, but with the other tribe's leader (Trump) in negative context.

Fig. 1 Twitter Word Cloud generated from 18,000 tweets about "pizzagate" (words in red have negative sentiment)

Since the 2016 US Presidential Elections fake news have achieved new prominence, with right- and left-wing journalists accusing each other to spread them. Fact checking news Web sites have been set up, where paid staff and volunteers manually check the accuracy of news (Allcott and Gentzkow 2017). In earlier work, researchers have identified fake tweets by cross-checking them with trusted news sources such as Reuters or Bloomberg (Gupta et al. 2013a, b, 2014). Additionally, Jimmy Wales, the founder of Wikipedia, has also created a community-based initiative to fact-check fake news.

In this paper, we take the declaration of news by different tribes as "fake" or not as one of the main motivations for our tribe detection and classification system.

3 Our Solution

A tribe can be described as a concept, idea or a thing that its members believe or like. To define the tribes we created a system named "TribeCreator", this system automatically help the user to find people that belong to a defined tribe. The TribeCreator

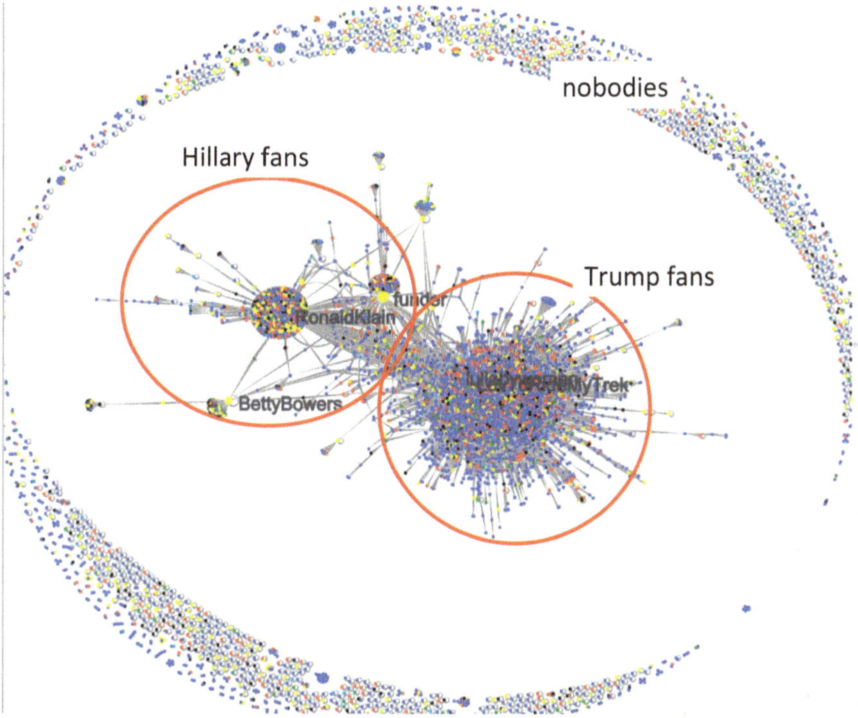

Fig. 2 Twitter retweet network generated from 18,000 tweets about “pizzagate”

does this by using four different search functions: Profile description, tweets, followers, and friends.

The “profile description” can be used to find a user that has a description that matches with the tribe (for example “I love nature” is a description that matches with the concept of a Treehugger). Search for tweets can be useful to identify people that are tweeting about a certain topic or hashtag, like #ArtificialIntelligence or #blockchain for the “nerd” tribe (Becker et al. 2011). The “followers” and “friends” functions can be used to find users that follow or are followed by a Twitter account, using this function we can find users that are connected with an account that post tweets related to the tribe, showing an interest in the subject (Fig. 3).

Once we have identified members of each tribe we can collect their Twitter timeline, those tweets allow us to create a tribal vocabulary and our machine-learning model to find the tribes of a given user. We now also have the data to analyze what those tribe members are posting about. To understand the context of a trive, we created three visualizations: First, a network view that allows us to see the top 50 nodes by reach2 for the tribe. Second, a hashtag word cloud view to identify the top hashtags for the tribe, and finally a table with the most frequent links posted by it members (Figs. 4 and 5).

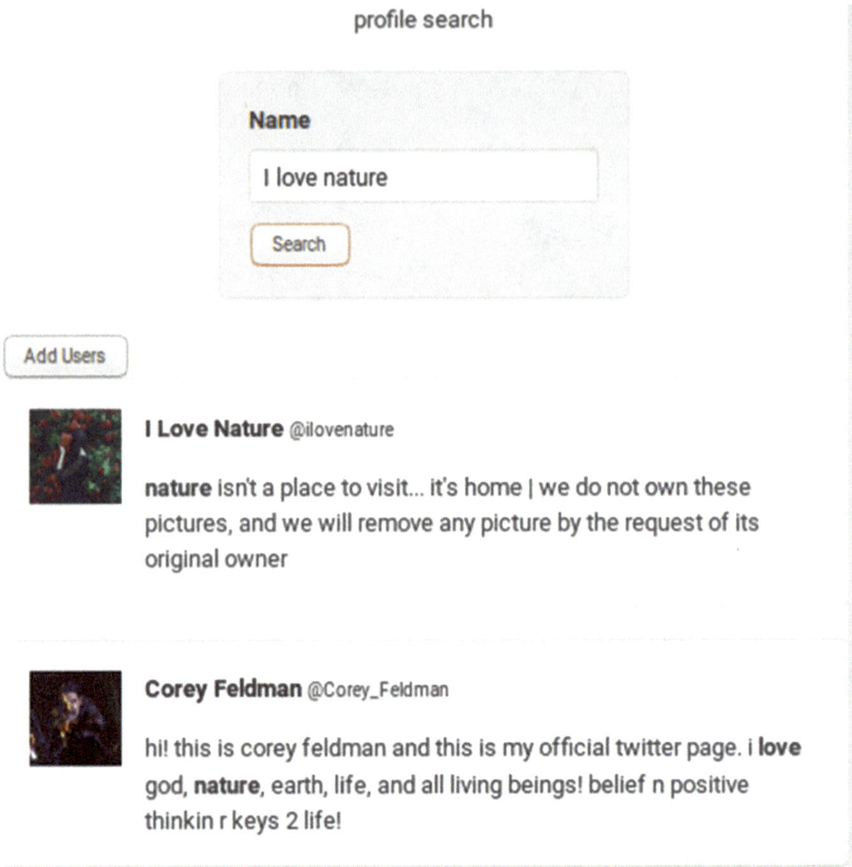

Fig. 3 Example of a profile search for "I love nature"

To identify the most influential leaders overall, we are using Wikipedia. One of the most popular categories in Wikipedia are the people pages. Wikipedia editors have put together "notability criteria" that clearly define if a person deserves inclusion into Wikipedia or not. We use the people pages in Wikipedia to identify the most influential people as well as the tribes they belong to through their links to the most central concept pages such as "veganism", "liberalism", "socialism", etc. At the same time we construct co-occurrence links for the most significant pages for a person found by a subject-driven centrality-measuring algorithm similar to Google's page rank. While Google's page rank is fixed for each website, giving them a determined value, our ranking algorithm is topic-related. E.g. the "Huffington Post" has very high relevance for debates about politics, but a low relevance for conversations about "pet food" (Gloor et al. 2016).

Table 1 illustrates the most influential tribal leaders, based on Wikipedia's people pages. We measure the importance of people through calculating their reach-2 metric

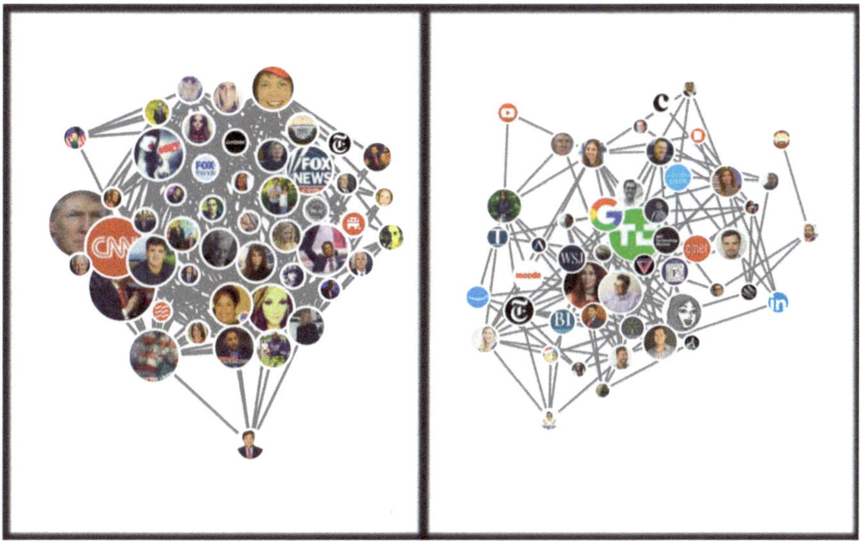

Fig. 4 Network view illustrating that different actors have a different influence in each tribe, for example the size of Donald Trump in the fatherlander tribe is bigger than his size on the nerd tribe

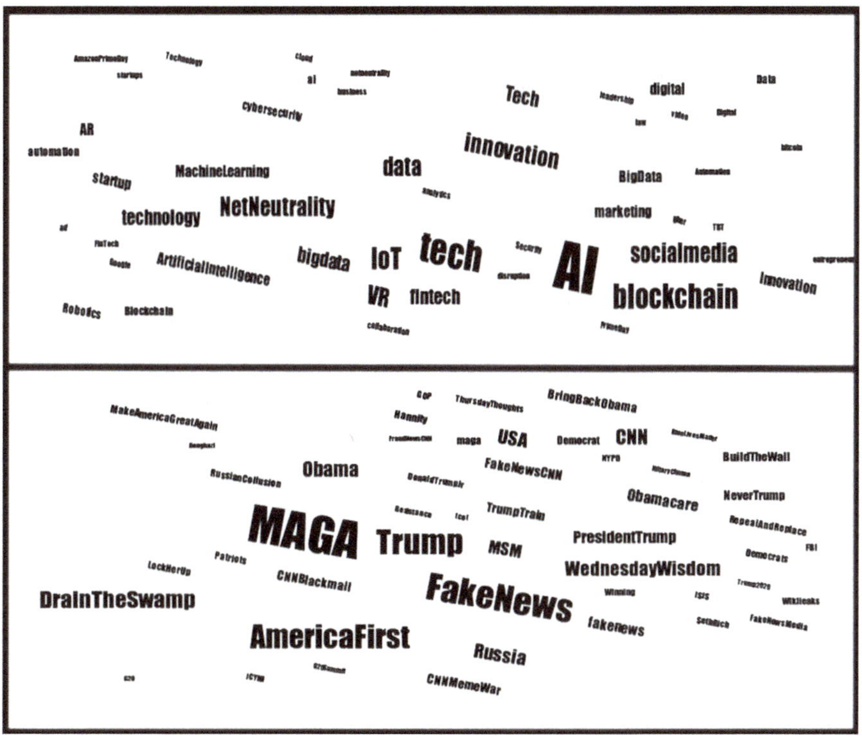

Fig. 5 Twitter hashtags for Fatherlander and Nerd tribe in TribeCreator

on Wikipedia, i.e. the number of other Wikipedia people pages than can be reached within two degrees of separation from a particular people page. Reach-2 is a proxy for social capital, as it basically measures the influence of the people a person is connected to.

As Table 1 illustrates, the most influential people are the most recent US presidents plus Hillary Clinton, followed by two musicians and two celebrities from the film industry. Figure 6 shows the distribution of the different professions among the top 100 most influential people by reach-2. Show business celebrities dominate the list, as 73 out of the top 100 are actors and musicians.

The first spiritual leaders, Pope Francis (position 107), and the Dalai Lama (270) come much further down in the ranking. The same is true for business leaders, with Bill Gates being the most highly ranked leader coming at position 132. Philosophers and other thinkers of big ideas are even further down the list.

Figure 7 illustrates the Wikipedia link network collected with the category fetcher of Condor (Gloor 2017), which constructs a link network for all pages belonging to a particular category. The network in Fig. 3 includes all pages belonging to the category "Ideologies". The size of a node is its betweenness in the network. As we can see, the most influential concepts, and thus a candidate for a tribe are "Socialism", "Capitalism", "Liberalism", and "Feminism". The same process has been repeated for the Wikipedia categories "Lifestyles" and "Cultures" (renamed "recreation" for clarity in Fig. 6).

Table 1 Top most influential living people in the English Wikipedia, sorted by reach-2

Name	Reach2
Barack Obama	111,398
George W. Bush	89,476
Donald Trump	73,081
Bill Clinton	68,839
Hillary Clinton	66,538
Bob Dylan	51,433
Elton John	49,950
Barbra Streisand	49,514
Steven Spielberg	48,903

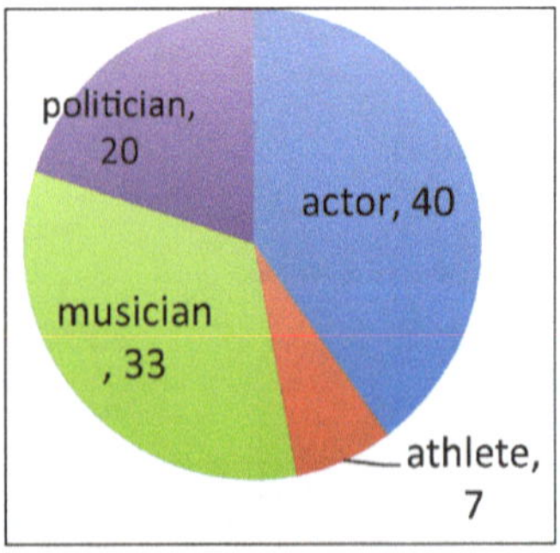

Fig. 6 Percentage of domains of top 100 most influential people in English Wikipedia

Our final approach combines the pieces described above, using dynamic semantic social network analysis, NLP (natural language processing) and machine learning. Figure 8 illustrates the main component of our system. We calculate a bipartite graph

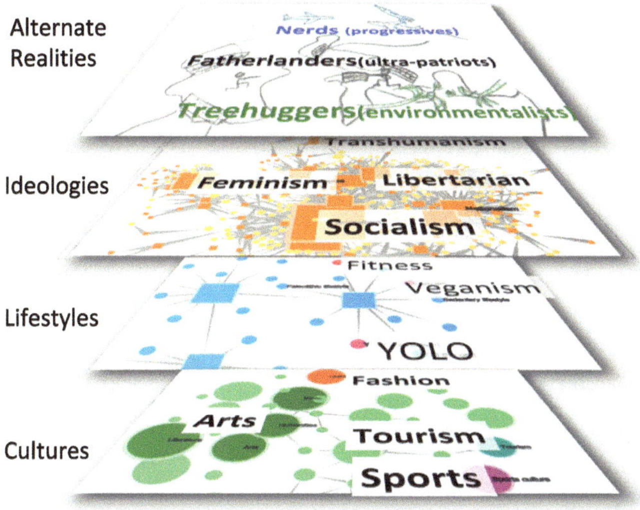

Fig. 7 Four tribal categorizations derived from Wikipedia categories

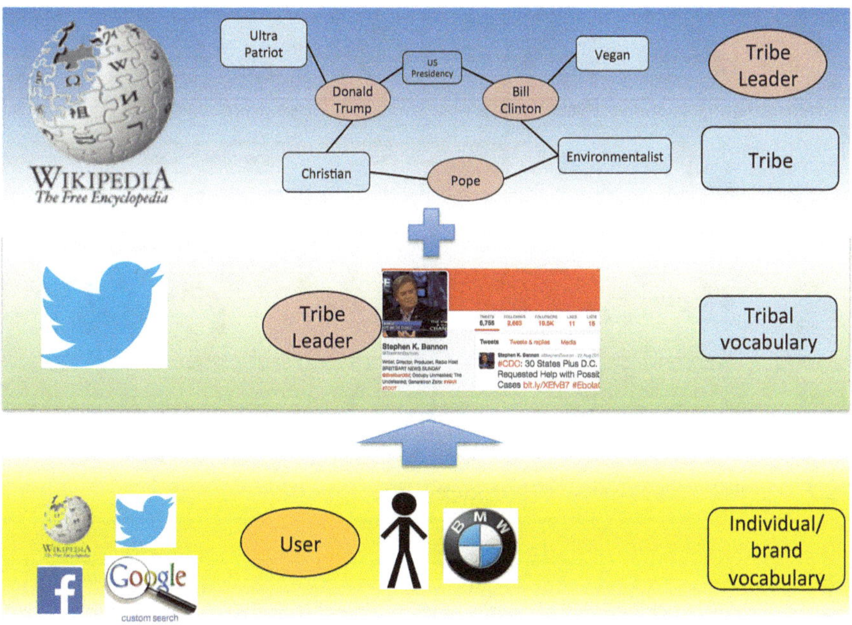

Fig. 8 Key components of GalaxyScope

of all Wikipedia concepts, linking them by the people sharing the same concept. For example, Bill Clinton is connected to the three concepts "vegan", "environmentalism" and "US president". By ranking the most important concepts we identify the tribes.

In the last step, we assign an individual person through their word usage on the Facebook wall, or the Twitter feed to a particular tribe based on similar word usage to the tribal vocabulary. To match a certain brain, or a certain news item to a tribe, we can do a similar word matching to the bag of words calculated for the tribe.

Figure 9 illustrates the tribefinder component of GalaxyScope, Entering the Twitter id of a person (US Vice President Pence, and Elon Musk in the examples below) shows their tribal affiliations, Pence is a big fatherlander, while Musk comes out as a nerd. Similarly we can see their lifestyles where both are members of the "YOLO" ("You Only Life Once") tribe, while Musk also has a large transhumanist affiliation.

Fig. 9 Tribefinder components of GalaxyScope

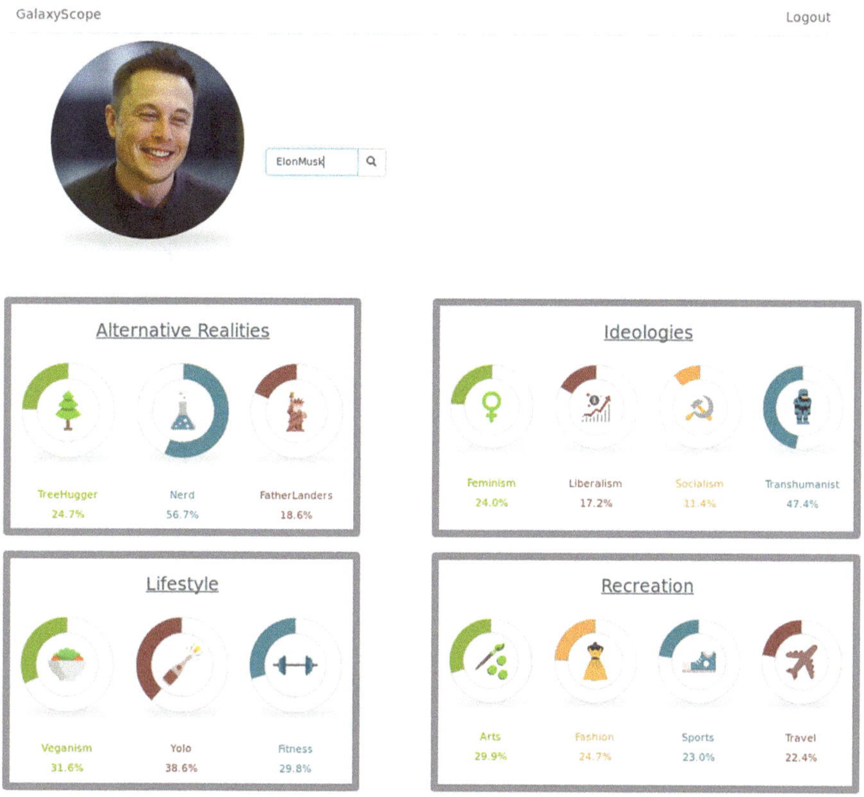

Fig. 9 (continued)

4 Conclusion

We have introduced a new way of measuring "truth" for different segments of society. We identify the most influential tribes, through their tribal leaders on Wikipedia, as well as their vocabulary on Twitter. This allows us to assign other people, brands, ideas, and news items to tribes. While first results are encouraging, much more work is needed to make this a useful and scalable system.

References

Allcott, H., & Gentzkow, M. (2017). *Social media and fake news in the 2016 election.* http://www.nber.org/papers/w23089

Becker, H., Naaman, M., & Gravano, L. (2011). Beyond trending topics: Real-world event identification on Twitter. *ICWSM, 11*, 438–441.

Gloor, P. (2017). *Sociometrics and human relationships: Analyzing social networks to manage brands, predict trends, and improve organizational performance*. London: Emerald.

Gloor, P., Marcos, J., de Boer, P., Fuehres, H., Lo, W., & Nemoto, K. (2016, October). Cultural anthropology through the lens of Wikipedia In X. Fu, J.-D. Luo, M. Boos (Eds.), *Social network analysis: Interdisciplinary approaches and case*, Chapter 10. Boca Raton, FL: CRC Press, Taylor & Francis Group. isbn 1498736645.

Gupta, A., Lamba, H., & Kumaraguru, P. (2013a). *$1.00 per RT #BostonMarathon #PrayForBoston: Analyzing fake content on Twitter, 2013*. APWG eCrime Researchers Summit, San Francisco, CA, pp. 1–12.

Gupta, A., Lamba, H., Kumaraguru, P., & Joshi, A. (2013b). Faking Sandy: Characterizing and identifying fake images on Twitter during Hurricane Sandy. In *Proceedings of the 22nd International Conference on World Wide Web (WWW'13 Companion)* (pp. 729–736). ACM, New York, NY, USA.

Gupta, A., Kumaraguru, P., Castillo, C., & Meier, P. (2014). TweetCred: Real-time credibility assessment of content on Twitter. In L. M. Aiello & D. McFarland (Eds.), *Social informatics. SocInfo 2014. Lecture notes in computer science* (Vol. 8851). Cham: Springer.

Petrovic, S., Osborne, M., McCreadie, R., Macdonald, C., Ounis, I., & Shrimpton, L. (2013, June). Can Twitter replace newswire for breaking news? In *Seventh International AAAI Conference on Weblogs and Social Media*.

Wuity as Higher Cognition Combining Intuitive and Deliberate Judgments for Creativity: Analyzing Elon Musk's Way to Innovate

Xin Wang and Peter A. Gloor

Abstract Derived from unifying dual-process theories of cognitive psychology, we propose a new concept of deliberate intuition as a construct of higher-level cognition that integrates intuitive and deliberate judgments. We introduce "Wuity" cognition embedded into Chinese philosophy, which is defined by the capability of deliberate intuition and intuitive insights, based on imagery reasoning and non-dualistic thinking and manifested as mindful observation and visual analogy. We develop a framework of five features of Wuity and six steps of Wuity-based innovation. As a case study illustrating our method, we analyze Elon Musk's way to innovate and discuss common aspects of Wuity as a higher cognition and creative thinking way of innovators in East and West.

1 Introduction

Psychological and cognitive theories and management science enjoy the longevity of William James's suggestion that human reasoning involves two distinct processing systems: one that is quick, effortless, associative, and intuitive; the other that is slow, effortful, analytic, and deliberate. Nisbett and his colleagues find that Westerners tend to engage in context-independent, analytic and conceptual processes by focusing on a salient object independently of its context, whereas Asians tend to engage in context-dependent, holistic and intuitive perceptual processes by attending to the relationship between the object and the context in which the object is situated (Peng and Nisbett 1999; Nisbett et al. 2001).

This paper is sponsored by China National Social Science Fund Project (16BTQ058).

X. Wang (✉)
Beijing Institute of Technology, Beijing, China
e-mail: wang_xin@bit.edu.cn

P. A. Gloor
MIT Center for Collective Intelligence, Cambridge, MA, USA
e-mail: pgloor@mit.edu

F. Grippa et al. (eds.), *Collaborative Innovation Networks*, Studies on Entrepreneurship, Structural Change and Industrial Dynamics,
https://doi.org/10.1007/978-3-319-74295-3_14

A wealth of psychological and management research has been conducted in an effort to resolve the debate whether those two systems obey dual-processes theories or whether there is an overall framework of humans integrating the two conflicting ones. Bird (1988) claims that entrepreneurial intentions are structured by both rational/analytic thinking (goal-directed behavior) and holistic/intuitive thinking (vision). Evans and Stanovich hold a default-interventionist and parallel-competitive assumption, which means that intuitive (Type 1) answers are often prompted rapidly and with little effort when people are confronted with novel problems. Where they lack relevant experience, however, these answers may be biased, inappropriate and fail to meet the goals set. Thus reflective (Type 2) reasoning intervenes and replaces default intuition slowly and delicately (Evans and Stanovich 2013; Thompson 2009; Thompson et al. 2011). Sowden et al. (2015) propose that creative thinking may rest on the parallel and serial combination between type 1 and type 2. (Kruglanski and Gigerenzer 2011) provide convergent arguments away from dual-processes theories and evidences for a unified theoretical approach to both intuitive and deliberative judgments. They propose that the very same rules can underlie both intuitive and deliberate judgments, and believe that deliberate judgments are not generally more accurate than intuitive judgments. Less effort can lead to higher accuracy.

The conceptual and empirical difficulties entailed by the partition between intuitive and deliberate judgments, and their alignment with multiple similar dichotomies have impeded a deeper examination of the psychology of judgment, it is therefore time to move beyond imprecise dualisms and toward specific models of the judgmental process (Kruglanski and Gigerenzer 2011). In this paper, we introduce a new concept which we term "Wuity" cognition, embedded into the context of Chinese philosophy. "Wuity" is the capability of developing sensible intuition into intuitive insights through imagining and reasoning based on imagery rather than logic, rooted in a non-dualistic opposite view of Daoism and Zen culture. We integrate research results from cognitive science to explore its role as a higher-level cognition to harmonize intuitive and analytic processes. We also provide evidence how the higher-level Wuity cognition synthesizes deliberative intuition and visual analogy reasoning for creativity, through a six-step Wuity-based innovation process model and a case study of Elon Musk's innovation process.

2 Related Work

2.1 Higher Cognition

Cognition is the mental action or process of acquiring knowledge and understanding through thought, experience, and the senses (Oxford Dictionary 2016). It encompasses processes such as knowledge, attention, memory and working memory, judgment and evaluation, reasoning and "computation", problem solving and decision making, comprehension and production of language. Human cognition is conscious and unconscious, concrete and abstract, as well as intuitive and conceptual.

Cognitive processes use existing knowledge to generate new knowledge. A higher and creative cognition can bind and harmonize intuitive and delicate information processing, from a non-dualistic opposite view, as is held by Daoism which believes that the true nature of reality is non-dual (yang and yin interact with each other and create new insights), and all binary opposites are either unrealistic or inaccurate descriptions. Kruglanski and Gigerenzer (2011) propose that deliberation can become intuitive (intuitive deliberation), for example a novice piano player engaged in 10,000 h of training would perform perfectly (assuming some talent). On the other hand, intuition can become deliberate (deliberate intuition), through training the mind to be attentive and through reasoning by imagery.

2.2 Deliberate Intuition

Francisco and Burnett (2008) propose deliberate intuition as the intentional engagement of intuitive skills in the service of uncovering hidden relationships, ideas and insights to harmonize intuitive and deliberate information processing while generating creative changes. This paper explores how intuitive insights can be legitimized, and how intuition can be actively encouraged in creative problem solving. How to systematically gain intuitive insights is not discussed in this paper and is left for further research. Rationality and analysis are the dominant thinking models in the Western scientific world. The Eastern thinking model on the other hand builds on deliberative intuition and reflection. We introduce "Wuity" cognition embedded into Chinese philosophy, medicine and practices, which is defined by the capability of deliberate intuition and intuitive insights. Subsequently we analyze the three parts of Wuity thinking: (1) features, (2) cognitive model and (3) processes to explore how new ideas might be developed through deliberate intuition.

3 "Wuity" Cognition

Informally, Wuity cognition is embedded into Chinese philosophy, medicine and practices, which is defined by deliberate intuition and intuitive insights, based on imagery reasoning and non-dualistic thinking, the core of which is the "Qu Xiang Bi Lei" cognitive model (Zhang and Cheng 1991; Fengli 2010), which manifests as mindful observation and visual analogy.

3.1 Definition

Wuity (悟*wù* intuitive insights 性*xìng* nature) is the capability of developing sensible intuition into intuitive insights based on non-binary opposing views and visual thinking, relative to achieving a deep understanding, higher cognition and insights into essence through intuitive perceiving, observing with awareness, visual analyzing and knowing previously undiscovered relationships and opportunities in the process of cognitive dynamics. It emphasizes returning to the heart, going back to the origin of the problem and putting aside the dualistic opposition (for example yin and yang, black and white). It has its base on intuition, imagination, metaphor, and analogy reasoning. Wuity cognition featured by the "Qu Xiang Bi Lei" cognitive model is the collective subconscious of Chinese people. It is rooted in the traditional culture and religions of Daoism, Zen, and Confucianism, but it transcends the religious meaning of mindfulness or Vipassana. It evolved into the "Qu Xiang Bi Lei" cognitive model and has been applied to philosophy, literature, medicine, mathematics, engineering, agriculture and so on, since Daoist philosopher Zhuangzi first mentioned Wuity 2000 years ago (Zhuangzi 21,Tianzifang, line 33; Liu 2003). Yang Yi believes that Wuity is the advantage of the Chinese traditional way of thinking; Oriental Wuity and Western rationality are two important achievements in the history of human thought, they can compare with and complement each other (Yang 2008).

3.2 Five Features of Wuity Cognition

Based on earlier work, adopting the case study method of management science in the context of a Chinese aerospace innovation team, we propose a framework of Wuity thinking consisting of four elements and a Wuity-based innovation process with six specific steps. From a cognitive perspective, we find that Wuity thinking helps innovators to distill insights into essence through the process of entering the deliberate intuition thinking process after getting stuck in analytic thinking, and thus gaining innovative solutions through rational reconstruction with a rigorous scientific methodology (Wang and Li 2017).

Wuity cognition is composed of five characteristics, the (1) mindful inquiry to deeply dig into the essence of a question; (2) zero mentality to put down the bounds of previous experience and knowledge; the (3) non-binary mindful observation method to see things as a whole; the (4) between- domain inspiration by visual analogy; and (5) to finally get insights.

3.2.1 Mindful Inquiry

Mindfulness is a state of mind that permits insight, presence, and reflection, in which one focuses on experience in the present moment in a non-judgemental way (Kabat-Zinn 1994; Marlatt and Kristeller 1999). A non-judgmental way means suspension of existing experience and knowledge on the impact of observation. Mindfulness includes both formal type meditation practice (e.g., sitting meditation, walking meditation, and so on) and informal type mindful practice in everyday life (e.g., mindfulness of eating, mindfulness of driving, and so forth) (Kabat-Zinn 1990).

Mindful inquiry offers a holistic reconstruction of reflective thinking, which holds mindfulness and inquiry in a dialectic inter-relationship. "Mindful inquiry combines the Buddhist concept of mindfulness with phenomenology, critical theory, and hermeneutics in a process that puts the inquirer in the center" (Bentz and Shapiro 1998). Mindful inquiry of Zoan is the tradition of Zen Buddhism to get the source and the nature of the problem and oneself. This is the process of reconstructing the problem (Goel 1997). "Grasping the difficulty in its depth is what is hard. For if you interpret it in a shallow way the difficulty just remains. It has to be pulled out by the root; that means, you have to start thinking about these things in a new way. The change is as decisive as that from the alchemical to the chemical way of thinking. The new way of thinking is what is so hard to establish. Once it is established the old problems disappear" (Wittgenstein and von Wright 1998).

3.2.2 Letting Go

Letting go, or zero mentality or beginner's mind or "empty cup" mentality, is the most familiar and convenient strategy to prepare and clarify the mind. It is the preparation for mindful observation. If an innovator is getting stuck in the routine thinking model, past hurts and old injustices might prevent her/him from observing clearly and attentively, s/he would be unable to move forward or to experience joy. A let-go attitude and behavior might lead to a radical reboot to get past yesterday's thinking (Smallwood and O'Connor 2011; Smallwood et al. 2013).

3.2.3 Mindful Observation

Dekeyser et al. (2008) point out four aspects of mindfulness: mindful observation, non-aversion, non-judgment, and letting go; Epstein (2003) thinks mindful practice includes core features: attentive observation, critical curiosity, "beginner's mind" and presence. All descriptions of mindfulness emphasize the importance of observing, noticing, or attending to a variety of stimuli, including internal phenomena, such as bodily sensations, cognitions, and emotions, and external phenomena, such as sounds and smells (Dimidjian and Linehan 2003; Kabat-Zinn 1990; Segal et al. 2002). Mindful observation means observing and seeing with awareness, which is the careful attending to internal and external phenomena (e.g., thoughts, emotions, sounds, smells, or proprioceptive sensations) (Dimidjian and Linehan 2003; Linehan 1993; Baer et al. 2004). As Schwartz et al. (2005) state, 'Perhaps the essential characteristic of mindful observation is that you are just watching, observing all facts, both inner and outer, very calmly, clearly and closely'. This implies a detachment from the 'things' being observed. Learning, therefore, is not solely a matter of what one knows, but also of whom learners become (Borgo 2007; Pavlovich and Krahnke 2012).

Scientific observation usually refers to the observation from binary opposing views, or outward observation, in which subjective observers are separated from the object observed. The effects of observation depend on certain tools, such as eyes, telescopes or microscopes to observe the external world. Observers have to maintain an objective attitude to avoid any personal subjective assumptions affecting results. The limitation of this approach is that it can't apply to observing a person's mind and sub-consciousness. On the contrary, mindful observation is from the non-binary opposing view, also known as inward observation in Daoism or Vipassana (Insight Meditation) in Buddhist tradition, emphasizing that the observer and the observed are whole or unified. There is no need to distinguish between subjects and objects, observers have to carefully perceive and scan what is observing or seeing intuitively to keep a seamless observation and achieve deep understandings of relationships of overall structure and detailed parts. The cognitive results depend on the status of the observer, just as revealed by the principle of physical uncertainty. So the observer makes himself/herself to be an accurate and reliable observation tool, just as a mirror, through training their mind, reflecting images or phenomena or mental images by imagery-based thinking, and eliminating the influence of the subjective status. Mindful observation is not against scientific observation, whose purpose is to find undiscovered parts that have never been attended to with careful awareness and non-judgment. Rather it complements or hints at the findings of scientific observation.

3.2.4 Visual Analogy/Metaphor

Visual analogy is an analogical reasoning process based on the similarity and connection among dynamic perceptual imagery and mental images. Visual mental images have led many people to liken it to "seeing with the mind's eye" (Pylyshyn 1973); however, for a long time researchers have failed to evidence its role in information processing and imagery-based reasoning, and hold an argument that all mental activity relies on symbolic, propositional representations, and the experience of imagery is like "the heat thrown off". Based on new findings from neuroscience many researchers have revived the idea that mental imagery involves a special format of thought, one that is pictorial in nature (Pylyshyn 2003). In 2011, Lewis et al. (2011) successfully integrated visual mental images and visual percepts in two experiments, which provide new evidence for imagery-based thinking as depictive representations. Goldschmidt (2001) proposes that the use of visual analogy in problem solving is an example of similarity-based reasoning, cognitively facilitated by imagistic operations. These findings provide evidence for the hypothesis that certain analogical reasoning processes can be imagery based. Wang and Lawson (2015) show a dual representation position that takes visual mental imagery as a key representational format, suggesting complementary and integrating roles for verbal and pictorial representations in accounting for certain cognitive phenomena.

A faculty for analogical reasoning is an innate part of human cognition, while the concept of a sound, inferentially useful analogy is universal (Gavetti and Rivkin 2005). Therefore visual analogy and metaphors have been used at different points in the history of Western scientific thought (Gentner and Jeziorski 1993). The Chinese Daoism Schemas of Yin and Yang, Five Agents and Ba Gua are all visual analogies based on non-dualistic thinking. Analogical reasoning can be used to classify two or more types of objects in terms of structure, function, causality, symmetry, and model, among others. Analogical reasoning is a kind of probabilistic reasoning, the similarity or connection between objects makes it possible to obtain the correct conclusion while the difference between them leads to the conclusion with probabilities. Normal analogy reasoning is a kind of reasoning method developed by conceptual logic, its intermediary for reasoning is attributes, with strict connotation and extension. However the intermediary of visual analogy is images, including both images of objects or phenomena and mental images. With multidimensional features and contents of images, contrary to a single attribute of conceptual logic, connections between two analogical images are multidimensional, dynamic and easy to imagine. Visual analogy is often applied to solve non-routine problems. The type of analogy is known as 'between-domain', where the analogical source, and the target problem belong to different and distant domains. In cases in which source and target are embedded in the same or very close domain, the analogy is called 'within-domain' (Casakin 2004). Dejong (1989) claims that within-domain analogies are mainly based on surface similarities, and therefore are easier to establish. Vosniadou (1989) proves that successful analogical reasoning can be employed between any two objects that belong to the same domain provided it involves transferring an explanatory structure from one item to the other. Visual displays belonging to a remote domain (between-domain sources). Researchers such as Holyoak and Thagard (1989), and Keane (1988) have found that novices and experts show different preference in establishing structural analogies, which lead to different results.

3.2.5 Gaining Insight

Gaining a clear and deep insight is the most productive result of Wuity thinking. Once good analogy between different domains is found, confusion and contradiction caused by superficial observation will be swept away, and one will enter a transparent state with a clear mind and insights into essence. The study of insights started in the 1970s as a branch of cognitive psychology. Researchers pointed out that people tend to encounter an obstacle, commonly known as "getting stuck" on their way to insight. At the same time, insight is considered to be gained through a cognitive restructuring process, which is the only way to the right answer (Epstein 1984). We provide evidence that insights are gained through putting full attention to the target, developing visual analogy, and mapping integration between two domains: one domain is the resource domain, the other is the target domain, the relationship between them is called within-domain or between-domain. If an innovator could find good analogies from unrelated between-domain and build undiscovered relationships between them, the probability of gaining sudden insight is much higher. Especially, innovators build visual analogies between the knowledge world and the action world.

3.3 Cognitive Model of Wuity-Based Thinking

"Qu Xiang Bi Lei" means integrating mindful observation and visual analogy/metaphor, especially adopting dynamic images by mindful observation and visual analogizing/metaphoring between images of different domains. "Qu" means "adopting or selecting"; "Xiang"/ "象xiàng" is a general term for images, mental images, and phenomena, which means xiang-based thinking or imagery-based thinking; "Bi Lei" means reasoning by visual analogy or natural metaphors (Wang 1997). It is a kind of cognitive thinking model used by the ancient Chinese to study the laws of nature, which is based on the similarity of different images and the leveraging of mindful observation and visual analogy/metaphors. As a core feature of classical Chinese visual thinking, these images are dynamic and changeable, resulting from mindful observation at different time points in the process of cognitive dynamics. There is also a similar connection along the evolution of different images. These forms of images are not only the images of phenomena seen by the eye, but also the mental images that reflect what is perceived, even a grand or whole image as a rule or law. The purpose of adopting dynamic images is to realize the transformation from what has been seen to what is to be known, from the surface to the nature. Visual analogizing is based on the dynamic images to illustrate not the superficial association between two types of those images, but the deep level association or innate relationship, even if these connections or similarities are not off-the-shelf or ever used by others, but alien linkages that have not been discovered or explored until now.

It was through the "Qu Xiang Bi Lei" cognitive model that China's ancient people mastered the laws of nature, thus creating the important structural relationship diagram of the yin and yang, five agents, Ba Gua, and then applying them to multi-disciplines such as ancient literature, arts, Chinese medicine, geography, mathematics, chemistry, engineering and other fields, embodied in the traditional culture of Taoism, Confucianism and Zen culture and religions and Gong Fu such as Taiji. Once good "Qu Xiang Bi Lei" is found, confusion and contradiction caused by superficial observation will be swept away, and one will enter a "transparent" state with an enlightened mind (Ren et al. 2011). Its purpose is to realize the transformation of something seen into something known, fuzzy intuitive insights into a clear theoretical concept (Wang and Liu 1993).

3.4 Six Steps of Wuity-Based Innovation

We proposed the framework of the Wuity-based innovation process consisting six steps and adopted the case study method to verify it on the team level in the China aerospace context (Wang and Li 2017). The six steps include: (1) getting stuck—in the thematic knowledge domain; (2) letting go—returning to the original source as the restarting point; (3) mindful observation—toward getting a whole picture of the associated objects; (4) visual analogy—triggering inspirations of the underlying link

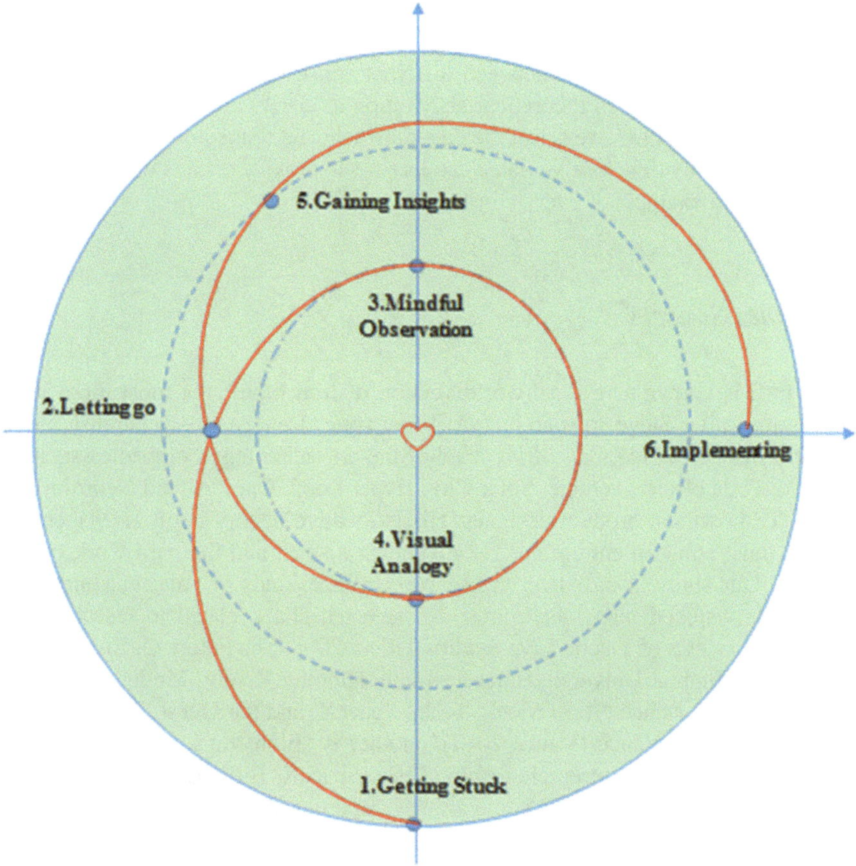

Fig. 1 Six steps of Wuity-based innovation

between the two mapping domains; (5) gaining insight—clear and deep, into the complex context, and (6) implementing—obtaining innovative solutions based on rational reconstruction with a rigorous scientific methodology (Fig. 1).

4 Case Study

4.1 Case Study Method

We illustrate the Wuity-based innovation method in a case study related to Western innovators. Our goal is to verify the applicability of the theoretical model and provide a relevant competitive interpretation through learning transfer theory (Simmons 2016). Since the framework of Wuity cognition is rooted in Eastern culture, we propose to make it clear in a case study to verify it in the Western innovation context

(Eisenhardt 1989; Eisenhardt and Graebner 2007). We chose the case of Elon Musk, because it is highly enlightening and provides a rare opportunity to light up and expand the relation and logic between different constructs (Siggelkow 2007). We provide self-sufficiency in theoretical elaboration to clarify all the constructs mentioned. At the same time, we select the data most relevant to theoretical constructs in the case study and offer closely related details so as to provide readers with a concrete and convincing example of every construct.

4.2 *Data Sources*

Elon Musk is known as a "real-world version of Iron Man", the most innovative businessman after Steve Jobs and a "Da Vinci style" Renaissance generalist. He is currently the CEO/Chairman of six state-of-the-art technology companies such as Space X, Tesla electric vehicle, Solar City, Hyper Loop, Open AI and Neurolink as well as Tesla's main product designer. His innovative history is of an "American dream", illustrating an entrepreneur's adventurous spirit and the hard work of the engineer. Our study is based on the following three kinds of data: (1) Interview videos. We watched many interviews and selected chats related to research, for example interviews of Tiecon Live Studios TiEcon2008, The Future Of Energy And Transport, Qsinghua University Interview and Timothy Kenny. Modeling Report. (2) Books. For instance "Elon Musk: Tesla, SpaceX, and the Quest for a Fantastic Future" by Ashlee Vance (Vance 2017), another is "Elon Musk: A Biography of Business, Success and Entrepreneurship (Tesla, SpaceX, Billionaire)" by B Storm. (3) Media papers and websites. Some articles, reports and e-courses related to Elon Musk and his companies and so have been retrieved and studied.

4.3 *Case Analysis*

In this case study, we analyze those data points in the spatial and temporal dimensions. On one hand, we find four metaphors that Elon Musk mentioned and that are cited by media frequently, and compare them with the four features of Wuity cognition. On the other hand, we sorted out the process that Elon Musk developed when experimenting with the Space X rockets and motors and analyze it from the six steps view.

4.3.1 Elon Musk's Five Metaphors

1. *The tough thing versus mindful inquiry*
   "The Hitchhiker's Guide to the Galaxy" was one of Elon Musk's favorite books when he was a teenager. He said, "I read The Hitchhiker's Guide to the Galaxy, which was quite positive. It taught me that the tough thing is figuring out what

questions to ask, but that once you do that, the rest is really easy. I came to the conclusion that we should aspire to increase the scope and scale of human consciousness in order to better understand what questions to ask. Really, the only thing that makes sense is to strive for greater collective enlightment" (Easto 2017). Before starting Space X, one question that Musk often thought about was why couldn't persons go to Mars to live? By constantly inquiring, he believed that people did not do it, not because no one thought of it, but because people thought it was impossible to succeed and because for the individual the cost was too expensive. In this case, the problem became how to find a practical path to transport individuals to Mars. He further asked the question, "Why can't I enter the domain of space flight to help people reduce the cost of going to space?" Eventually, he took "greatly reduce the total cost of the rocket" as a fundamental issue of development. So, through mindful inquiry Elon Musk began to change the rules of space travel (Mosher 2016).

2. *Glasses + abyss versus Letting go*

   Elon Musk said, "A friend of mine has a saying: 'Starting a company is like chewing glass and staring into the abyss.' You have to do lots of things you don't like" (Musk 2017). "Failure is an option here. If things are not failing, you are not innovating enough; Optimism, pessimism; we're going to make it happen. As God is my bloody witness, I'm hell-bent on making it work" (Zachary 2016). Judging from those quotes, it seems that Musk knows how to keep a beginner's mind and letting go pessimistic emotion. His most traumatic years were around 2008–2009; he desperately needed financing for electric car venture Tesla during the global economic recession. "It was the last hour of the last day that financing needed to be closed, or the company would go bankrupt," he said (Musk 2012). The stock market had gone into a free fall, and investors kept changing the terms. Musk took over the reins as CEO and funneled millions of his own money into Tesla. He not only is staying in the mode of continuous exploration, but also always starts again after a failure, without being interrupted by his negative emotions. In 2008 after the first three rocket tests failed, he faced the risk of bankruptcy, however he persisted on the last day and never gave up, reviving the raising of funds and launched successfully in the fourth rocket test.

3. *Knowledge as a semantic tree versus mindful observation*

   In Musk's Reddit AMA interview, when answering how he learned so much so fast and took it (learning) to a whole new level, Musk wrote, "It is important to view knowledge as sort of a semantic tree—make sure you understand the fundamental principles, i.e. the trunk and big branches, before you get into the leaves/details or there is nothing for them to hang onto"(Musk 2015b). As a cross-spanning expert-generalist, Elon Musk enjoys reading, "his ability to master several different fields isn't magic. At first, Musk's reading spanned science fiction, philosophy, religion, programming, and biographies of scientists, engineers, and entrepreneurs. As he got older, his reading and career interests spread to physics, engineering, product design, business, technology, and energy. This thirst for knowledge allowed him to be exposed to a variety of subjects he had never necessarily learned about in school"(Simmons 2016). With the focus of his interests changing and experiencing new business practices, Musk constantly obtains new concepts of different disciplines of the knowledge world, it is mindful observation strategy that helps him arrange the priority sequence between all kinds of knowledge based on sematic understanding and sense-making in a deliberate and intuitive way, he builds a dynamic and holistic semantic tree of different disciplines, which reflects his own knowledge view as a knowledge map. He builds an integrated view of his knowledge tree intuitively by observing his own mind and sub-consciousness inwardly.

4. *Cross-specialization connection versus visual analogy*

   Facing problem-solving in the business world, Elon Musk did not copy routines that others made, but broke the path dependence, gained inspiration through creatively connecting two domains and observed them together as a whole. He could then visually analyze the advantages of one domain and disadvantages of the other domain, and thus found insightful new innovative opportunity that had never been discovered before. When Elon Musk was asked "if time could be reversed how will you redesign and select your career, and your life to maximum and to perfect, and what's your advice to students in Tsinghua University?" he answered, "I think it is a good idea to study a broad range of subjects, a lot of innovation comes through cross-specialization from one area to another, because increasingly as the knowledge basis grows we become quite captured in the siloes of our knowledge. Maybe someone is specialized in one area or another area, and if you can combine these specialties and create some composites of the parts, there are a lot of innovation opportunities by doing that. I think to have general knowledge of domains is very important. Even specializing in two areas, I think there are great opportunities. If you look and see what has been done in one domain, and what parts of that domain could be transferable to another domain. If you can combine them, that would be quite helpful" (Musk 2015a).

5. *First principle versus insights into essence*

   Elon Musk mentioned the first principle several times in different circumstances. "If we put in the time and learn core concepts across fields and always relate those concepts back to our life and the world, transferring between areas becomes much easier and faster. As we build up a reservoir of 'first principles' and associate those principles with different fields, we suddenly gain the superpower of being able to go into a new field we've never learned before, and quickly make unique contributions" (Musk 2015a). It was in a brainstorming session that he suddenly realized that the first principle would help him solve the question of rocket improvement and low cost strategy, he disclosed it in "The Future Of Energy And Transport interview" (Musk 2012). Actually, the first principle is insight that he gained through connecting the two domains of the knowledge world and the action world. At the same time, he applied this insight to provide rules both for communicating with employees and for logical analytic thinking in the business world. To resume, the first principle is multifunctional, it is an insightful common principle that could be applied to the knowledge world as the premise of logical analysis and to the action world as a simple rule to communicate with people (Kruglanski and Gigerenzer 2011; Bingham and Eisenhardt 2011).

4.3.2 The Process of Innovation in Developing Space X

In this section we analyze the process that Elon Musk developed to experiment with the Space X rockets and motors and analyze them using the six steps view. His innovation process is divided into six steps:

1. *getting stuck*

   "Unwilling to pay what U.S. rocket companies were charging, Elon Musk made three trips to Russia and tried to buy a refurbished Dnepr missile, but found deal-making in the wild west of Russian capitalism too risky financially" (Chaikin 2012).
2. *letting go*

   When the Russians refused to negotiate, Elon decided to build the rocket himself—the modern Falcon 9 in 2002 (Cantrell 2015). Robert Zubrin, president of Pioneer Astronautics said "When I first met him in 2001, he knew absolutely nothing about rockets, though he clearly had a scientific mind, By 2004, he had learned a fair amount, and by 2007 he knew everything" (Hull et al. 2014). "Musk also keeps a small collection of books on his desk—a sort of autodidact's guide on how to build rockets: Huzel and Huang on the fundamentals of liquid propellants, Sutton and Biblarz on propulsion elements, J.E. Gordon's Structures: Or Why Things Don't Fall Down" (Kluger 2012).
3. *mindful observation*

   "Elon can get to near mastery level on a subject in a pretty short amount of time through sheer will. What he's very good at is processing complex information for a wide variety of fields very well." "There's little in his educational background that should have made him ready to make cars and rockets. He largely learned aerospace by reading textbooks given to him by a friend and interviewing experts and his own employees. He does—and this is true—help design the rockets" (Vance 2016).
4. *visual analogy*

   Elon said, "If we put in the time and learn core concepts across fields and always relate those concepts back to our life and the world, transferring between areas becomes much easier and faster". "I think it is a good idea to study a broad range of subjects, a lot of innovations come through cross-specialization from one area to another, because increasingly as a knowledge basis grows we become quite adept through the siloes in our knowledge. I think to have general knowledge of domains is very important. Even specializing in two areas, I think there are great opportunities" (Musk 2015a).
5. *gaining insight*

   "For example with rockets and cars, the auto industry is very good at producing large complex mechanical objects at low cost. It is remarkable how little the car costs this way, and applying those manufacturing technologies to rocketry is very helpful. Going the other direction, rocketry is very good at making things very light. Because if it is not this way, it could not be sent to the orbit. So if you apply those techniques to cars, you can help with making lighter cars, and it allows cars have greater range. So this is an example of cross-specialization" (Musk 2015a).

6. *implementing*

   For the rocket industry, Elon Musk combined the advantages of low-cost pipelines and thrust-adjustable engines in the automotive industry with the high cost and non-reusable disadvantages of the rocket industry. First, the Space X Company took the lead in the field of aerospace in assembly line production mode. Second, Space X Falcon Rockets achieved a smooth landing and a successful recovery, the "gray falcon" rocket engine is the key to success (Musk 2015a; Tesla News 2015).

5 Discussion and Conclusions

Applying the case study method, we find that Elon Musk's four innovation metaphors of "The tough thing", "glasses+abyss", "knowledge as a semantic tree", "cross-specialization connection" and "first principle" correspond to four features of Wuity thinking (zero mentality, mindful observation, visual analogy, and insights into essence). His innovative process of developing and testing Space X corresponds to the six steps of Wuity-based innovation. Wuity-based innovation is used to interpret Elon Musk's way to innovate through learning transfer (Simmons 2016). Wang Shuren believe that, imagery-based thinking and the Wuity method are the source of original innovation, to innovate is to break the bondage of conceptual thinking, return to the original and natural thinking (Wang and Li 2006; Wang 2012). We have shown that Wuity is a way to combine common cognition and creative thinking of innovators in East and West, although more discussion and rigorous empirical studies are needed in the future.

From the perspective of unifying dual-processes theories of cognitive psychology, we proposed a new concept of deliberate intuition as higher-level cognition of integrating intuitive and deliberate judgments, and introduced Wuity cognition derived from the context of Chinese culture. We used the framework of the five features of Wuity, "Qu Xiang Bi Lei" thinking Model and the six steps of Wuity-based innovation to uncover the mechanism to gain deliberate intuition and insights through Wuity cognition. The case study methodology was adopted to illustrate Elon Musk's Wuity-based thinking, deliberate intuition and the process of innovation. From Wuity to deliberate intuition, we find three premises are very important to pay attention to and to explore further, which are mindfulness (mindful inquiry, letting go and mindful observation), imagery-based thinking (visual analogy and 'Qu Xiang Bi Lei' cognitive model) and Non-dualistic thinking (deliberation and intuition, conceptual thinking and imagery-based thinking).

In The Innovator's DNA, authors Jeff Dyer, Hal Gergersen, and Clayton M. Christensen build on the idea of disruptive innovation to outline the five discovery skills that distinguish the Steve Jobses and Jeff Bezoses of the world from the run-of-the-mill corporate managers. Those five skills are questioning, experimenting, observing, associating, and networking. Comparing with our five features of Wuity-based innovation, which includes mindful inquiry, letting go, mindful observation, visual analogy, and insights, we believe our five features play a complimentary role to the five skills for innovators above. Mindful inquiry is a process of reconstructing a problem to find the nature of the question, which is connected to the innovators' spirituality and inner call, it is different from critical questioning the outside world. Letting go is of great importance for innovators, especially entrepreneurs, to clear the negative effects and try other alternatives and experiments. A better combination of mindful observation and visual analogy/metaphor, which is the thinking model of Eastern philosophy might help develop insights that lead to simple rules, maybe even a roadmap for the next steps.

References

Baer, R. A., Smith, G. T., & Allen, K. B. (2004). Assessment of mindfulness by self-report: The Kentucky inventory of mindfulness skills. *Assessment, 11*(3), 191–206.

Bentz, V. M., & Shapiro, J. J. (1998). *Mindful inquiry in social research*. Thousand Oaks, CA: Sage.

Bingham, C. B., & Eisenhardt, K. M. (2011). Rational heuristics: the 'simple rules' that strategists learn from process experience. *Strategic Management Journal, 32*(13), 1437–1464.

Bird, B. (1988). Implementing entrepreneurial ideas: The case for intention. *Academy of Management Review, 13*(3), 442–453.

Borgo, D. (2007). Free jazz in the classroom: An ecological approach to music education. *Jazz Perspectives, 1*(1), 61–88.

Cantrell, J. (2015). *Why did Elon Musk ask Jim Cantrell and Adeo Ressi, in particular, to travel to Russia with him in 2001?* Retrieved June 10, 2017, from https://www.quora.com/Why-did-Elon-Musk-ask-Jim-Cantrell-and-Adeo-Ressi-in-particular-to-travel-to-Russia-with-him-in-2001

Casakin, H. (2004). Visual analogy as a cognitive strategy in the design process: Expert versus novice performance. *Journal of Design Research, 4*(2), 124–141.

Chaikin, A. (2012, January). Is SpaceX changing the rocket equation? *Air and Space Magazine*. Retrieved July 1, 2017, from http://www.airspacemag.com/space/is-spacex-changing-the-rocket-equation-132285884/

Dejong, G. (1989). The role of explanation in analogy; or, the curse of an alluring name. In *Similarity and analogical reasoning* (pp. 346–365). Cambridge, MA: Cambridge University Press.

Dekeyser, M., Raes, F., Leijssen, M., Leysen, S., & Dewulf, D. (2008). Mindfulness skills and interpersonal behaviour. *Personality and Individual Differences, 44*(5), 1235–1245.

Dimidjian, S., & Linehan, M. M. (2003). Defining an agenda for future research on the clinical application of mindfulness practice. *Clinical Psychology: Science and Practice, 10*(2), 166–171.

Easto, J. (Ed.). (2017). *Rocket man: Elon Musk in his own words*. Evanston, IL: Agate Publishing.

Eisenhardt, K. M. (1989). Agency theory: An assessment and review. *Academy of management review, 14*(1), 57–74.

Eisenhardt, K. M., & Graebner, M. E. (2007). Theory building from cases: Opportunities and challenges. *Academy of management journal, 50*(1), 25–32.

Epstein, R. A. (1984). In defense of the contract at will. *The University of Chicago Law Review, 51*(4), 947–982.

Epstein, R. M. (2003). Mindful practice in action (I): Technical competence, evidence-based medicine, and relationship-centered care. *Families, Systems, and Health, 21*(1), 1–9.

Evans, J. S. B., & Stanovich, K. E. (2013). Dual-process theories of higher cognition: Advancing the debate. *Perspectives on Psychological Science, 8*(3), 223–241.

Fengli, L. (2010). Metaphor, Qu-Xiang Bi-Lei and Chinese Medicine. *The way of thinking: Theory, methodology and structure of Traditional Chinese Medicine*. (pp. 63–88).

Francisco, J. M., & Burnett, C. A. (2008). Deliberate intuition: Giving intuitive insights their rightful place in the creative problem solving thinking skills model. In K. J. Lewis (Ed.), *Creativity and innovation, management journal conference* (pp. 236–253).

Gavetti, G., & Rivkin, J. W. (2005). How strategists really think: Tapping the power of analogy. *Harvard Business Review, 83*(4), 54–63.

Gentner, D., & Jeziorski, M. (1993). The shift from metaphor to analogy in western science. In A. Ortony (Ed.), *Metaphor and thought* (2nd ed., pp. 447–480). Cambridge, England: Cambridge University Press.

Goel, A. K. (1997). Design, analogy, and creativity. *IEEE Expert, 12*(3), 62–70.

Goldschmidt, G. (2001). Visual analogy: A strategy for design reasoning and learning. In *Design knowing and learning: Cognition in design education* (pp. 199–220). Amsterdam: Elsevier.

Holyoak, K. J., & Thagard, P. (1989). Analogical mapping by constraint satisfaction. *Cognitive Science, 13*(3), 295–355.

Hull, D., News, B., & May, P. (2014). *Rocket Man: The otherworldly ambitions of Elon Musk*. Retrieved May 28, 2017, from http://www.mercurynews.com/2014/04/14/rocket-man-the-otherworldly-ambitions-of-elon-musk/

Kabat-Zinn, J. (1990). *Full catastrophe living: The program of the stress reduction clinic at the university of Massachusetts medical center*. New York: Delta.

Kabat-Zinn, J. (1994). *Wherever you go, there you are*. New York: Hyperion Books.

Kabat-Zinn, J. (2009). *Wherever you go, there you are: Mindfulness meditation in everyday life*. New York: Hachette Books.

Keane, J. (1988). *Civil society and the state: New European perspectives*. New York: Verso Books.

Kluger, J. (2012). *Rocket man: Billionaire Elon Musk is getting America back in the space game*. Retrieved May 20, 2017, from http://content.time.com/time/subscriber/article/0,33009,2116714-2,00.html

Kruglanski, A. W., & Gigerenzer, G. (2011). Intuitive and deliberate judgments are based on common principles. *Psychological Review, 118*(1), 97–109.

Lewis, K. J., Borst, G., & Kosslyn, S. M. (2011). Integrating visual mental images and visual percepts: New evidence for depictive representations. *Psychological Research, 75*(4), 259–271.

Linehan, M. (1993). *Cognitive-behavioral treatment of borderline personality disorder*. New York: Guilford Press.

Liu, X. G. (2003). *Classifying the Zhuangzi chapters (No. 65)*. Ann Arbor: University of Michigan Center for Chinese.

Marlatt, G. A., & Kristeller, J. L. (1999). Mindfulness and meditation. In W. R. Miller (Ed.), *Integrating spirituality into treatment: Resources for practitioners* (pp. 67–84). Washington, DC: American Psychological Association.

Mosher, D. (2016). *Elon Musk's full Mars rocket and spaceship talk*. Retrieved September 29, 2016, from http://www.businessinsider.com/elonmusk-mars-speech-transcript-2016-9

Musk, E. (2012). *The future of energy and transport (Interview)*. Retrieved May 23, 2017, from https://www.youtube.com/watch?v=pKHyZxSCseE&list=PL2Sr-npLuQliTbJboBPVg-N2yEbzE4bhE

Musk, E. (2015a). *Qing Hua university China interview (Interview)*. Retrieved May 23, 2017, from https://www.tesla.cn/videos/dialogue-qianyingyielon-full-1022

Musk, E. (2015b). *Knowledge as a semantic tree (Interview)*. Retrieved June 20, 2017, from https://www.reddit.com/r/IAmA/comments/2rgsan/i_am_elon_musk_ceocto_of_a_rocket_company_ama/

Musk, E. (2017). *Elon Musk on how to start up a business* (Interview). Retrieved April 10, 2017, from https://www.youtube.com/watch?v=gg23Y9Ua4qE

Nisbett, R. E., Peng, K., Choi, I., & Norenzayan, A. (2001). Culture and systems of thought: Holistic versus analytic cognition. *Psychological Review, 108*(2), 291–310.

Oxford Dictionary. (2016). Cognition. In *Oxford dictionary* (online). Oxford Press. Accessed February 4, 2016, from https://en.oxforddictionaries.com/definition/cognition
Pavlovich, K., & Krahnke, K. (2012). Empathy, connectedness and organisation. *Journal of Business Ethics, 105*(1), 131–137.
Peng, K., & Nisbett, R. E. (1999). Culture, dialectics, and reasoning about contradiction. *American Psychologist, 54*(9), 741–754.
Pylyshyn, Z. W. (1973). What the mind's eye tells the mind's brain: A critique of mental imagery. *Psychological Bulletin, 80*(1), 1–12. 164.
Pylyshyn, Z. (2003). Return of the mental image: Are there really pictures in the brain? *Trends in Cognitive Sciences, 7*(3), 113–118.
Ren, J., Huang, Z., Luo, J., Wei, G., Ying, X., Ding, Z., Wu, Y., & Luo, F. (2011). Meditation promotes insightful problem-solving by keeping people in a mindful and alert conscious state. *Science China Life Sciences, 54*(10), 961–965.
Schwartz, J. M., Stapp, H. P., & Beauregard, M. (2005). Quantum physics in neuroscience and psychology: A neurophysical model of mind-brain interaction. *Philosophical Transactions of the Royal Society B: Biological Sciences, 360*(1458), 1309–1327.
Segal, Z. V., Teasdale, J. D., Williams, J. M., & Gemar, M. C. (2002). The mindfulness-based cognitive therapy adherence scale: Inter-rater reliability, adherence to protocol and treatment distinctiveness. *Clinical Psychology and Psychotherapy, 9*(2), 131–138.
Siggelkow, N. (2007). Persuasion with case studies. *The Academy of Management Journal, 50*(1), 20–24.
Simmons, M. (2016). *How Elon Musk learns faster and better than everyone else*. Retrieved July 20, 2017, from https://medium.com/@michaeldsimmons/how-elon-musk-learns-faster-and-better-than-everyone-else-104806b23df8#.9kjo7z3x9
Smallwood, J., & O'Connor, R. C. (2011). Imprisoned by the past: Unhappy moods lead to a retrospective bias to mind wandering. *Cognition and Emotion, 25*(8), 1481–1490.
Smallwood, J., Ruby, F. J., & Singer, T. (2013). Letting go of the present: Mind-wandering is associated with reduced delay discounting. *Consciousness and Cognition, 22*(1), 1–7.
Sowden, P. T., Pringle, A., & Gabora, L. (2015). The shifting sands of creative thinking: Connections to dual-process theory. *Thinking and Reasoning, 21*(1), 40–60.
Tesla News (2015). Retrieved April 3, 2017, from https://www.tesla.cn/en/node/23354
Thompson, V. A. (2009). Dual process theories: A metacognitive perspective. In *Two minds: Dual processes and beyond*. Oxford: Oxford University Press.
Thompson, V. A., Turner, J. A. P., & Pennycook, G. (2011). Intuition, reason, and metacognition. *Cognitive Psychology, 63*(3), 107–140.
Vance, A. (2016). *Is Elon Musk an expert generalist or specialist?* Retrieved July 26, 2017, from https://www.quora.com/Is-Elon-Musk-an-expertgeneralist-or-specialist
Vance, A. (2017). *Elon Musk: Tesla, SpaceX, and the quest for a fantastic future*. New York: Ecco, an imprint of HarperCollins Publishers.
Vosniadou, S. (1989). Analogical reasoning as a mechanism in knowledge acquisition: A developmental perspective. *Similarity and analogical reasoning*, 413–437.
Wang, Q. (1997). The essence and significance of "Qu Xiang Bi Lei" in Chinese traditional science. *History of Natural Science, 16*(4), 297–303.
Wang, S. (2012). *Return to the original thinking – The wisdom of China from Xiang thinking perspective*. Nanjing: Jiangsu People's Publishing House.
Wang, L., & Lawson, M. J. (2015). Visual mental imagery: A key representational format. In H. Askell-Williams (Ed.), *Transforming the future of learning with educational research* (pp. 36–50). Hershey, PA: IGI Global.
Wang, S., & Li, M. (2006). *Percept Zhuangzi with intuitive Wuity: From Xiang thinking perspective*. Nanjing: Jiangsu People's Publishing House.
Wang, X., & Li, P. P. (2017). A conceptual framework of "Wu"-based innovation at the team level: A case study on indigenous innovation in the context of aerospace projects. *Foreign Economy and Management, 39*(3), 3–23.

Wang, Q., & Liu, G. (1993). Chinese traditional abstract thinking from Chinese medicine adopting "xiang". *Journal of Philosophy, 1993*(4), 45–50.
Wittgenstein, L., & von Wright, G. H. (1998). *Wittgenstein's Nachlass the Bergen Electronic Edition*. Charlottesville, VA: InteLex Corporation.
Yang, Y. (2008). *The general theory of sentiment and wuity*. Beijing: People's Publishing House.
Zachary, K. D. (2016). *Elon Musk's best quotes on business & innovation*. Retrieved July 20, 2017, from https://elonmusknews.org/blog/elon-musk-business-innovation-quotes
Zhang, D. N., & Cheng, Z. Y. (1991). *The preference of Chinese thinking*. Beijing: China Social Sciences Press.

A Method of Generating Societal Vision Based on the Social Systems Theory

Norihiko Kimura, Haruka Mori, Yuzuki Oka, Wataru Murakami, Rio Nitta, and Takashi Iba

Abstract In this paper, we propose a method of generating societal vision based on the social systems theory. When trying to generate innovation for the future society by some kind of new technology, we must have a vision of how the technology will spread in the society and change it. It is quite difficult to imagine how a new technology will spread to and influence the whole society, considering the high complexity and opaqueness of the modern society. To generate innovation and design a better future, some frameworks to understand society as a whole are necessary. In this paper, we first refer to some existing methods for thinking about the future and indicate how they are not appropriate to our research question due to the lack of a framework to understand the societal wholeness. Second, to create the framework, we (1) refer to the social systems theory that considers society as an autopoietic system whose elements are communication, (2) utilise the perspective of a functionally differentiated society and (3) refer to the functional method to analyse the social systems. Further, on the basis of the theory, we propose a method of generating societal visions, and also show the worksheet that is used to practice the method. Through this work, we enable a user to think about the network of the functional systems of the society and its change, and then to imagine the influence or

N. Kimura (✉)
Graduate School of Media and Governance, Keio University, Fujisawa, Kanagawa, Japan
e-mail: nkimura@sfc.keio.ac.jp

H. Mori · R. Nitta
Faculty of Policy and Management, Keio University, Fujisawa, Kanagawa, Japan
e-mail: s14856hm@sfc.keio.ac.jp; s1665rn@sfc.keio.ac.jp

Y. Oka · W. Murakami
Faculty of Environment and Information Studies, Keio University, Fujisawa, Kanagawa, Japan
e-mail: t16163yo@sfc.keio.ac.jp; t16853wm@sfc.keio.ac.jp

T. Iba
Graduate School of Media and Governance, Keio University, Fujisawa, Kanagawa, Japan

Faculty of Policy and Management, Keio University, Fujisawa, Kanagawa, Japan
e-mail: iba@sfc.keio.ac.jp

F. Grippa et al. (eds.), *Collaborative Innovation Networks*, Studies on Entrepreneurship, Structural Change and Industrial Dynamics,
https://doi.org/10.1007/978-3-319-74295-3_15

spreading diffusion of the innovation to various areas outside the target domain of the innovation.

1 Introduction

Since the beginning of the twenty-first century, several kinds of technological innovations have been generated in various fields. When trying to generate innovation for our future society by some kind of new technology, we must have an image or vision of how the technology will spread in the society and change it. If the image or vision is attractive and persuasive, we can pursue an innovation on the basis of the vision and gather collaborators or funds.

Even though such a future vision is necessary for innovation, it is quite difficult to imagine that a new technology will spread to and influence the whole society. As the modern society is highly complex and opaque, we can only imagine the change around the technology or its domain and cannot imagine how the technology changes the whole society. In such a situation, some frameworks to understand the society are necessary in order to imagine the society and design a better future society.

In this context, this research proposes a method of generating the future vision for understanding society, by referring to social systems theory, which has abundant concepts and theories for grasping a complex society.

2 Studies About the Methods of Thinking for the Future

There are some methods of predicting and thinking about the future in several fields.

In the field of organisation management, there is a method called Scenario Planning, wherein managers (1) set two axes of the scenario, which will cause changes in future, (2) consider the extreme situation of each axis and (3) combine them to create multiple scenarios (Heijden et al. 2002). Organisations use this method to formulate their business strategy in preparation for those scenarios.

In the field of design, future-oriented design methodologies such as Speculative Design and Design Fiction are proposed. Speculative design considers designing 'a means of speculating how things could be' and inspires 'people's imaginations to flow freely'. In this method, designers design some futuristic products, and based on them, they debate and think with audiences about people's desired future (Dunne and Raby 2013). Similarly, design fiction is the method of exploring the future by writing the fiction in which there are some futuristic products that do not currently exist (Sterling 2009; Bosch 2012).

We, authors, have also developed and practiced the method called Future Language that transforms the visions of the desired future into words (Iba 2016b; Kimura et al. 2016). Future Language comprises Future Words, which are vocabularies written about the desired future. By making these words, this method enables us to talk about the future and share the vision in the communities or organisations, for instance.

These methods are useful for discussing the future and deciding how organisations and communities should behave on the basis of the foreseen future. However, although those methods can inspire the visions around products and technologies, or the organisations and communities, they are not suited to inspire 'societal' visions because the methods do not provide us the framework to understand the society in its entirety. In this complex society, we want whole societal visions and not just visions about technologies or communities.

Therefore, in this research, referring to the social system theory proposed by the sociologist Niklas Luhmann, we will extract a framework to understand the society as a whole, and based on that understanding, we will propose a method to generate a future vision of the society.

3 Social Systems Theory

The social systems theory considers (1) society as an autopoietic system whose elements are communication and (2) the modern society as a set of functional systems. To analyse the society, we also refer to his functional method.

3.1 Social Systems

Luhmann (1927–1998) was a sociologist who applied the system theory of autopoiesis to sociology in order to tackle the fundamental question of 'how society is possible'.

The system theory of autopoiesis is advocated in biology, which defines a system as the network of the recursive production process of the elements (Maturana 1981). Luhmann generalised this theory and applied it to his own sociology as the social systems theory; the theory considers society an autopoietic system whose elements are communication. Communication, in this theory, is not understood as a transfer-model, but as a triple selection—a selection of information, utterance and understanding (Luhmann 1984). As communications are events that vanish instantly, the continuous recursive reproduction of communication is crucial to social systems. Autopoietic systems are closed in operational levels, and hence, they cannot procure their elements from the environment, including other systems; in other words, the systems need to self-reproduce their own elements.

Luhmann emphasised that the autopoietic system theory reformulated the central problem of the system theory from the difference between whole and part to system differentiation and built it into the new paradigm (Luhmann 1984). The former sees a system as comprising a certain number of parts and the relations among them, which

Fig. 1 Three types of social systems (Luhmann 1984)

means that it only consider the internal aspects of a system; the latter considers a system as the difference between a system and its environment, which means that in order to generate and maintain a system, the system needs to continue making a difference from its environment and other systems by reproducing its own elements constantly. According to Luhmann,

> System differentiation is nothing more than the repetition within systems of the difference between system and environment. (Luhmann 1984)

For example, to generate and maintain a social system, it needs to be differentiated from the psychic system by reproducing communication constantly.

Luhmann divided social systems in three types: interactions, organisations and societies (Fig. 1) (Luhmann 1984). These types are distinguished on the basis of the level of complexity of communication that systems could handle. Interactive systems could handle only communication that has a limitation of the number of topics or people, for instance, face-to-face communication. Organisation systems could deal with communication 'that extend far realm of co-present people' (Borch 2011) but have a limit for membership. The type of societies is the sum of all communication, according to Luhmann, and, in his career, he particularly explored this type of social systems.

3.2 *Modern Society as a Set of Functionally Differentiated Systems*

According to Luhmann, human society has had several societal structures to form social order; he defined the structure of the modern society as a functionally differentiated society.

The functionally differentiated society is the society divided into subsystems that fulfil necessary specific functions for society; for example, politics, economics, law, science, art, religion, education, etc. (Fig. 2). In previous research, one of the authors, Iba, suggests to add the co-creation system as the vision of creative society (Iba 2016a).

Each functional system is differentiated from the type of societies-system; and each system has its own way to reproduce continuous communication to maintain its autopoietic system, in other words, to continue distinguishing itself from its environment (including other systems), so that it is quite probable that each system differentiates from the whole society. As mentioned above, a system can only exist

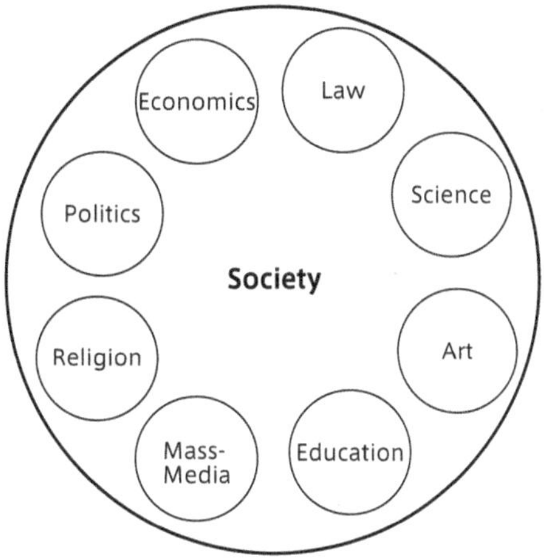

Fig. 2 Functionally differentiated society

when it has something different from the environment. To maintain its own communication system, each system has a specific function in society, communication media, binary code and programmes (Table 1).

As mentioned above, each functional system has a specific function that is necessary for society; for instance, the function of the politics system is procuring the capacity to enforce collective building of decisions, and the function of the economics system is ensuring future supply under scarcity (Luhmann and Kieserling 1998; Luhmann 1988) (Table 1, second column).

To fulfil these functions and maintain a nexus of communication, functional systems have their own communication mediums. Communication media provides support to increase the probability of communications, such as power in the politics system or money in the economics system (Luhmann and Kieserling 1998; Luhmann 1988) (Table 1, third column).

Moreover, functional systems have their own binary code, a two-sided form (positive side and negative side, like A/not-A) as a way to describe society, in order to structure communication, such as government/opposition in the politics system and payment/not-payment in the economics system (Luhmann and Kieserling 1998; Luhmann 1988) (Table 1, fourth column).

To assign each target to a positive side or a negative side of the binary code, functional systems have programmes. Programmes express the decision rules to structure communication codes, such as manifests, constitutions and elections in the politics system or prices and investment programmes in the economics system (Luhmann and Kieserling 1998; Luhmann 1988) (Table 1, fifth column).

Understanding society as a functionally differentiated system means that the modern society 'has no central agency' (Luhmann 1981); in other words, the society is decentred and 'there is no central perspective from to which to observe social phenomena' (Borch 2011). Therefore, when analysing and solving social problems, it is necessary for each functional system to present its own solution based on its function and communication.

Table 1 Examples of functional systems

Functional system	Function	Media	Code	Programme
Politics	Procuring the capacity to enforce collective building of decisions	Power	Government/ opposition	Manifests, constitutions election
Economics	Ensuring future supply under the condition of scarcity	Money	Payment/ not-payment	Prices, investment programmes

3.3 The Functional Method

Analysing society using the social systems theory, Luhmann adopts the functional method, which is used in anthropology and sociology. The functional method of Luhmann is characterised as equivalent functionalism and is the method for (1) analysing an actual solution of some social issue and (2) seeking and comparing other virtually functionally equivalent alternatives. The equivalent functional method emphasises seeing that actual solutions are contingent and comparing possible functionally alternative ways to solve problems and not just to clarify the linkage between the cause and the result of the societal problem, which is previous functional method. According to Luhmann,

> The relation between the problem and its solution will thus not be grasped for its own sake; rather, it serves as a connecting thread to questions about other possibilities, as a connecting thread in the search for functional equivalences. (Luhmann 1984)

The equivalent functional method (i) establishes an abstract problem for comparison, called a functional reference point and (ii) defines the range of functionally equivalent and substitutable alternatives to solve problems, called equivalent area (Luhmann 1970) (Fig. 3). The functional method is a comparative method, i.e. the method is a heuristic way to shift our attention from the actual solution to still virtual better different solutions.

According to Luhmann, the functional method will be effective when it is used with the system theory because the system limits the possibilities of choices (Luhmann 1970). If there are no limits, the functional reference points could be defined arbitrarily and the possibilities of equivalent alternatives within the equivalent area would be infinite. Referencing a system, we could define the functional reference points as a problem of maintaining the system and could think of other solutions within the limited equivalent area that are possible ways only in the system. Thus, if there are some societal problems, each functionally differentiated system thinks of the solutions and handles them within a limited range within its own system. Then, if necessary, we could compare each solution and choose a better one; in other words, in the modern society, there is no choice but to do so (Luhmann 1986).

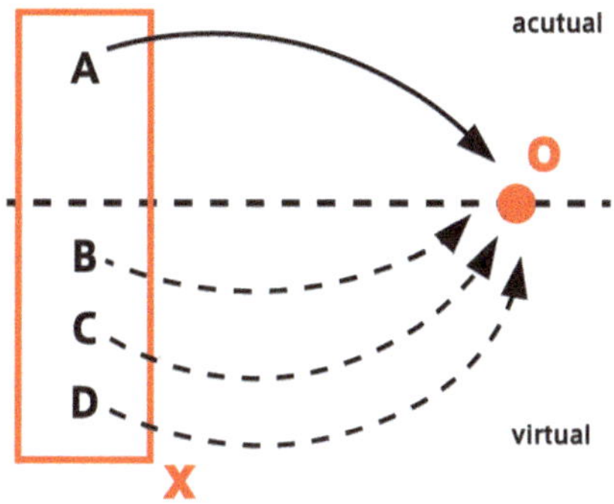

Fig. 3 The equivalent functional method (O = functional reference point, X = equivalent area, A–D = functionally equivalent alternatives)

4 Vision Generation Method

On the basis of the social system theory, we propose a method to draw visions of the future society. In the following, we will introduce the method and the worksheet using that method, which is currently being created.

4.1 Generate Functionally Equivalent Alternatives

Paraphrasing the perspective into drawing a societal vision, we need to present the visions on the basis of the functions and communication of each functionally differentiated system. Drawing visions of a decentred modern society will be possible by analysing the problem from the viewpoint of each functional system, drawing visions of each functional system and comparing or integrating the visions. The equivalent functional method such as finding functional equivalents is effective for analysing and generating new ideas of each system.

However, there remains the question of how to discover new functional equivalents. Although generated ideas are based on the present societal premises and existing technologies, it is not certain whether the ideas will be applicable in future. For the rapidly changing future society, it is necessary to consider solutions (functional equivalent alternatives) that are not still actualised.

Therefore, in this research, we propose a method of generating functional equivalent alternatives by expanding the equivalent area based on new technologies (Fig. 4); in other words, this method aims to make us imagine the expanded equivalent area, and, on the a basis of the new generated equivalent alternatives, draw visions of the future society. However, without any trigger, the equivalent area could not be expanded; hence, some factors are required to expand the equivalent area to areas where possible virtual solutions exist. Examples of such factors are new technologies, tools or philosophy. The triggers to expand equivalent area are depending on those who use this new method. After selecting the factors and expanding the equivalent area, we can generate the ideas.

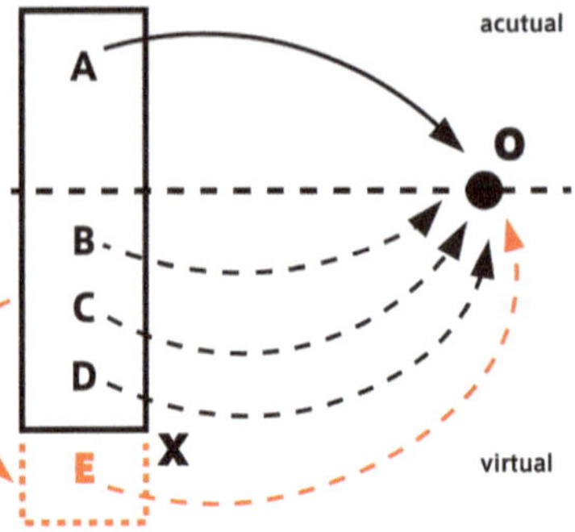

Fig. 4 Expanding equivalent area by new technologies (O = functional reference point, X = equivalent area, A–D = functionally equivalent alternatives, T = some new technologies, E = generated new functionally equivalent alternatives, new ideas)

Therefore, the process of the method proposed by this research is as follows: (1) imagine a social system whose element is the nexus of communications, (2) assign a certain functional system, (3) analyse and list current actual functional equivalent alternatives needed to maintain the system, (4) select some factors to expand their equivalent areas and generate new ideas of functionally equivalent alternatives and (5) draw the vision from the perspective of the functional system based on the new ideas. Then, (6) repeat this process in other functional systems and (7) draw a whole societal vision by comparing and integrating the each system's visions (Fig. 5).

4.2 *Vision Generation Worksheet*

We are now developing a worksheet that applies this method to use in workshops; we call it a 'vision generation worksheet'. Each worksheet corresponds to each functional system. Participants of the workshop proceed on the steps above from (1) to (5) in one sheet, draw the vision of the system and then change to another worksheet of another system. Working on each sheet and each system, we could compare and integrate the visions from each system's viewpoint, and then, we could get the vision of the society as a whole.

Below, as an example of the worksheet, we show the vision generation worksheet of the politics system (Fig. 6) and some examples of it in practice (Fig. 7).

These worksheets are developed on the basis of the books written by Luhmann—a series of books that he wrote after the late 1980s. Each book is about each functional differentiated system and is titled 'X as a social system' (X, for instance, stands for economy, law or science). He wrote these books on the basis of the social systems theory and the functional method and revealed the mechanism of each system. We researched these books and other related books about each functional differentiated system and extracted the essences of each system.

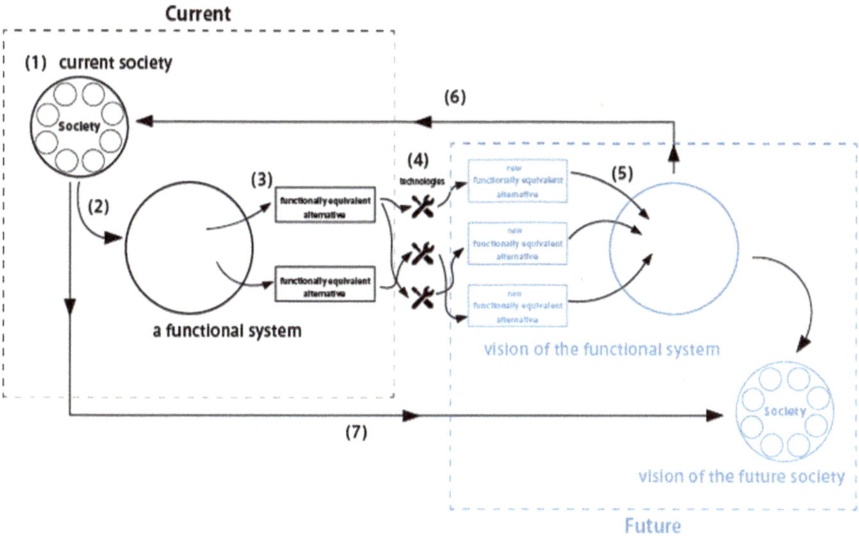

Fig. 5 The process of vision generation method

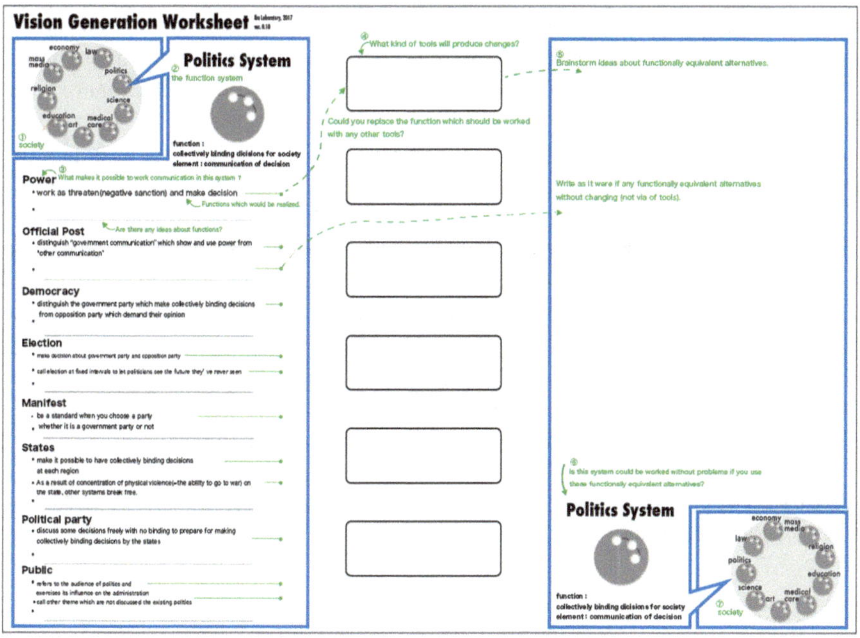

Fig. 6 Vision generation worksheet of the politics system

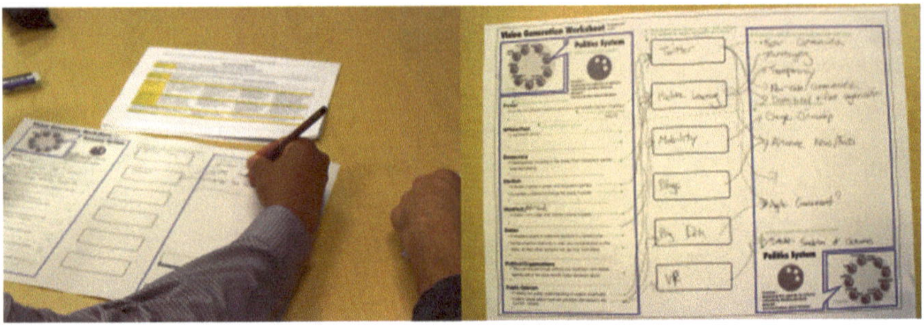

Fig. 7 Examples of practiced worksheets

5 Conclusion

In this paper, we proposed a method of generating the societal visions on the basis of the social systems theory that provide us a framework to understand the society and generate ideas; we also presented worksheets that apply the method to use in workshops. Thus far, we have developed two worksheets, corresponding to the politics system and the economics system. In future research, we will develop other worksheets, corresponding to other functional systems that Luhmann presents, for e.g. the law system, science system, education system and mass media system.

Through this work, we aim to be able to imagine the influence of an innovation spreading over various areas outside the target domain of the intended innovation. An innovation will change not only the domain in which it occurs (for example, the technological innovation of autonomous cars will certainly change the future of driving and traffic) but will also cause changes in the law system and economics system, which will further influence the politics system and other systems. The functional systems of the society are mutually influential and constitute a network of functional systems within themselves (Fig. 8). Thus, a change in one system will influence the other systems through the network. In the systems theory, the mutual influence between the systems is called structural coupling. By those worksheets, we could (1) track the vision under the consideration of the network of functional systems and its change and (2) imagine the spreading of the innovation.

Acknowledgements We want to acknowledge Yuma Akado, and Konomi Munakata for the help in designing and improving our method and worksheets.

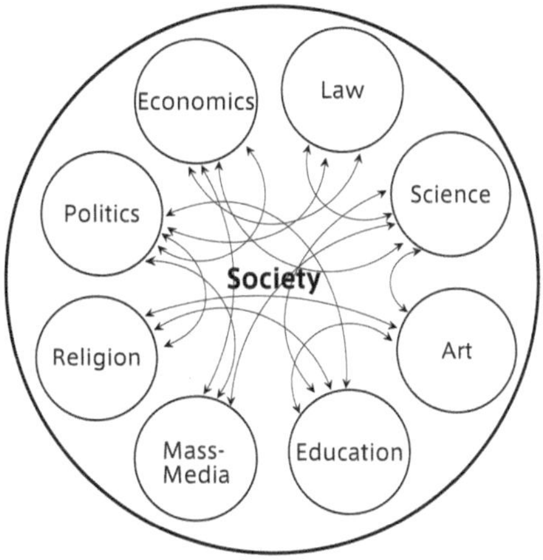

Fig. 8 The network of the functional systems: a change in one system will influence the other systems through the network

References

Borch, C. (2011). *Niklas Luhmann*. London: Routledge.

Bosch, T. (2012). *Sci-Fi writer Bruce Sterling explains the intriguing new concept of design fiction*. http://www.slate.com/blogs/future_tense/2012/03/02/bruce_sterling_on_design_fictions_.html

Dunne, A., & Raby, F. (2013). *Speculative everything: Design, fiction, and social dreaming*. Cambridge: MIT Press.

Heijden, K. V. D., Bradfield, R., Burt, G., Cairns, G., & Wright, G. (2002). *The sixth sense: Accelerating organizational learning with scenarios*. Chichester: Wiley.

Iba, T. (2016a). Sociological perspective of the creative society. In M. P. Zylka, H. Fuehres, A. Fronzetti Colladon, & P. A. Gloor (Eds.), *Designing networks for innovation and improvisation* (pp. 29–428). Cham: Springer International Publishing.

Iba, T. (2016b). *Future language for collaborative design*. Paper presented at 2016 International PUARL conference, University of San Francisco, California, 28–30 October 2016.

Kimura, N., Akado, Y., & Iba, T. (2016). *The future vision of productive city: Where pattern languages are used*. Poster presented at 2016 International PUARL conference, University of San Francisco, California, 28–30 October 2016.

Luhmann, N. (1970). Funktionale Methode und Systemtheorie. In *Soziologische Aufklärung* (Bd. 1, pp. 31–53) *Aufsätze zur Theorie sozialer Systeme*, Köln-Opladen: Westdeutscher Verlag.

Luhmann, N. (1981). *Politische Theorie im Wohlfahrtsstaat*. München: Olzog. (English edition: Luhmann, N. (1990). *Political theory in the welfare state* (J. Bednarz, Trans.). Berlin/New York: De Gruyter.

Luhmann, N. (1984). *Soziale Systeme: Grundriß einer allgemeinen Theorie*. Frankfurt: Suhrkamp. (English edition: Luhmann, N. (1995). *Social systems* (J. Bednerz, & D. Baecker, Trans.). California: Stanford University Press.

Luhmann, N. (1986). *Ökologische Kommunikation: Kann die moderne Gesellschaft sich auf ökologische Gefährdungen einstellen?*. Opladen: Westdeutscher Verlag. (English edition: Luhman, N. (1989). *Ecological communication* (J. Bednarz, Trans.). Cambridge: Polity Press.

Luhmann, N. (1988). *Die Wirtschaft der Gesellschaft*. Frankfurt: Suhrkamp.

Luhmann, N., & Kieserling, V. A. (Eds.). (1998). *Die Politik der Gesellschaft*. Frankfurt: Suhrkamp.

Maturana, H. (1981). Autopoiesis. In M. Zeleny (Ed.), *Autopoiesis: A theory of living organization* (pp. 21–33). New York: Elsevier North Holland.

Sterling, B. (2009). COVER STORY: Design fiction. *Interactions, 16*(3), 20–24. https://doi.org/10.1145/1516016.1516021. ACM, New York.

Part IV
Open Dialogue and Creativity

Peer Learning via Dialogue with a Pattern Language

Takashi Iba

Abstract In this paper, we study the way of peer learning via dialogue that uses a pattern language. Pattern languages are a collection of patterns to describe design knowledge that exists in particular areas of a profession. For the past 7 years, we have been holding workshops for dialogue with a pattern language in order to realise peer learning. In this paper, we introduce the dialogue workshop using the Learning Patterns, a pattern language for creative learning, and analyse the data of our survey. The results of 710 valid responses show that 92.4% of participants learned something new about the way of learning, when they read the book of the Learning Patterns; 91.5% reflected that the dialogue was important to learn the ways of learning; 95.7% of participants considered this activity of listening to others significant for various reasons; 90.3% thought the pattern language was helpful for sharing their experience with peers; 88.3% were able to imagine how they can actually take actions of the patterns they chose; and 96.5% of participants thought reading the pattern language and participating in the dialogue workshop was enjoyable.

1 Introduction

Our society is becoming more complex and diverse day by day. In such a society, identifying problems by ourselves and creatively thinking of solutions from various perspectives is essential. People need to learn by constructing their own living knowledge based on their situation and not by merely memorizing existing ideas; Learning how to generate new ideas and how to think is also necessary. In addition, in such fluid and dynamic changing age, the fixed textbook is a limited learning tool because of the cost and time required to collect and update the diverse knowledge and write it down into a textbook.

T. Iba (✉)
Faculty of Policy Management, Keio University, Fujisawa, Kanagawa, Japan
e-mail: iba@sfc.keio.ac.jp

F. Grippa et al. (eds.), *Collaborative Innovation Networks*, Studies on Entrepreneurship, Structural Change and Industrial Dynamics,
https://doi.org/10.1007/978-3-319-74295-3_16

On the other hand, you can find people who have different experience from you just by looking around you. That is, different people have different practical knowledge in various domains. In such environment, peer learning—learning from peers—is paying attention not only in schools but also outside them.

In this paper, we introduce pattern languages as media for peer learning, present how to use them in a dialogue for exchanging narratives of experience, and demonstrate a dialogue workshop using a pattern language. Because we have already published qualitative feedbacks from participants of the dialogue workshop (Iba 2015), this paper focuses on the quantitative survey results of our practices.

2 Pattern Language as Media for Peer Learning

Pattern language is collection of patterns that describe practical knowledge in a certain domain. Each pattern is written in a format of Context, Problem, Solution, and Consequence, and has a name, which can be used as common words among people. The pattern language we present in this paper is the Learning Patterns, which is a pattern language for creative learning. It has 40 patterns for rules of thumb and tips for learning in a creative way, as shown later.

The originator of the pattern language was Christopher Alexander, the architect who proposed it in order to develop design knowledge of building and town (Alexander et al. 1977; Alexander 1979). Ten years after the book was published, Alexander's idea of pattern language was adopted in the field of software design (Beck and Cunningham 1987; Gamma et al. 1994).

Since the 1990s, an increasing number of fields have adopted the methods of pattern language (Manns and Rising 2005, 2015; Hoover and Oshineye 2009; Pedagogical Patterns Editorial Board 2012). On the basis of this background, we have been creating pattern languages in a new area of knowledge concerning human actions such as learning (Iba and Iba Laboratory 2014a), presentation (Iba and Iba Laboratory 2014b), collaboration (Iba and Iba Laboratory 2014c), education, business, social innovation, policy-making, and even beauty in daily life.

The Learning Patterns, on which we focus in this paper, consists of 40 patterns (Fig. 1). At the centre of the pattern language is the pattern *Creative Learning*, and the three main patterns for such learning: *Opportunity for Learning*, *Learning by Creating*, and *Open Learning* surround the *Creative Learning*. The subsequent patterns are grouped into three categories. The first group, patterns Nos. 4–15, relates to *Opportunity for Learning*. The second group of patterns, Nos. 16–27 shows patterns related to *Learning by Creating*. The third group, pattern Nos. 28–No. 39 relates to *Open Learning*. These patterns help learner achieve a *Creative Learning* through their interactions.

Figure 2 shows the format of a pattern in the Learning Patterns. The left-hand page gives you a brief idea of the pattern's meaning. On the top left side of the page, you will see the Pattern Number, Pattern Name, One-liners to explain the pattern, and Illustration. At the bottom of the page are Quotes related to the pattern. The

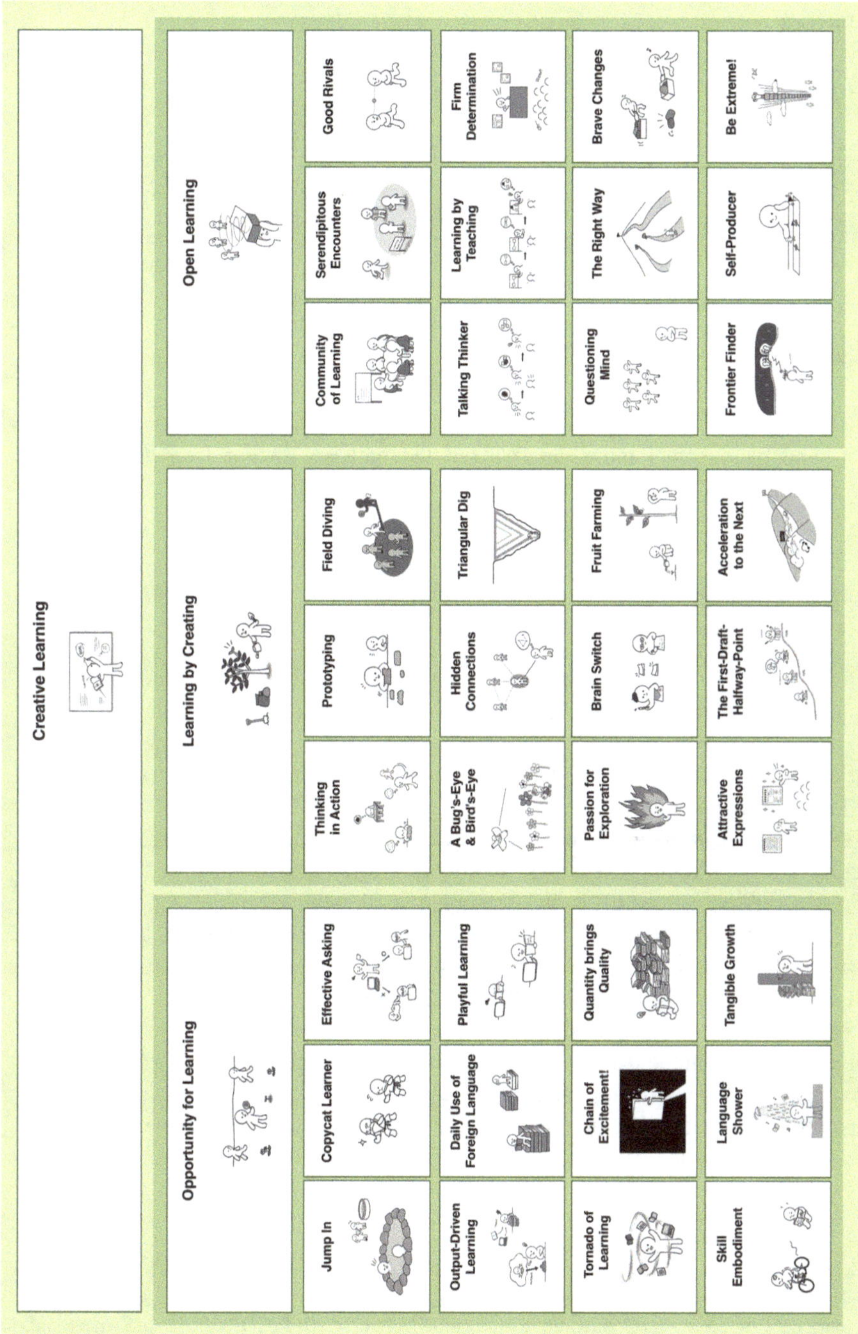

Fig. 1 Pattern name and its illustration of the Learning Patterns

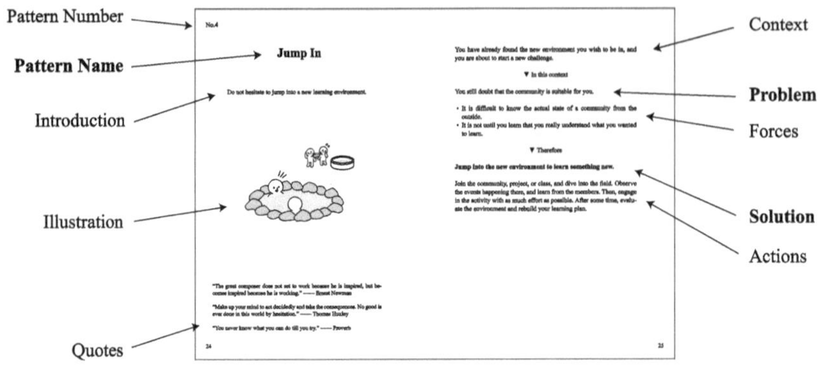

Fig. 2 Format of a pattern in the Learning Patterns

right-hand page offers more detail about the pattern. Listing from the top, the Context, Problem, Forces, Solution, and Actions are all described.

3 Dialogue Workshop for Peer Learning

Pattern languages are used in dialogue for reflecting on the speaker's experiences, talking about them with others, and making a plan for future actions using the pattern language.[1] Note that Iba (2012) presents a pattern language for designing this type of workshop. In what follows, we show our practices of the dialogue workshop using the Learning Patterns.

The dialogue workshops using the Learning Patterns have been held at the Faculty of Policy Management and Faculty of Environment and Information Studies, Keio University, since 2011. All freshmen at the two faculties, approximately 900 students, have participated in these workshops and talked about their experiences of learning in light of the patterns (Fig. 2). About 6500 students have participated in the workshops over the past 7 years.

The main aim of the workshop is to change the mindset of students, who often define "learning" in the narrow sense by limiting it to studies in school. Another aim is to provide them with an opportunity to learn from their peers (other students), and to make them realise that they can learn by peer learning. We also expected the workshop to be an ice-breaking event for freshmen to kick off their campus lives.

[1]We held similar dialogue with the Learning Patterns in several international conference: 3rd International Conference on Collaborative Innovation Networks 2011 (COINs2011) in Switzerland, 2nd Asian Conference on Pattern Languages of Programs (AsianPLoP2011) in Japan, and 19th Conference on Pattern Languages of Programs (PLoP2012) in US.

The workshop was held as part of an obligatory class for freshmen, where the names of classes were "Policy Management Studies" and "Environment and Information Studies". Each class had approximately 450 participants. In the first class, we handed out the booklet of the Learning Patterns to all participants, and explained the homework they needed to complete to prepare for the workshop. Specifically, the students were asked to read the booklet, think about their experience with the patterns, and make marks on the Dialogue Workshop Preparation Sheet (Fig. 3) in the following manner: first, circle the patterns that they have experienced before, noticing that the learning experience is not limited to traditional "learning" in a school setting; it may include experiences in sports, music, extracurricular activities, and hobbies; second, choose five patterns that they would like to incorporate into their learning in the future, and put a star mark beside them.

In the next class, which took place 1 week after assigning the homework, we had a dialogue workshop with the pattern language. In the workshop, participants were free to mingle and to find and talk with other participants for about 45 min. We set a rule that participants must talk only to people they do not know, so participants could easily talk to people whom they have never talked to before. This rule makes the dialogue setting feasible even if participants are shy and hesitating to talk with new people. In the workshop, when they find someone who has experienced a pattern they want to master, they listen to the other participant's story. The workshops were held twice a year in April, with about 450 participants at in each workshop (Fig. 4).

After the workshop, students were asked to submit a second homework: Their first task was to reflect on what they learned from other students in the workshop and write it down. Second, they had to write a plan for learning to gain five patterns they'd chosen. In addition, we ask them to give us feedbacks about the workshop experience, and the analysis of this paper is the results of this survey.

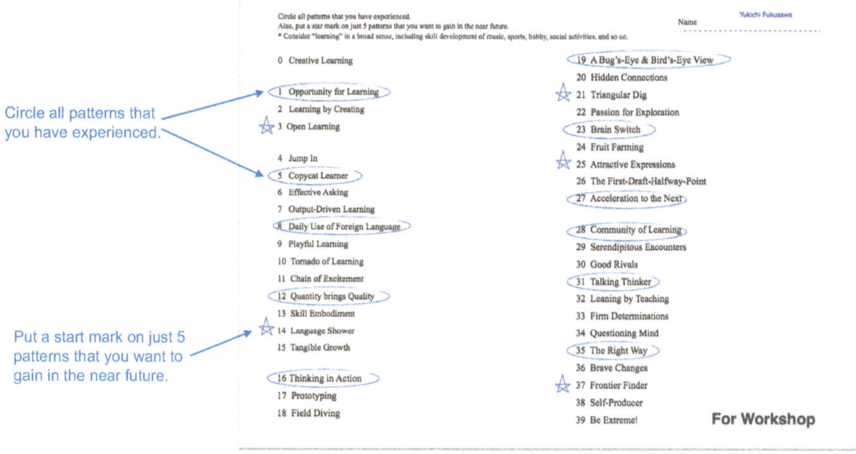

Fig. 3 Dialogue workshop preparation sheet (for the Learning Patterns)

Fig. 4 Dialogue workshop using a pattern language (Keio University, 2017)

To understand the experience of participants in the dialogue workshop, Iba (2015) analysed qualitative feedback from the participants and got the following results. First, participants said they enjoyed talking to people to whom they have never talked before (one of the rules was that participants must talk only to people they did not know). Moreover, most participants said the workshop was fun and interesting and they even made new friends, although the main goal of the dialogue was learning.

Second, to actualize the patterns they wanted to implement, the participants gained ideas about specific actions they could take and also learned that the same pattern can have various applications. In the workshop, participants were often motivated by other people's attitudes and experiences of learning in the case of Learning Patterns, and by seeing the diversity of the experiences of others. Through the workshop, the participants gained a broader viewpoint of the world and themselves and were better able to share and solve problems they were facing.

Third, the workshops not only allowed participants to learn something unique about others, but also to discover new aspects in themselves by using the pattern language to talk about themselves. In the dialogue, they also sometimes discovered that they had experience with a pattern that they did not realize they had experienced before.

In a different study, Iba (2014) demonstrates a bar chart of aggregated data about how many patterns participants have already experienced, and Iba (2015) further shows the growth of individual experience in terms of the Learning Patterns on a radar chart. However, so far there are no studies that examine the feedback of participants quantitatively. In the next section, we present the quantitative survey results about the experience of the dialogue workshop.

4 A Survey on Dialogue Workshops with the Learning Patterns

We conducted the survey on dialogue workshops with the Learning Patterns among the students who participated in the workshop at Keio University in 2017. The survey covers everything starting from the students' experience of reading the pattern booklet to their experience of the workshop itself. The number of valid responses of this survey is 710. Note that the survey was conducted in Japanese, with the results shown below translated into English for the purposes this paper.

To measure the students' grasp of the premise to the workshop, we asked the participants how many patterns they had already experienced among the 40 patterns of the Learning Patterns. The answers are shown in Fig. 5.

In addition, we asked whether they had learned something new about the way of learning when reading the book of the Learning Patterns. The result in Fig. 6 shows that 92.4% of participants, in total, gained new insights about the way of learning when they read the book of the Learning Patterns.

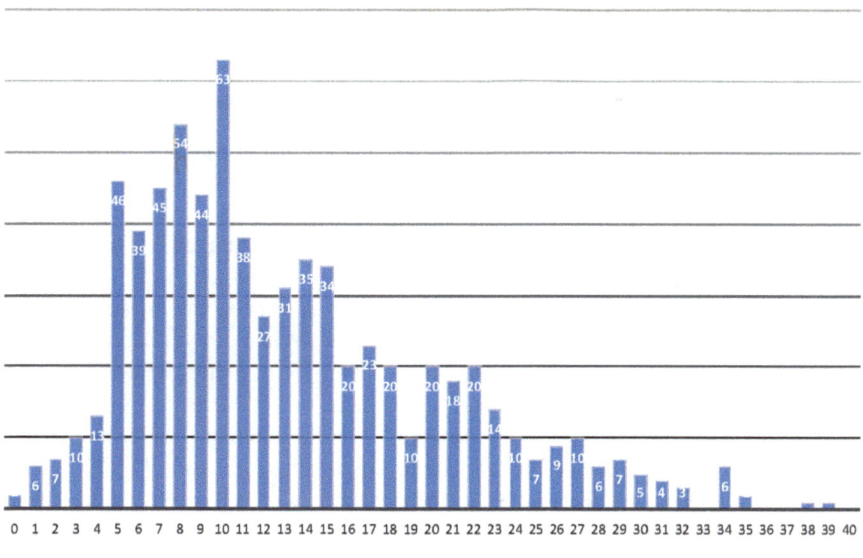

Fig. 5 Answer for the question "How many patterns you have already experienced in 40 patterns of the Learning Patterns?" [N = 710]

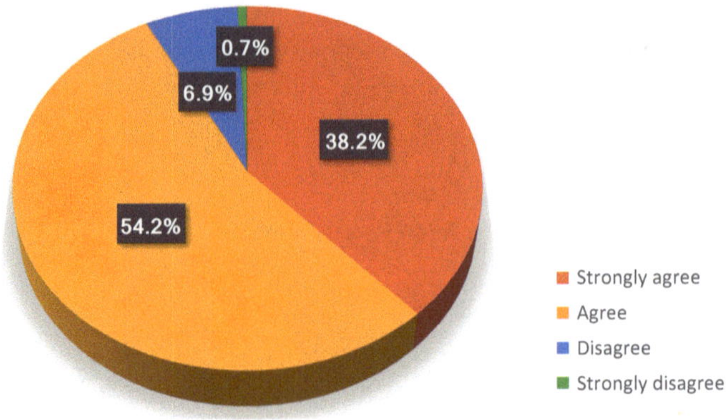

Fig. 6 Answer for the question "Did you learn something new about the way of learning, when you read the book of the Learning Patterns?" [N = 710]

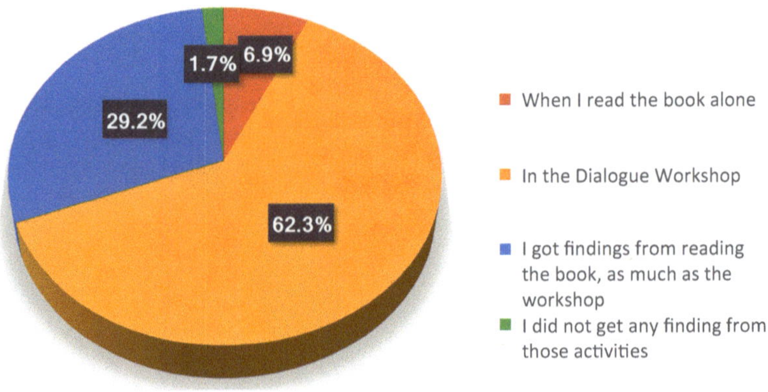

Fig. 7 Answer for the question "After reading the book, you joined the Dialogue Workshop. When did you learn the most about the way of learning?" [N = 710]

As shown above, most participants gained new insights when reading the book of the Learning Patterns. Furthermore, most of them learned new things in the dialogue workshop as well. Figure 7 shows the result of the answer to the question "After reading the book, you joined the Dialogue Workshop. When did you learn the most about the way of learning?". This result shows that 91.5% of participants in total said the dialogue was important in their learning process.

In questions about the workshop, we asked them how many people they talked with in the 45 min of the dialogue workshop. The result is shown in Fig. 8.

Further, Fig. 9 shows the answer to the question, whether they thought it was important for them to listen to the learning experiences of others, and whether it helped them to think about their own way of learning. This result shows that 95.7% of participants in total consider the activity of listening to others important.

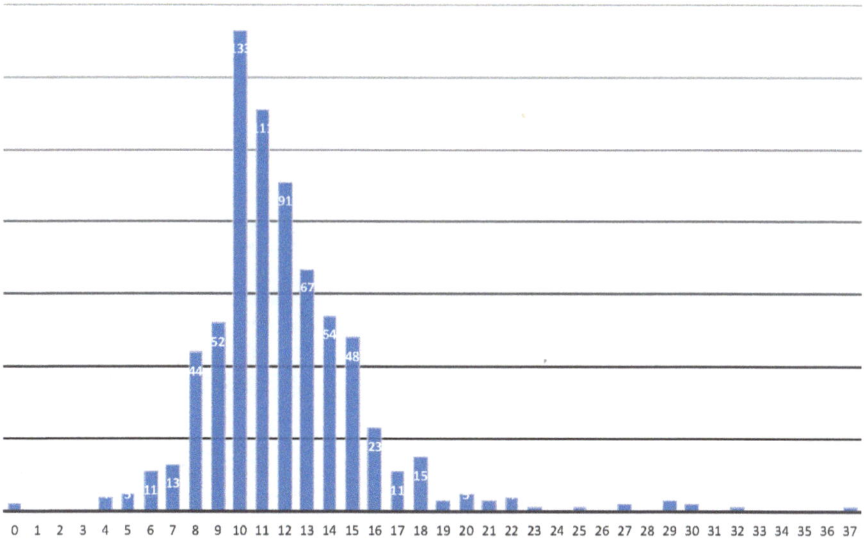

Fig. 8 Answer for the question "How many people did you talk with in the Dialogue Workshop?" [N = 710]

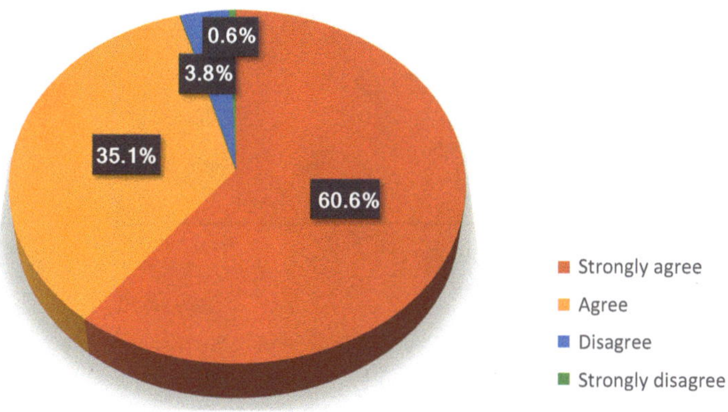

Fig. 9 Answer for the question "Do you think it was important for you to listen to the learning experiences of others, in order to help you think about your own way of learning?" [N = 710]

Related to this question, the participants who answered that the activity of listening to others was important, were then asked, what was good about the dialogue workshop using the Learning Patterns, Multiple replies were allowed here. The results in Fig. 10 show that there are various reasons why the participants considered this workshop significant.

In our past qualitative study of dialogue workshops (Iba 2015), participants said that pattern languages helped them share their experiences. This time, all participants were asked the question "Did you feel that the Learning Patterns helped you to tell

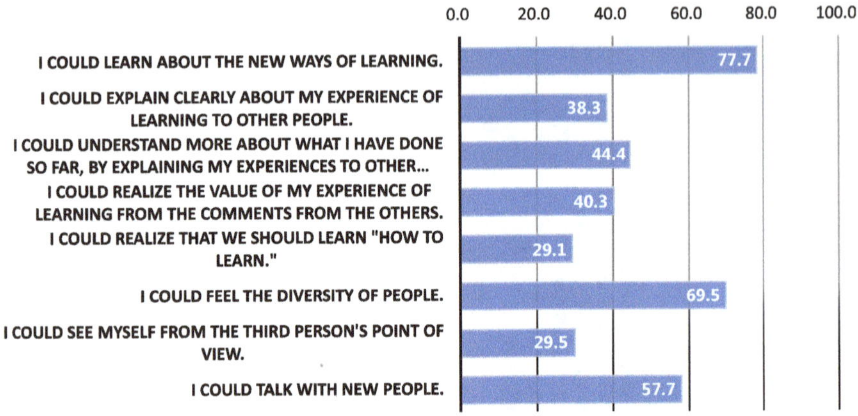

Fig. 10 Answer to the question "If you chose "Strongly agree" or "Agree" in the previous question, please answer this question. What was good about this dialogue workshop where we have shared our own learning experiences using the Learning Patterns? Please check all that apply"

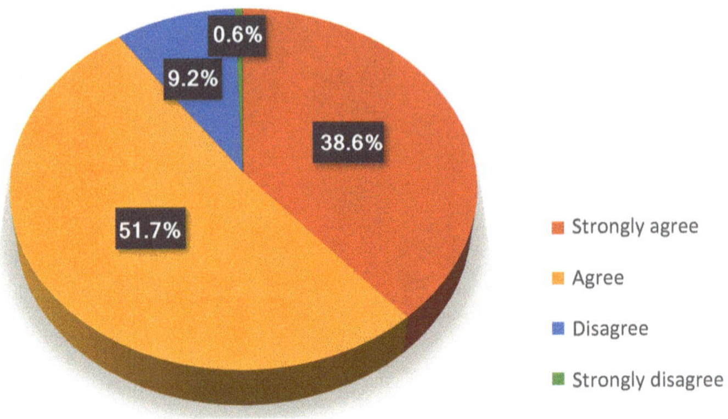

Fig. 11 Answer to the question "Did you feel that the Learning Patterns helped you to tell someone your own stories of learning in the dialogue?" [N = 710]

someone your own stories of learning in the dialogue?". The result in Fig. 11 shows that 90.3% of all participants thought that the pattern language was helpful in sharing their experience with peers.

One of the purposes of holding a dialogue workshop with pattern languages is to be able to imagine a future scenario when the participants will apply the patterns into practice based on what they learned from their peers. Figure 12 shows the answer to the question "About the five patterns you have chosen; are you now able to imagine clearly how you can actually take action?". The results demonstrate that 88.3% of participants thought that after the workshop they were able to imagine how they could take actions of the patterns they chose.

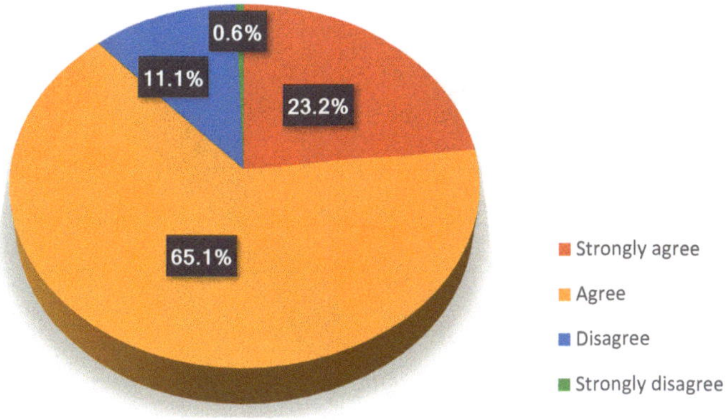

Fig. 12 Answer to the question "About the five patters you have chosen; are you now able to imagine clearly how you can actually take action?" [N = 710]

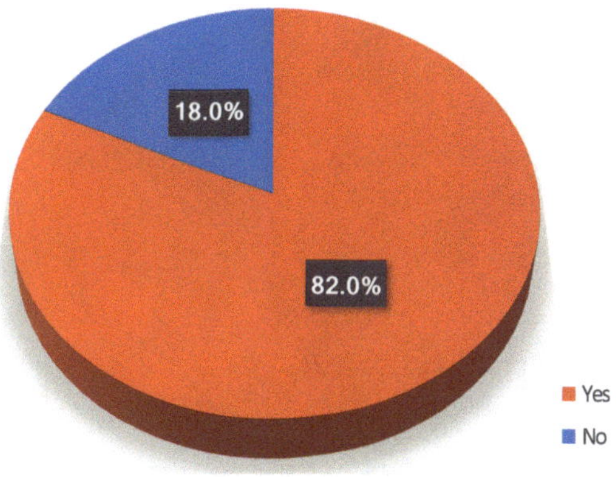

Fig. 13 Answer to the question "Were there any patterns you realised, during the workshop, that you already had experience of, even though you had chosen them as "no experience" when reading the book of the Learning Patterns?" [N = 710]

According to our past qualitative survey (Iba 2015), some participants said they realized, during the workshop, that they already had experience of patterns that they had marked as "no experience" when first reading the book of the Learning Patterns. We were interested in how many people found this to be true, so this time we included this question in the survey. Figure 13 shows the answer, demonstrating that 82.0% of participants realised, during the workshop, that they already had experience of patterns that they had originally chosen as "no experience" when reading the book of the Learning Patterns.

Figure 14 shows answer to the question about the experience of reading the Learning Patterns book and participating in the dialogue workshop, "All in all, was it enjoyable for you to read the Learning Patterns and to have the dialogue with

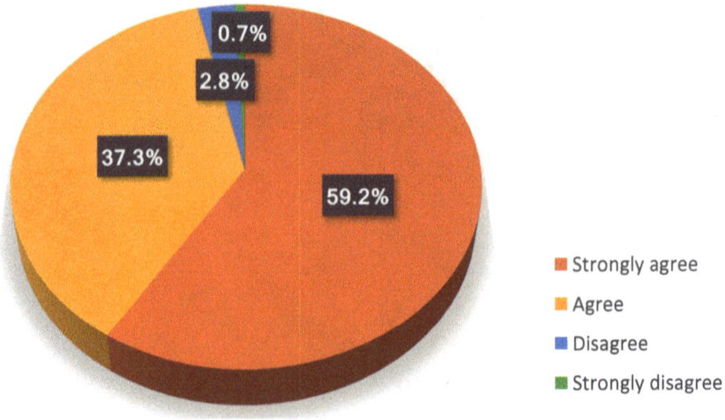

Fig. 14 Answer to the question "All in all, was it enjoyable for you to read the Learning Patterns and to have the dialogue with others?" [N = 710]

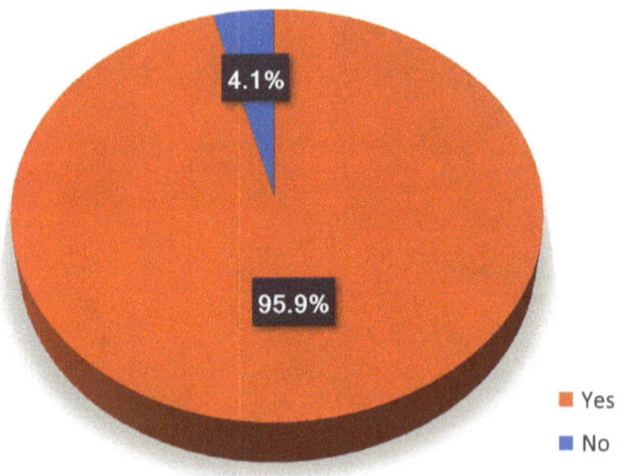

Fig. 15 Answer to the question "Would you recommend this workshop about the Learning Patterns to the freshmen coming next year?" [N = 710]

others?". Figure 14 shows that 96.5% of participants thought it was enjoyable. Finally, Fig. 15 shows the result of the answer to the question, "Would you recommend this workshop about the Learning Patterns to the freshmen coming next year?". It shows that 95.9% of participants would recommend this workshop.

5 Conclusion

In this paper, we introduced the dialogue workshops with pattern languages, examined one case of a dialogue workshop using the Learning Patterns, and studied the result of the survey completed by workshop participants. The results presented in this preliminary study reflect a subjective response to the workshop experience. In order to confirm the effectiveness of the dialogue with a pattern language, a wider study with experimental and control groups is necessary, and is planned for the future.

References

Alexander, C., Ishikawa, S., Silverstein, M., Jacobson, M., Fiksdahl-King, I., & Angel, S. (1977). *A pattern language: Towns, buildings, construction*. New York: Oxford University Press.

Alexander, C. (1979). *The timeless way of building*. New York: Oxford University Press.

Beck, K., & Cunningham, W. (1987). Using pattern languages for object-oriented programs. In *OOPSLA-87 workshop on the specification and design for object-oriented programming*.

Gamma, E., Helm, R., Johnson, R., & Vlissides, J. (1994). *Design patterns: Elements of reusable object-oriented software*. New Delhi: Addison-Wesley.

Hoover, D., & Oshineye, A. (2009). *Apprenticeship patterns: Guidance for the aspiring software craftsman*. Sebastopol, CA: O'Reilly Media.

Iba, T. (2012). A pattern language for designing workshop to introduce a pattern language. In *17th European conference on pattern languages of programs (EuroPLoP2012)*.

Iba, T. (2014). Using pattern languages as media for mining, analysing, and visualising experiences. *International Journal of Organisational Design and Engineering: Special Issue on Creative Networks, 3*(3/4), 278–301.

Iba, T. (2015). Pattern languages as media for creative dialogue: Functional analysis of dialogue workshops. In P. Baumgartner & R. Sickinger (Eds.), *PURPLSOC: The workshop 2014* (pp. 236–255).

Iba, T., & Iba Laboratory. (2014a). *Learning patterns: A pattern language for creative learning*. Yokohama: CreativeShift.

Iba, T., & Iba Laboratory. (2014b). *Presentation patterns: A pattern language for creative presentations*. Yokohama: CreativeShift.

Iba, T., & Iba Laboratory. (2014c). *Collaboration patterns: A pattern language for creative collaborations*. Yokohama: CreativeShift.

Manns, M. L., & Rising, L. (2005). *Fearless change: Patterns for introducing new ideas*. New York: Addison-Wesley.

Manns, M. L., & Rising, L. (2015). *More fearless change: Strategies for making your ideas happen*. New York: Addison-Wesley.

Pedagogical Patterns Editorial Board. (2012). *Pedagogical patterns: Advice for educators*. USA: Createspace.

Using Open Dialogue Patterns to Improve Conversation in Daily Life

Masafumi Nagai and Takashi Iba

Abstract This study explores a novel way of using Open Dialogue Patterns to improve everyday communication. Open Dialogue is a dialogue-based approach frequently utilised in psychotherapy and has been proposed to apply to other situations. We organised the essence of Open Dialogue by using pattern language so as not to be limited to the field of psychotherapy (Iba et al., Open dialogue patterns: a pattern language for collaborative problem dissolving. Viking Conference on Pattern Languages of Programs, 2017; Nagai et al., Basic patterns for dialogical meeting: open dialogue patterns, Part2. 22st European Conference on Pattern Languages of Programs (EuroPLoP2017), 2017). In this study, we employed a learning programme to improve everyday conversation using Open Dialogue Patterns and confirmed four participants and ten cases. The results reported herein suggest that these patterns are effective through 'utilisation to deepen understanding of interpersonal relations', 'induction of the inquiry of effective dialogue' and 'recognition of the dialogue as a design issue.'

1 Introduction

Many problems in modern society occur due to complications associated with human relationships. Issues such as bullying and power harassment arising from problems in human relationships are constantly occurring in workplaces and schools, and dilution of human relations is becoming a noticed problem in people's everyday lives.

When trying to resolve these problems, the common approach is to seek the causes in the individual involved. The problem is considered to reside within the

M. Nagai (✉)
Graduate School of Media and Governance, Keio University, Fujisawa, Kanagawa, Japan
e-mail: mnagai@sfc.keio.ac.jp

T. Iba
Graduate School of Media and Governance, Keio University, Fujisawa, Kanagawa, Japan

Faculty of Policy Management, Keio University, Fujisawa, Kanagawa, Japan
e-mail: iba@sfc.keio.ac.jp

F. Grippa et al. (eds.), *Collaborative Innovation Networks*, Studies on Entrepreneurship, Structural Change and Industrial Dynamics,
https://doi.org/10.1007/978-3-319-74295-3_17

individual, and thus the problem could be solved if the person's behaviour is improved. Some may even blame the individual, saying that 'The problem happened because of your behaviour', or 'this would not have happened if you had done better'. Although the guidelines for improvement of such an approach are easy to understand, they ignore the fact that all individuals exist within a continuum of various relationships. In a certain relationship, he/she may have been forced to take the action that resulted in problems.

Under these circumstances, it is necessary not only to find the causal factors that reside within the individuals who are involved but also to gain perspective from surrounding relationships. By improving these relationships with the surrounding people, it becomes possible to create situations where problems do not occur. In this investigation, we aim to solve problems or prevent problems beforehand by urging improvements in daily communication and human relationships.

2 Open Dialogue Patterns

The purpose of Open Dialogue Patterns is to solve individuals' problems by inducing dialogue that involves various people related to the situation (Iba et al. 2017; Nagai et al. 2017). We referred to the method of Open Dialogue, a dialogue-based approach with a proven track record of effectiveness in the field of psychotherapy. Additionally, we organised the essence of Open Dialogue by using pattern language so as not to be limited to the field of psychotherapy.

2.1 Open Dialogue

Open Dialogue is a family therapy method developed by a team led by Mr. Jaakko Seikkula of Jyväskylä University, which has been implemented at Keropudas Hospital in the West Lapland region of Finland since the 1980s (Seikkula and Arnkil 2014).

Historically, medical doctors would diagnose conditions such as schizophrenia and then would employ approaches such as medical treatment and hospitalisation. The Open Dialogue approach, however, is a treatment in which open dialogical meetings with people related to the situation are performed. In other words, it treats patients as part of a larger social network, rather than isolating them as an independent individual. Therefore, these dialogical meetings convene important people from around the patient as well as the necessary medical professionals, rather than having a one-on-one medical examination with the patient. Furthermore, this technique does not utilise a one-way conversational approach for diagnosis; rather, it is an interactive two-way conversation. By repeatedly conducting dialogical meetings and trying to talk about experiences that had been difficult for the patient alone to express, the symptoms abate and causal behaviours gradually cease to exist.

The effectiveness of this approach has already been demonstrated in Finland where the recurrence-prevention rate is high, and the hospitalisation period is shorter than that of the patient receiving normal treatment such as pharmacotherapy (Seikkula and Olson 2003).

2.2 *Pattern Language for Describing Practical Knowledge*

In organising the knowledge of Open Dialogue, we used a method called pattern language. Pattern language was originally created by the architect Christopher Alexander, as a method of knowledge documentation to ease resident participation in the design of urban buildings and towns (Alexander et al. 1977). A pattern language consists of patterns, which each pattern containing a piece of knowledge that is labelled with a 'pattern name', and is described in the order of 'context', 'problem', 'solution' and 'consequence'. It is a method that has also been applied outside of the architecture domain, including software design and human action (Helm et al. 1994; Iba 2013).

2.3 *Overview of Open Dialogue Patterns*

The Open Dialogue Patterns consist of 30 patterns in total. The core patterns consist of *Experienced World*, *Various Voices* and *Co-Created Understanding*, supplemented by nine patterns for each core pattern that provide suggestions of specific practices (Fig. 1). Each category, along with a brief description of the pattern name and contents, will be provided in the upcoming paragraphs.

1. Experienced World	**2. Various Voices**	**3. Co-Created Understanding**
4. As a Living Person	13. Significant Others	22. First Meeting in Crisis
5. Deep Listening	14. Working as a Team	23. Everyday Meeting
6. Exact Same Words	15. Sitting in the Circle	24. Continuous Engagement
7. Open Question	16. Invitation for Utterances	25. Diverse Understanding
8. Pause for Thinking	17. Slow-Paced Conversation	26. Ambiguous Situation
9. Response to What is Said	18. Chain of Responce	27. Transformation of Meaning
10. Inner Viewpoint	19. Tiny Sign	28. Ever-Widening Perspectives
11. Tunnel of Emotion	20. Emotional Resonance	29. Finding Together
12. Respectful Mind	21. Reflecting Talk	30. Community for the Future

Fig. 1 The whole structure of Open Dialogue Patterns

The first core pattern, *Experienced World* is about understanding the speakers' way of perceiving things through dialogue and using this frame to grasp their experiences. To effectively practice this method, nine patterns can be employed as illustrated below. Labels and expertise are to stop the individual from being *As a Living Person*. This also means recognising others *As a Living Person* too. It is important to have a *Deep Listening* to their pace of thoughts and utterance as well as a choice of words so that you can use the *Exact Same Words*.

Simple yes/no questions should not be utilised during the dialogue. Thus, practice question that will enable the individual to answer in his/her own words, known as *Open Question* should be used. Also, take a *Pause for Thinking* so that the person you are having a dialogue with has ample time to think about what they want to say. When they have fully answered your question, make sure you also appropriately *Respond to What is Said*.

To understand their *Experienced World*, it is imperative to use not only your point of view but also their *Inner Viewpoint*. Sometimes there may be a strong emotional expression, which is a great opportunity to put those experiences that could not be expressed in words through a *Tunnel of Emotion*. In case of this situation, make sure you settle a *Respectful Mind* towards dark and tough experiences they may have faced in the past.

The second core pattern, *Various Voices* means to carry on a dialogue with people who surrounding situation. The aim is to share a variety of narratives from the person and the various interpretations from the surrounding people. To effectively practise this pattern, the practitioner can follow the nine patterns as below. First, we must have our identified *Significant Others* join in and have everybody *Working as a Team*. Then, gather those members in one place and request them to arrange themselves as *Sitting in a Circle*.

As for dialogue, send out *Invitation for Utterances* from the beginning and ask them questions. Rather than trying to summarise the story, it is important to proceed with a *Slow-Paced Conversation* and to create a welcoming atmosphere in which everyone can speak frankly. Also, make sure to appropriately respond to any comments so that a *Chain of Responses* is created.

Also, be sure to not only pay attention to words but also focus on the *Tiny Sign* that each person gives, such as a little expression or tension. Moreover, thinking that the move of your feelings is more natural *As a Living Person*, express it and let *Emotional Resonance* happen. Showing *Reflecting Talk* with the supporting team members will prompt the individuals to think for themselves, which may lead to a new thought process.

The third core pattern *Co-Created Understanding* refers to the capture of circumstances responsible for the generation of the problem, and through re-speaking in dialogue, we will start to gain a new understanding, which will enable us to dissolve the problem itself. To correctly practice this method, the nine patterns listed below can be utilised. Initially, there is a *First Meeting in Crisis*; a meeting in which the person's emotions and speech are easy to elevate. Also, because it is an unstable period, an *Everyday Meeting* and *Continuous Engagement* with the same members are required as this will bring psychological continuity and security.

Through this dialogue, we grasp and share our *Diverse Understanding*, rather than defining who is right or wrong. Tolerating an *Ambiguous Situation* will occur throughout this process; however, rather than trying to quickly summarise it, it is necessary to endure this uncertain state. By doing so, you and *Significant Others* will experience *Transformation of Meaning* of the situation.

A further important aspect is to direct the dialogue towards an *Ever-Widening Perspective* rather than converging on one agreement point. And then you should do *Finding Together*, rather than giving advice from the standpoint of a specialist. The experience of such a dialogue will bring about a common language and important experience among participants, and the group will begin to form a *Community for the Future*.

3 The Application of Open Dialogue Patterns in Daily Life-Conversation

We curried out a learning programme to improving everyday conversation by using Open Dialogue Patterns. In this instance, we confirmed a total of four people and ten cases in which the patterns were utilised and feedback was collected from participants after the programme.

3.1 Outline of Dialogue Class: A Learning Programme of Dialogue

To discern the efficacy of the Open Dialogue Patterns when applied in other contexts, such as collaboration or human relationship in everyday life, we held a dialogue class, which is a programme targeted towards those who want to improve their general dialogue skills.

A Dialogue Class is a learning programme with the purpose of acquiring general knowledge and skills to conduct effective dialogue by using Open Dialogue Patterns as a support tool for learning. Participants learn Open Dialogue Patterns and practise them in daily life. This programme consists of four sessions. Participants learn about Open Dialogue Patterns in each session, practise the patterns in daily life, and learn from each other's practice in the next session (Fig. 2).

This time, a total of four people aged 20–30 years old with interest in dialogue participated, and the first author of this paper assumed the role of the generator (Nagai et al. 2016). Each session was conducted in one and a half hours once every other week using an online video call.

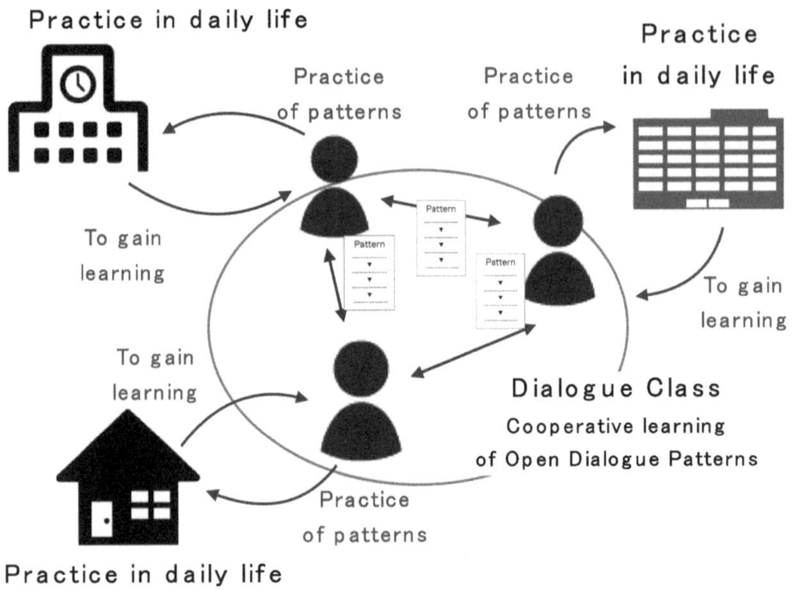

Fig. 2 The image of dialogue class

3.2 Utilisation Examples of Each Pattern

During the Dialogue Class, a total of ten cases in which the patterns were utilised were confirmed. The utilisation results of the patterns are summarised in the form of 'patterns performed', 'area of practice', 'what was practised', 'consequence' and 'what is learned'. These criteria aim to make participants aware of the influence of their actions and to gain discoveries from them. Since a detailed description of the contents is listed in the appendix in a table; here we briefly introduce the contents.

The breakdown of 'patterns performed' is as follows; seven patterns from the category of *Experienced World* were performed. These included *Experienced World*, *As a Living Person*, *Deep Listening*, *Exact Same Words*, *Open Question* and *Response to What is Said*. The *Emotional Resonance* from the category of *Various Voices* was performed and two patterns from the *Co-Created Understanding* category were also employed, which were *Diverse Understanding* and *Finding Together*.

The 'area of practice' is diverse. For instance, dialogue around 'when to advice colleagues', 'relationship with girlfriend', 'about human relationships within shared house', 'relationship with friends from the same project', 'at events to hold' and so on.

Regarding 'what was practised', basically participants practise a solution and action of patterns according to the situation at that time. For instance, there were examples of participants practising the patterns' solutions and actions according to their circumstances, such as one participant who performed *As a Living Person* noted, 'I had always been advising my colleague in the form of 'you should try ~~', but this time I consciously talked to him in a way that encouraged him to determine what he wanted to do'. Another participant who performed *Response to What is Said* noted, 'even when we are fighting, I brought myself to respond to what my girlfriend was saying'. There were also results that did not work. For example, for *Diverse Understanding*, although they are behaving according to the 'solution', which is 'talk while distinguishing each other's opinions and perceptions consciously, it resulted in them only claiming their perceptions, and thus their opinions never matched up, resulting in a negative outcome.'

In the 'what is learned' phase, there was also 'learning about the pattern itself' and 'learning about the relations of each pattern'. With regards to the 'learning about the pattern itself', the participant who performed *Response to What is Said* noted, 'by being conscious of responding to what she says, I could listen carefully to what she meant'. Regarding 'learning about the relations of each pattern', there was evidence of learning from a participant who noted, 'sometimes, I said "It is better for you to do this". I think it would have been better to practise *Deep Listening* or *Pause for Thinking.*'

3.3 Impressions from Participants

As written below, we collected feedback from participants after completion of the programme. The participants were asked through a free description questionnaire about the Open Dialogue Patterns and Dialogue Class.

Answers to the questions on the Open Dialogue Patterns revealed comments about triggers for learning about dialogue and hints for understanding others.

The comments regarding triggers for learning about dialogue are listed below. One specific comment stated 'Although it is difficult to actually use the patterns as written, it is quite effective in applying to many cases and getting to know the open dialogue. I learned more from patterns that I could not practice than those I was able to practice', while another stated, 'Since it is possible to recognise the method of each dialogue as a pattern, I think it will be easier to judge what I am doing right or not doing right'.

The comment providing hints for understanding others stated that 'I thought the Open Dialogue Patterns are a way to show the direction of communication to deepen understanding of others'.

With regards to the Dialogue Class, there were comments about the effectiveness of learning with others, a period of the programme and suggestions to improve the programme content.

The comment about the goodness of learning stated that 'I think that if you talk about what you have experienced, you will discover more things because others will refer to it from a different viewpoint. However, we may spend too much time for one episode, which is inevitable since I think that it will depend on the flow of the conversation'.

One comment about the period of the programme stated 'I think that the dialogue is also influenced by the relationship with others. I think that it was good to do it in a period of 1 month because it is possible to see others only from my sense of values since the other participants were people who I met only once or twice', while another said that 'I thought that it is better to have 2 week intervals between the classes. I feel like 1 week is a bit short to put what I learned into practice'.

Finally, one constructive comment which provided a means to improve the programme content stated that 'there were difficulties due to the short duration of the programme. I think that I could have learned more deeply if I got a double structure of having a look at the actual opportunity of dialogue and observed it'.

4 Consideration

Collectively, it was suggested that Open Dialogue Patterns are effective in the following three ways: 'utilisation to deepen understanding of interpersonal relations', 'induction of the inquiry of effective dialogue' and 'recognition of the dialogue as a design issue'.

4.1 Utilisation to Deepen Understanding of Interpersonal Relations

The first consideration is utilisation to deepen understanding of interpersonal relations. This investigation determined that it is relatively easy to utilise the Open Dialogue Patterns in everyday life to deepen the understanding of an individual.

The patterns employed were included from the sections known as 'experiencing the world' where 'context' assumes one-on-one conversation. There was also one specific feedback comment, which said, 'I thought the Open Dialogue Patterns are a direction of communication to deepen understanding of others'.

From these results, it can be concluded that the Open Dialogue Patterns are useful in deepening interpersonal understanding of others in daily life. The Open Dialogue itself is intended to resolve symptoms through the dialogue with stakeholders, but the aspect of having common words to share with others seems to have made it more useful in everyday life.

4.2 Induction of the Inquiry of Effective Dialogue

The second consideration is to induce the inquiry of effective dialogue. Using patterns, an individual becomes aware of his/her actions that were completed unconsciously before. From this, the individual can discern what kind of influence their actions impart.

For example, when the dialogue practice goes reasonably well, there is learning about the effect of a pattern, for example 'by being conscious of responding to what she says, I could listen carefully to what she meant'. In contrast, even if the participant feels that he/she did not do well, for example in *Diverse Understanding* or *Experienced World*, the participant still says, 'I often learned from the patterns I could not practice'.

These results suggest that the significance is not about whether the pattern is exactly feasible, but that the guidance of exploration and learning is directed by the patterns.

4.3 Recognition of the Dialogue as a Design Issue

The third consideration is utilisation to recognise the dialogue as a design issue. Although dialogue is an act that is not physically visible, participants were able to think about how to combine different patterns to design a better dialogue.

For example, one participant noted that 'not only claiming *Diverse Understanding* but also *Deep Listening* and *Tunnel of Emotion* must be carried out at the same time.' And the other noted that 'In some timing, I said "It is better for you to do this." I think it would have been better to practice *Deep Listening* or *Pause for Thinking*.'

These comments suggest that the participants concluded that combining and using the patterns can improve the quality of his/her dialogue. Collectively, we can conclude that the use of Open Dialogue Patterns enables people to think about dialogue, as something that can be designed upon will.

5 Conclusion

This research suggests that the Open Dialogue Patterns are an effective means in the following three points: 'utilisation to deepen understanding of interpersonal relations', 'induction of the inquiry of effective dialogue' and 'recognition of the dialogue as a design issue'.

Conversely, due to bias in some patterns, we also saw the possibility that there may be patterns that are difficult to practice in an everyday context. For this reason, we would like to continue implementing these patterns and closely examine the utilisation possibilities of each.

Furthermore, it is expected that the program curriculum we designed for people to learn about the Open Dialogue Patterns could be applied as a method of learning other pattern languages. This was supported by the comment 'I think that if you talk about what you have experienced, you will discover many things because others will refer to it from a different viewpoint', which suggests that this method of pattern language acquisition has the potential for future applications.

Acknowledgements We thank Ayaka Yoshikawa, Haruka Mori and Konomi Munakata for their assistance in writing this paper, and all members of the Open Dialogue Patterns Project.

Appendix

All utilisation examples of each pattern

Patterns performed	Area of practice	What was practised	Consequence	What is learned
As a Living Person	When giving advice to colleague	I had always been advising my colleague in the form of 'you should try ~~,' but this time I consciously talked to him in a way that encouraged him to determine what he wanted to do.	The intention like 'Let's take action' appeared to his mind.	At some timings, I said 'It is better for you to do this'. I think it would have been better to practice *Deep Listening* or *Pause for Thinking*.
Response to What is Said	Relationship with girlfriend	Even when we are fighting, I brought myself to respond to what my girlfriend was saying.	I was able to reconcile because I could understand what she was trying to express and avoided emotionally replying.	By being conscious to respond to what she says, I could listen carefully to what she meant.
Experienced World	About human relationships within shared house	When she said, 'I cannot understand the meaning of the story', I listened deeply to her opinion.	I noticed the difference in our viewpoints. I talked from the viewpoint of 'How does he get better' and she talked from the viewpoint of 'her emotions'.	If there is a difference in the viewpoint, the discussion will be inconsistent.
Deep Listening	About human relationships within shared house	When I heard from her that 'I cannot understand the meaning of the story', I listened deeply to her opinion.	I understood her argument, 'I cannot understand anything he is doing. I think he is strange.'	
Open Question	The opportunity to learn about World Cafe	When the discussion was dead, I asked an open question 'What do we want to deepen in the first place?'	A voice, 'I wanted to do something like this,' came out from other participants and the question was deepened.	When I speak out what I felt, the others might have felt the same sense of incongruity. In that case, the questions will get deeper.

Response to What is Said	Relationship with girlfriend	I tried to respond to what she is saying.	I could listen to her story but I lost the timing to say what I want to say.	When saying important things, it is easier for me to make the context in advance, for example 'I have something to talk about'.
Emotional Resonance	Relationship with the partner of a project	I listened to her story with calmness and empathy.	For the first time, the trouble that she could not talk to people so far was put into words.	The result of politely repeating the dialogue did not cause change as an action, but it was occurring inside her.
Exact Same Words	At the workshop I held	I got close to the opponent's idea with a smooth attitude. Specifically, I asked using his words and context.		I noticed that the members who also act as mother are good at doing 'same words' naturally.
Diverse Understanding	About human relationships within shared house	Talking while distinguishing each other's opinions and perceptions consciously.	Talk while distinguishing each other's opinions and perceptions consciously, it resulted in them only claimed their own perceptions and their opinions never matching up, ending up in negative outcome.	Not only claiming *Diverse Understanding* but also *Deep Listening* and *Tunnel of Emotion* must be carried out at the same time.
Finding Together	Relationship with girlfriend	Regarding our relationship, we found another option, 'We will not meet for a while'.	The possibility of seeing her someday in our lives will be influenced by whether I experience this or not. There still is a room to meet her as a friend in the future.	I decided to 'end the partnership' by myself, but we both were able to have the sense of ownership to the decision because there were opportunities to exchange each other's opinions.

References

Alexander, C., Ishikawa, S., & Silverstein, M. (1977). *A pattern language: Towns, buildings, construction*. New York: Oxford University Press.

Helm, E., Johnson, R., Vlissides, R., & Gamma, J. (1994). *Design patterns: Elements of reusable object-oriented software*. New York: Addison-Wesley Professional.

Iba, T. (2013). *Pattern language as media for the creative society*. In 4th International Conference on Collaborative Innovation Networks (COINs2013).

Iba, T., Nagai, M., Asano, R., Ishida, T., Eguchi, M., & Matsumiya, A. (2017). *Open dialogue patterns: A pattern language for collaborative problem dissolving*. In Viking Conference on Pattern Languages of Programs.

Nagai, M., Isaku, T., Akado, Y., & Iba, T. (2016). *Generator patterns: A pattern language for collaborative inquiry*. In 21st European Conference on Pattern Languages of Programs (EuroPLoP2016).

Nagai, M., Asano, R., Eguchi, E., & Iba, T. (2017). *Basic patterns for dialogical meeting: Open dialogue patterns, Part 2*. In 22st European Conference on Pattern Languages of Programs (EuroPLoP2017).

Seikkula, J., & Arnkil, T. E. (2014). *Open dialogues and anticipations: Respecting otherness in the present moment*. Helsinki: National Institute for Health and Welfare.

Seikkula, J., & Olson, M. E. (2003). The open dialogue approach to acute psychosis: Its poetics and micropolitics. *Family Process, 42*(3), 403–418.

Open Dialogue as Coupling of Psychic, Social and Creative Systems

Takashi Iba, Masafumi Nagai, and Tsuyoshi Ishida

Abstract In this paper, we study Open Dialogue, a psychiatric programme developed in Western Lapland, Finland, with the theory of autopoietic systems. Although originally developed as a psychiatric programme, we anticipate that the approach can be applied to not only psychotherapy but also educational and organisational situations as a way of "collaborative problem dissolution," because it is based on the philosophy of dialogism, which is not limited to psychotherapy. In an attempt to apply it in a more general context, we study the function of Open Dialogue in a higher level of abstraction with concepts of systems theories, i.e. the Social Systems Theory and Creative Systems Theory. Our consideration implies that Open Dialogue can be understood well through a combination of chain of consciousness in the psychic system, chain of communication in the social system and chain of discovery in the creative system.

1 Introduction

Recently, Open Dialogue, a psychotherapy method, is attracting a lot attention in Japan. Open Dialogue is originally a psychiatric programme developed in Keropudas Hospital in Western Lapland, Finland. It was initiated by Jaako Seikkula, a Professor

T. Iba (✉)
Faculty of Policy Management, Keio University, Fujisawa, Kanagawa, Japan

Graduate School of Media and Governance, Keio University, Fujisawa, Kanagawa, Japan
e-mail: iba@sfc.keio.ac.jp

M. Nagai
Graduate School of Media and Governance, Keio University, Fujisawa, Kanagawa, Japan
e-mail: mnagai@sfc.keio.ac.jp

T. Ishida
Faculty of Environment and Information Studies, Keio University, Fujisawa, Kanagawa, Japan
e-mail: t14067ti@sfc.keio.ac.jp

F. Grippa et al. (eds.), *Collaborative Innovation Networks*, Studies on Entrepreneurship, Structural Change and Industrial Dynamics,
https://doi.org/10.1007/978-3-319-74295-3_18

at the Department of Psychology, University of Jyväskylä, who is a clinical psychologist and family therapy trainer.

Open Dialogue includes those involved in a crisis, namely the important people in the patient's life, such as family members and social networks, gathering them together to engage in meetings (Fig. 1) (Seikkula and Olson 2003; Seikkula and Trimble 2005; Seikkula and Arnkil 2006, 2014). The aim of the meetings is to develop a dialogue, giving a voice to all concerned, putting the person at the centre without strategically trying to change him/her. Surprisingly, the symptoms of a mental disease, such as schizophrenia, disappear through dialogue. In contrast, in the old system, appointments and interventions with the psychiatrist are the only way to seek solutions. The effectiveness of the measures adopted in Open Dialogues includes number of relapses, rating of psychotic symptoms and social functioning, employment status and hospital days.

Although the Open Dialogue approach was originally developed as a psychiatric programme, we anticipate that it has applicability to educational and organisational situations, because it is based on the philosophy of dialogism, which is not limited to psychotherapy. Indeed, the approach presented by Jaakko Seikkula has been discussed for wider consideration in communication and human relationship (Bakhtin 1981, 1990; Gergen 1999; Holquist 1990; Maturana and Varela 1972; Vygotsky 1978, 1986).

To understand the applicability from a different angle, we analyse the function of Open Dialogue in a higher level of abstraction with concepts of systems theories, including Social Systems Theory (Luhmann 1984, 1997) and Creative Systems Theory (Iba 2010).

Fig. 1 Dialogical meeting in the Open Dialogue approach

2 Overview of Open Dialogue

Here, we discuss the points that are to be conducted in the dialogical meeting of the Open Dialogue approach. We use a vocabulary proposed in the Open Dialogue Patterns (Iba et al. 2017; Nagai et al. 2017). The Open Dialogue Patterns is a pattern language for practising a dialogical meeting, in which each pattern expresses knowledge of what kind of *problem* frequently occurs in a certain *context* and what is a good *solution* to the problem. In this paper, however, we use only words (pattern names) to introduce what are conducted in the dialogical meeting. Note that the words (pattern names) are shown in bold.

There are 30 patterns in the Open Dialogue Patterns. In the top level, there are core patterns: **Experienced World**, **Various Voices** and **Co-Created Understanding** (Fig. 2). Related to each of these three words, nine words are defined to show what are important to realize them.

2.1 *Understanding 'Experienced World'*

Imagine a situation where you are trying to understand the problem (the symptom in the case of a psychiatric programme) the person (patient) of concern is facing. For truly understanding his/her **Experienced World**, you must not diagnose him/her, but listen to what he/she says **As a Living Person**. Then, it is important to engage in **Deep Listening**, receive his/her saying and use the **Exact Same Words** to respond without modifying them into words you are familiar with.

During the dialogue, your questions may better be **Open Questions** that allow him/her to think and give his/her own answer, rather than asking question that require only answers with Yes or No. Allowing for a **Pause for Thinking** is important, so that he/she can have time to think about what he/she wants to say. When he/she answers your question, it is important to give a **Response to What is Said**.

To understand his/her **Experienced World**, you need to feel from his/her **Inner Viewpoint**, not the objective or outsider's viewpoint. Sometimes there may be

Fig. 2 Core patterns in Open Dialogue Patterns

strong emotional expression; this is a great opportunity to go deeper through the **Tunnel of Emotion**, so that he/she will be able to put hidden and complex thoughts and experiences into words. It is also important to let you keep a **Respectful Mind** for him/her who lives with dark and tough experiences.

Consequently, it will not only be you having a deeper and better understanding of his/her **Experienced World**, but also, he/she can have the opportunity to talk about his/her experiences he/she could not express before. The summary of patterns in this category is shown in Fig. 3.

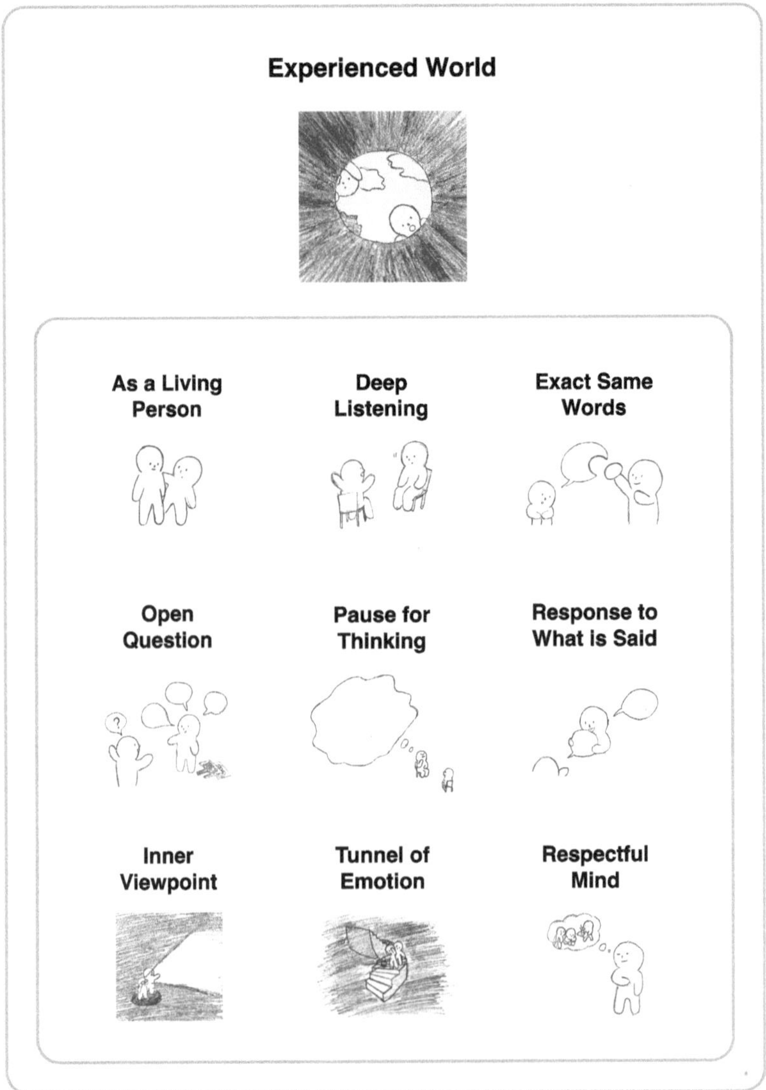

Fig. 3 'Experienced World' in the Open Dialogue Patterns

2.2 *Generating 'Various Voices'*

In the Open Dialogue approach, multiple people related to the person facing the problem are invited to the dialogical meeting to obtain multiple perspectives through **Various Voices**.

First of all, you invite **Significant Others** of the person facing with the problem and gather the member responsible for treatment so that you can be **Working as a Team**, not alone. Then, all participants will be **Sitting in the Circle**.

During the dialogical meeting, you keep sending an **Invitation for Utterances** to everybody. Rather than trying to quickly summarise the story, it is good to have a **Slow-Paced Conversation**, where anyone can start to speak frankly. Subsequently, you must make sure to respond to any utterance and realize a **Chain of Responses**.

It is important to pay attention to **Tiny Signs** that each person gives, such as a subtle expression or visible tension. When somebody expresses emotion, it can be beneficial to let **Emotional Resonance** develop and sometimes, it is important to have a **Reflecting Talk** with the supporting team members, where other participants can have a moment for thinking and producing a new voice.

Consequently, various narratives are drawn out from the participants and gradually the person facing the problem will release from his/her stiffened and self-contained thoughts, emerging from a dead-end situation and opening to new experiences. The summary of patterns in this category is shown in Fig. 4.

2.3 *Achieving 'Co-Created Understanding'*

Surprisingly, through dialogue meetings of the Open Dialogue approach, the problem disappears, because dialogue makes the participants express the problem with various words so that together, a new understanding can be created. To achieve this, the following points should be considered.

The **First Meeting in Crisis** is the meeting with the best timing because emotions and speech of participants come up easily. Since this is an unstable period, **Everyday Meetings** and **Continuous Engagement** with the same participants are necessary, bringing psychological continuity and security.

In the dialogue, we acknowledge and share the **Diverse Understanding** without judgement of right or wrong and tolerating **Ambiguous Situations.** Next, you will experience a **Transformation of Meaning** for the situation.

What is important is that a dialogue should be conducted for acquiring **Ever-Widening Perspectives** rather than converging to one point of agreement. It is also important to make sure to keep **Finding Together**, not giving advice from the

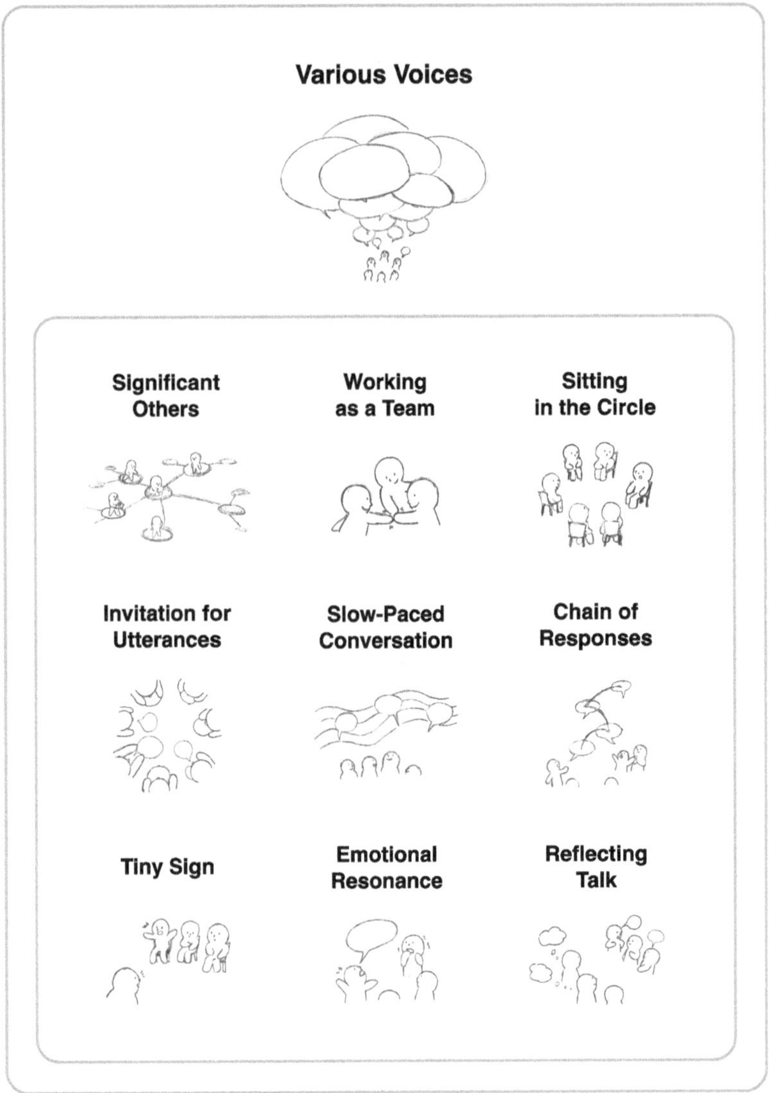

Fig. 4 'Various Voices' in the Open Dialogue Patterns

viewpoint of a specialist. The dialogue will provide a shared precious experience for the participants and the group will become a **Community for the Future**.

As a result, interpretations of the problem will change and new understandings will be generated and at the same time, the problem will dissolve naturally. The summary of patterns in this category is shown in Fig. 5.

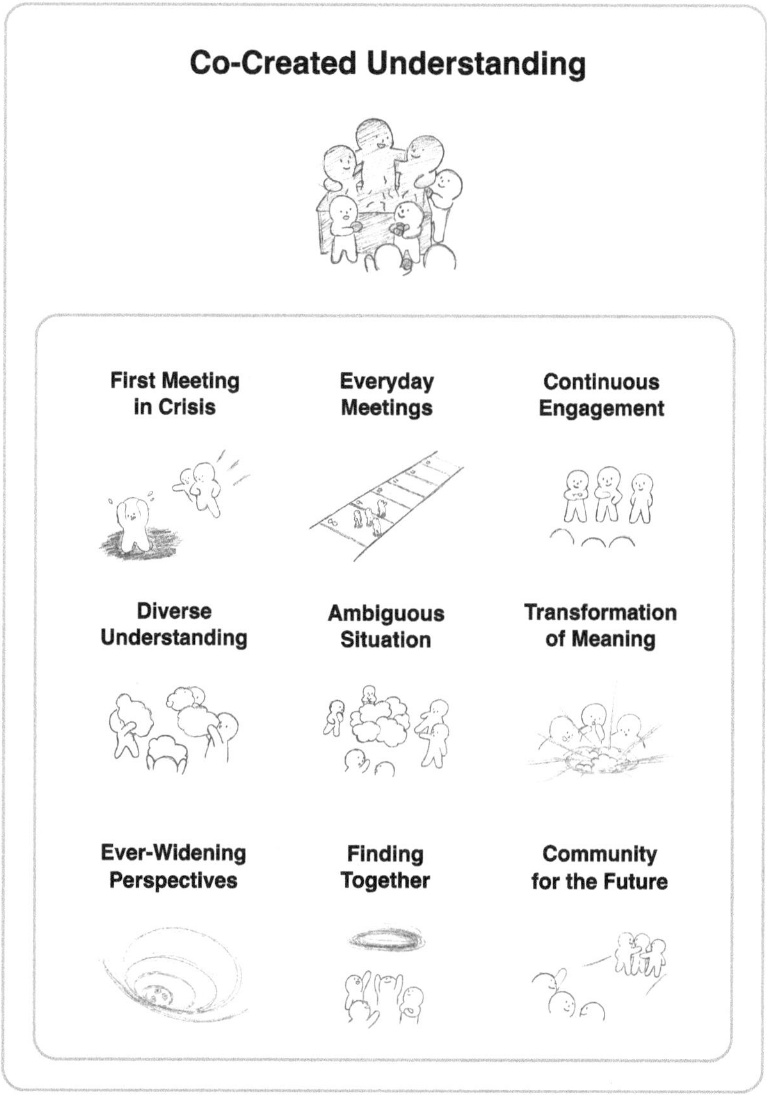

Fig. 5 'Co-Created Understanding' in the Open Dialogue Patterns

3 Autopoietic Systems Theory

Following, we analyse what happens in dialogical meeting of the Open Dialogue approach using the systems theory.[1] Autopoietic systems were proposed by Humberto Maturana and Francisco Varela in biology (Maturana and Varela 1972) as a unity

[1]It is reasonable to use autopoietic systems theory, because the theorists of autopoietic systems, Humberto Maturana, Francisco Varela and Niklas Luhmann, are referred in the literature on the Open Dialogue (Seikkula and Arnkil 2006).

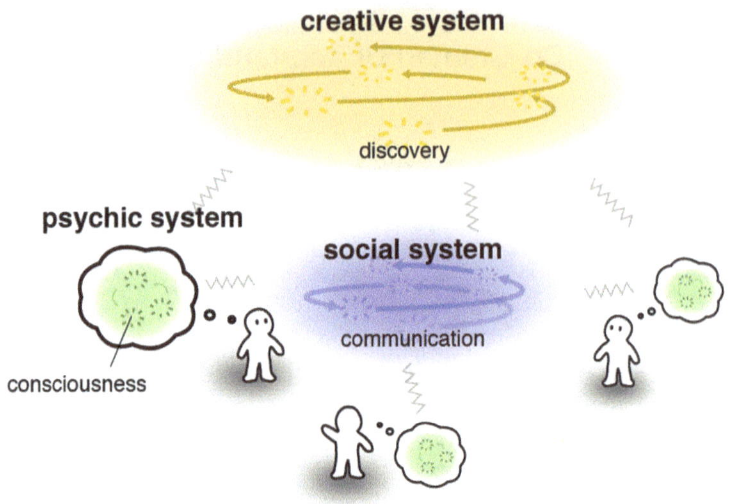

Fig. 6 Coupling psychic, social and creative systems

where the organisation is defined by a particular network of production processes of elements. Although the original area of autopoietic systems is biology, Luhmann generalised the theory and used it to enhance his theories of social systems that include *communication* as an element.

Based on these autopoietic systems theories, we suggest that what happens in dialogical meetings of the Open Dialogue approach can be explained by coupling *psychic, social* and *creative systems* (Fig. 6). To reach to this conclusion, we first outline the Social Systems Theory, focussing on the parts of theory to understand the function of Open Dialogue, then move on to the Creative Systems Theory, which is necessary to understand another side of the Open Dialogue. Note that from here, the technical terms used in the autopoietic systems theory are italicised.

In the Social Systems Theory, Luhmann formulates the human mind as an *autopoietic system*, which is called a *psychic system* and where the primary element is *consciousness*. The *psychic system* is a nexus of *consciousness* and the system reproduces *consciousness* by *consciousness*. The *consciousness* may have no duration due to its momentary operation and requirement to be reproduced constantly. Moreover, from an operational point of view, such a *psychic system* is a closed system as it cannot send or receive communication outside the system. Since the *psychic system* is operationally closed, you cannot directly access to its elements. *Psychic systems* are mutually inaccessible, therefore, *communication* is required.

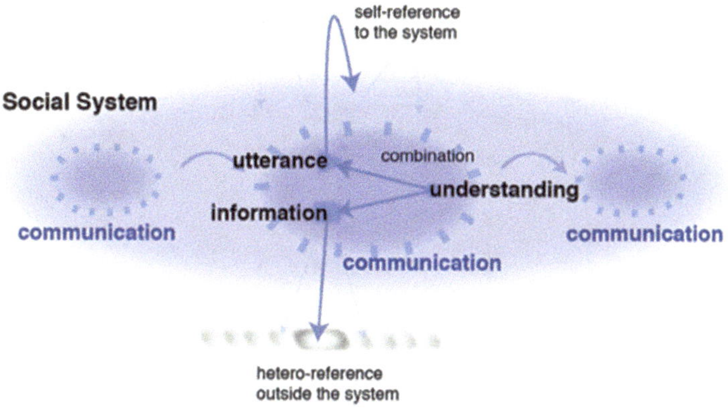

Fig. 7 Communication emerging from the synthesis of a three-part selection: information, utterance and understanding

In theory, *communication* is considered as the element of *social system* and emerges between people. According to Luhmann (1984), *communication* emerges from the synthesis of a three-part selection in social systems: selection of *information*, *utterance* and *understanding* (Fig. 7).

Note that such a definition of *communication* is much different from the conventional definition that is based on a metaphor of transference, where a sender passes a message (information) to a receiver and then, the information moves from the sender to the receiver. Luhmann pointed out that there is a limitation with this perspective, since it is prepossessed with the existence of the same information transferred between sender and receiver.

He claims that this perspective misses the understanding of the nature of *communication* as social phenomenon. Instead, *communication* should be considered as a social phenomenon related to *meaning*. Furthermore, I would like to emphasise that Luhmann's conceptualisation of *communication* is different from the so-called 'communicative act'; the concept of communicative act, as implied by the name, is based on the action theory rather than communication as mutual selection.

Communication can have no duration because it is a momentary operation that must be reproduced constantly. From an operations viewpoint, such a *social system* is a closed system as it cannot send or receive communication outside the system, even from psychic systems.

In the Creative Systems Theory (Iba 2010), a creative process is formulated as an autopoietic system, where elements are discoveries. In other words, a creative process is a reproduction network of *discoveries*. Each *discovery* emerges only when a synthesis of the following three selections occurs: *idea*, *association* and *finding* (Fig. 8).

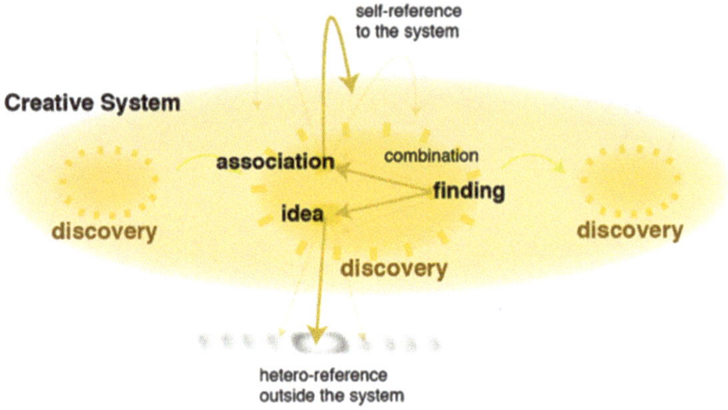

Fig. 8 Discovery emerging from the synthesis of a three-part selection: idea, association and finding

4 Understanding Open Dialogue with Autopoietic Systems Theory

Here, we present how Open Dialogue can be understood with the autopoietic systems theory, introduced in this last section, including the Social Systems Theory and Creative Systems Theory (Fig. 9). Note that pattern names of the Open Dialogue Patterns are shown in bold and the technical terms of the autopoietic systems theory are italicised.

4.1 Understanding 'Experienced World' in a Psychic System Through Communication

In the dialogical meeting, it is quite difficult to understand the **Experienced World** of people faced with the problem, because the *psychic system* (chain of *consciousness*) is operationally closed. Therefore, **Deep Listening, Inner Viewpoint** and sometimes the **Tunnel of Emotion** is necessary to understand the chain of *consciousness* of a person.

As mentioned above, however, *psychic systems* are mutually inaccessible; therefore an understanding can be achieved via a chain of *communication,* such as **Open Questions** and **Response to What is Said**. Due to closeness of *psychic systems* and *social systems*, there is no guarantee that what is said by one person will be the same of what is understood by another one, therefore, it is important to use the **Exact Same Words**. In addition, because the chain of *consciousness* and the speed of the process in a *psychic system* cannot be visible from outside, it is crucial to allow for the necessary **Pause for Thinking**.

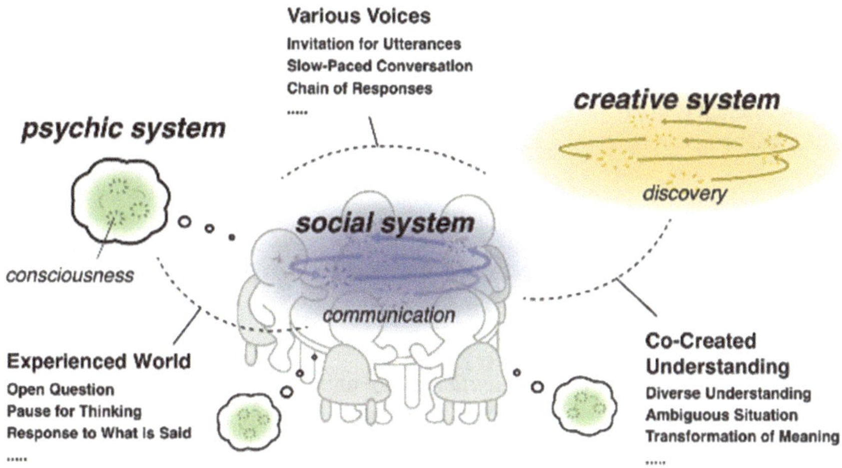

Fig. 9 Coupling psychic, social and creative systems in the Open Dialogue

Psychic systems observe the action of each other, thus, participating in the dialogue **As a Living Person** with a **Respectful Mind** can be recognised by the person facing the problem. As a result, he/she will *trust* that person and expect that what he/she says will be listened to carefully in the dialogue. Thus, *psychic systems,* which are mutually inaccessible in principle, can penetrate each other via the chain of *communication.*

4.2 Generating 'Various Voices' by Chain of Communication in a Social System

Dialogue is mainly conducted as a chain of *communication.* Unlike *communication* in functional systems of society, such as economy and science, the chain of *communication* with regard to a difficult problem hardly continues. Therefore, the Open Dialogue offers to set up an *environment* for dialogue by inviting the **Significant Others**, participating and **Working as a Team** and **Sitting in the Circle**. This is the *environment* for the dialogue in *social systems* and *creative systems.*

As introduced above, *communication* emerges when the *information* with intention of *utterance* is recognised (*understanding*) in the dialogue. Therefore, in the dialogue, the participants need to recognise the **Invitation for Utterances** in the precious chain of *communication* and not just think in a *psychic system.* **Slow-Paced Conversation** and **Chain of Responses**, which are also chains of *communication*, encourage participants to start to speak frankly, meaning that successive *communication* can emerge.

Furthermore, another *communication* emerges when the *information* with unconscious or hidden intention of *utterance* is recognised as **Tiny Signs**. **Emotional Resonance** makes the chain of *communication* to flow smoothly as the *environment.*

Reflecting Talk is making a sub-*social system* in the dialogical meeting; therefore, other *psychic systems* will *observe* the chain of *communication* from the outside of the dialogue.

Thus, where it is improbable to keep a certain type of *communication*, *social systems* can become probable by setting up the *environment* and chain of *communication*.

4.3 Achieving 'Co-Created Understanding' by Chain of Discovery in a Creative System

Achieving only a chain of *communication* is not enough for the Open Dialogue. In the dialogical meeting, a new shared understanding among participants of the meeting is generated. The **Co-Created Understanding** should be considered as phenomenon in the *creative system* (chain of *discovery*).

What happens in the dialogue towards **Co-Created Understanding** is **Transformation of Meaning** through **Ambiguous Situations** based on the **Diverse Understanding** from all participants. This occurs as chain of *discovery* in the *creative system* along the dialogue. As explained before, *discovery* emerges when *finding* an *association* of an *idea* to the on-going creation. In the dialogical meeting, new meaning is generated via the chain of *discovery*. Finally, a new understanding is created.

Intensive collaboration hardly occurs without any forces that make people concentrate in the creation. Thus, Open Dialogue offers to set up the *environment* and keep a tension for *creative systems*. The **First Meeting in Crisis** helps in the emergence of a chain of *discovery*, because the necessity of dialogue is very clear for everyone. The **Everyday Meetings** guarantee the continuation of the chain of *discovery* and the **Continuous Engagement** functions as a platform to generate the chain of *discovery*.

To truly dissolve the problem, the *discovery* with **Ever-Widening Perspectives** is significant for the participants to keep being creative also in their future. **Finding Together** through the generation of a chain of *discovery* along a chain of *communication* is very important in the Open Dialogue. A new understanding should be co-created by all participants, not just one part of them. This group will be able to become a **Community for the Future** for themselves, allowing to couple *psychic*, *social* and *creative systems* in the daily life.

5 Conclusion

In this paper, we studied the Open Dialogue approach with the theory of autopoietic systems. Open Dialogue can be understood well within the combined frame of the chain of *consciousness* in the *psychic system*, the chain of *communication* in the *social system* and the chain of *discovery* in the *creative system*. On one hand, this shows what happens in dialogical meetings of the Open Dialogue approach in the psychiatric programme. On the other hand, this also shows that the Open Dialogue can be considered as not only a psychiatric programme but also a collaboration method in a broader range of social domains, because the systems we discussed are not limited to psychotherapy as they consider fundamental systems of mind, communication and creation. In future, we would like to discuss about this possibility with readers.

References

Bakhtin, M. (1981). *Problems of Destojevskij's poetics: Theory and history of literature* (Vol. 8). Manchester: Manchester Univeristy Press.

Bakhtin, M. (1990). *The dialogic imagination* (M. Holquist, Ed., C. Emerson & M. Holoquist. Trans.). Austin, TX: University of Texas Press.

Gergen, K. (1999). *An invitation of social construction*. London: Sage.

Holquist, M. (1990). *Dialogism: Bakhtin and his world*. New York: Routledge.

Iba, T. (2010). An autopoietic systems theory for creativity. *Procedia – Social and Behavioral Sciences, 2*(4), 6610–6625.

Iba, T., Nagai, M., Asano, R., Ishida, T., Eguchi, M., & Matsumiya, A., (2017). Open dialogue patterns: A pattern language for collaborative problem dissolving. *VikingPLoP 2017*.

Luhmann, N. (1984). *Soziale Systeme: Grundriß einer allgemeinen Theorie*. Frankfurt: Suhrkamp (English translation: *Social systems*, John Bednarz Jr., Dirk Baecker (Trans.). Stanford: Stanford University Press, 1995).

Luhmann, N. (1997). *Die Gesellschaft der Gesellschaft*. Frankfurt: Suhrkamp (English translation: *Theory of society*, Vols. 1 & 2, Rhodes Barrett (Trans.). Stanford: Stanford University Press, 2012 & 2013).

Maturana, H., & Varela, F. (1972). *Autopoiesis and cognition: The realization of the living*. Holland: Reidel.

Nagai, M., Asano, R., Eguchi, M., & Iba, T. (2017). Basic patterns for dialogical meeting: Open dialogue patterns, Part II. In *22nd European conference on pattern languages of programs (EuroPLoP2017)*.

Seikkula, J., & Arnkil, T. E. (2006). *Dialogical meetings in social networks*. London: Karnac.

Seikkula, J., & Arnkil, T. E. (2014). *Open dialogues and anticipations: Respecting otherness in the present moment*. Helsinki, Finland: National Institute for Health and Welfare.

Seikkula, J., & Olson, M. E. (2003). The open dialogue approach to acute psychosis: Its poetics and micropolitics. *Family Process, 42*(3), 403–418.

Seikkula, J., & Trimble, D. (2005). Healing elements of therapeutic conversation: Dialogue as an embodiment of love. *Family Process, 44*(4), 461–475.

Vygotsky, L. S. (1978). *Mind in society: The development of higher psychological processes* (M. Cole, V. John-Steiner, S. Scribner, & E. Souberman, Trans. & Eds.). Cambridge, MA: Harvard University Press.

Vygotsky, L. S. (1986). *Thought and language*. (A. Kozulin, Trans. & Ed.). Cambridge, MA: MIT Press.

Story Writing for Creative Revising of Ideas

Konomi Munakata, Shuichiro Ando, and Takashi Iba

Abstract This paper presents the mechanism and methodology of creative revising in design processes. Creative revising is the process of concept development where brainstormed ideas are continuously expanded with many fresh insights and are layered with increasing complexity. This paper begins with a discussion on the factors that make the creative revising process difficult. It arrives at the conclusion that a fixed definition of ideas in the early stages hinders their development. Creative revising requires the practitioner to continuously obscure and redefine notions, and we found that designers could explore the different potentials of their ideas by writing stories. This method of creative revising ameliorates the coherence and complexity of the design as a whole. This paper therefore proposes that the writing of stories is an effective way of revising ideas and one that could prove to be a valuable method that would enable designers to ensure the sustainable improvement of their works.

1 Introduction

Csikszentmihalyi (1996) defined creativity as an act, an idea, or a product that changes an existing domain. A considerable number of studies have been conducted on creative processes in various fields, including business management. Studies on the mechanisms of the generation of new concepts and research on the methodologies for the creation of innovative ideas have especially caught public attention.

K. Munakata (✉)
Faculty of Environment and Information Studies, Keio University, Fujisawa, Kanagawa, Japan
e-mail: t15570km@sfc.keio.ac.jp

S. Ando · T. Iba
Faculty of Policy Management, Keio University, Fujisawa, Kanagawa, Japan
e-mail: s15045sa@sfc.keio.ac.jp; iba@sfc.keio.ac.jp

F. Grippa et al. (eds.), *Collaborative Innovation Networks*, Studies on Entrepreneurship, Structural Change and Industrial Dynamics,
https://doi.org/10.1007/978-3-319-74295-3_19

Although Csikszentmihalyi (1996) stated 'creative work is never done', the sustainable improvement of work is actually difficult at a practical level in the sense that we have to keep looking with fresh eyes at what has already been generated.

In this paper, we use the nomenclature *Creative Revising* to denote the continuous process of idea development and discuss the mechanism of how ideas can be elaborated in the design process after being generated. In addition, we suggest *Story Writing* as an effective way of achieving the aim of creative revising.

2 Creative Revising

The creative process has traditionally been described as taking a five-phased progression (Fig. 1): preparation, incubation, insight, evaluation and elaboration (Csikszentmihalyi 1996). Ideas are below the threshold of consciousness in the first two steps, and emerge in the insight phase. Only the ideas which are considered as valuable are then developed in the phase of elaboration in order to be produced in the form of a design.

Haruki Murakami, a Japanese writer, described in his book that he wrote a short story in three days and spent more than a year to rewrite it a dozen times (Ellis and Hirabayashi 2005). In re-exploring what he had already done, he discovered more '*right*' characters, found better expressions and even imagined a plot that he had not thought of before. His story became more complex and nuanced as the writing was processed, and ultimately, it became completely different from its first draft.

Christopher Alexander (1979), an architect, called such a process a creative 'Process of Repair'. It is the continuous course of improving the designs of buildings according to the real events which actually happen there, regardless of whether it is performed in the designer's mind or on the actual site. He says that repeating such acts of building generates a unified organic whole which is coherent and more complex.

The author of worldwide bestselling books, Stephen King (2000), described the method of revising as follows: 'I love this part of the process because I'm rediscovering my own book, and usually liking it. That changes. By the time a book is actually in print, I've been over it a dozen times or more, can quote whole passages'.

Therefore, it is evident that the process of elaborating ideas in the course of their creation often involves many fresh insights. It is not a process which takes place

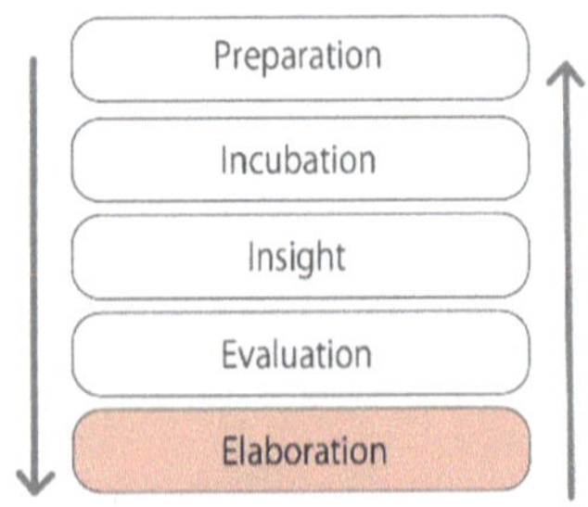

Fig. 1 Five phases of a creative process

under the creator's control but one where many new fresh insights could unintentionally emerge, even after one has just put in the finishing touches on the original ideas. In this way, it is less linear and more recursive with many loops involved (Csikszentmihalyi 1996). To emphasise such continuity and increased complexity with dynamic retouches on the initial ideas, we call the phase of idea elaboration in the creative process *Creative Revising* in this paper.

3 Story Writing as a Creative Revising Method

Creative Revising is actually very difficult in the sense that we have to reflect and redevelop the ideas which were just generated by us. We believe that *meaning* offers the key to solving this problem. Every single idea of design generated in our head has a *fixed meaning* with a sort of specific description when they are put into words to be mentioned and mulled over. This, however, removes the flexibility of ideas, makes it difficult for us to explore the other possibilities which they potentially possess and keeps us adhered to the initial definitions of ideas.

Niklas Luhmann, a prominent sociologist in the twentieth century, made several important statements on this *meaning* (Luhmann 1984). He explained that a function of *meaning* is to distinguish the actuality and the potentiality. *Meaning* makes it clear as to what was selected and what was not from all the other potentials in this complex world. Therefore, he says, 'meaning is a very potent technology to reduce the complexity of the society' (Baecker 2002, p. 172). From this passage, it can be understood that it is necessary to loosen the fixed *meaning* of existing ideas and make them ambiguous again to regain the complexity of ideas and explore their essences and hidden potentials.

Now a question arises: How can we make the generated ideas ambiguous again? According to Csikszentmihalyi (1996), whereas words transform fragile thoughts and feelings into concrete thoughts, 'poetry and literature allow the creation of experiences that we would otherwise not have access to; they take our lives to higher levels of complexity' (p. 238).

This indicates that writing a story about the brainstormed ideas would allow us to explore their hidden potentials, redefine them and enhance the coherence and complexity of the design as a whole. Therefore, we hypothesise that story writing would be an effective method for creative revising so as to elaborate and reconstruct the original ideas once generated for a better output of design.

3.1 Story Writing in Design Thinking

Although a story itself is usually recognised as a creative output, the concept of story writing has recently been brought to attention as a way of developing ideas, especially in the field of design thinking. It helps designers to predict the uncertain future and to prototype and evaluate their ideas in a costless way. *Design Fiction* (Sterling 2009), for instance, is an approach to explore and criticise future possibilities by creating speculative scenarios (Sterling 2009; Bosch 2012). *Scenario Planning* is also a method to think about the potential problems in the future and to develop the organisational skills to survive in this fast-changing society (Heijden et al. 2002).

Both methods indicate how creating stories during the designing process can maintain the flexibility of ideas and bring designers to divergent ways of thinking. Ideas are supposed to churn around in the specified context of a story, and they keep being developed in the process of creating stories. Therefore, in the beginning stage of writing a scenario, the ending is usually not planned, and there is usually no 'must' in this usage of story writing. It is very similar to how Murakami starts writing his story without any sketch or outline, and he just 'gives the characters a place to grow' and 'waits for the ending to come naturally' (Murakami and Kawai 2016, p. 62).

3.2 The Mechanism of Creative Revising with Story Writing

When the method of story writing is applied to the creative revising, it is expected that writers experience a dynamic change in their initial ideas. In this section, we explain the mechanism.

Creative revising should start with a set of clearly stated brainstormed ideas. Each idea has a *fixed meaning* with a specific description (Fig. 2a). Some ideas are then selected from the list to construct a story (Fig. 2b). In this way, they interact with each other in the specific context of the story so that they could lose their concrete definitions to some extent and get more ambiguous (Fig. 2c).

In developing a story, the essence of each idea keeps being questioned. Therefore, two ideas which have similar essences or functions may be integrated, whereas one which has multiple potentials could be differentiated (Fig. 3d). New alternative ideas might be discovered in this phase as well. This process of the adjustment of the story and its individual ideas is repeated until the transformation of ideas spontaneously comes to the end when the story obtains consistency as a whole (Fig. 3e). The framework of the story is then removed, and each idea has to be re-defined (Fig. 3f). It should be observed that the remaining list of ideas is somehow different from the first stage.

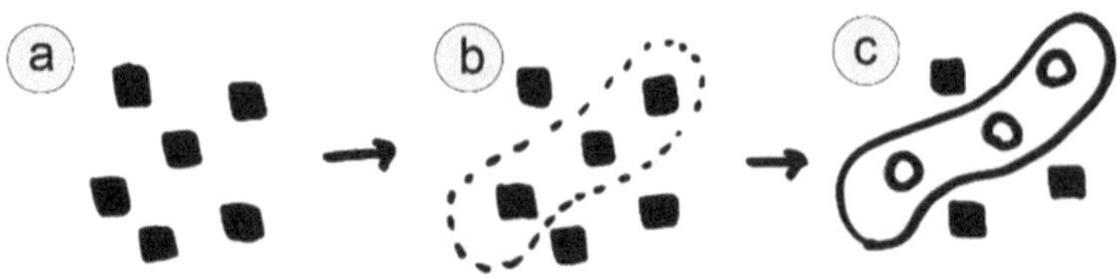

Fig. 2 Obfuscation of ideas

Fig. 3 Redefinition of ideas after integration, differentiation and generation

Fig. 4 Repetitions of story writing with different set of ideas

This process should be repeated, by choosing different sets of ideas or adding some other surrounding ideas (Fig. 4g), constructing different stories (Fig. 4h) and making their meanings ambiguous again (Fig. 4i).

In repeating these processes by writing various stories with different combinations of ideas and different contexts, the essence and potentials of ideas are deeply explored and rediscovered. Ideas thus get transformed into better definitions. In this repetition of the obfuscation and redefinition of ideas, we can switch divergent and convergent thinking so that we are able to keep reflecting on the initially generated ideas. Therefore, it would be reasonable to suppose that story writing is an effective method for the revising of ideas in creative processes.

4 Creative Revising in Student Residence Project

In this section, we discuss how story writing could be applied to the actual design process. We applied the method of story writing in the process of creative revising for the ideas generated in the Student Residence Project.

The Student Residence Project is a collaborative project with a Japanese architectural design company, UDS Ltd., conducted by four members of Iba Laboratory in 2016. Our goal in this project was to make the everyday life of university students more imaginative and creative. We conducted several workshops with other students in our campus to brainstorm new ideas to form a creative community (Fig. 5). Seventy-nine ideas were generated in total and forty among them were selected to be called 'Future Words' (Iba 2016) and put into the idea list.

Fig. 5 Workshops with campus students

4.1 Process

To conduct an investigation into the transformation of ideas in creative revising, it is first necessary to clearly state the definitions of the initial set of ideas. Therefore, we used a specific format to describe every single fragment of ideas, called Future Word, as shown in Fig. 6. This format aims to clarify exactly what each idea is about and why it is important, with a name that symbolises its essence (Iba 2016).

Second, in order to develop the future words on the list, each member worked independently for two months on writing various stories with the future words. This is what we call future stories. Here are two examples of future stories where future words were embedded and emphasised with the bold letters and brackets.

> . . .It was a Saturday morning, already half past nine. I had to be at my part time job by 10 am. As I ran through the first floor, I saw lots of new faces in the <**Floor Lounge**> today. Oh, we have the <**Welcome Party**> tonight. I remember we did the <**Self-Design of Welcome Party**> last year as well. I first thought it would be really challenging to plan the party ourselves and let the seniors follow the plan. But it was not, actually. I forced my <**Community Leader**> to sing a welcome song and it was supper funny. . . (‘*Saturday Morning in the Residence*’ by Shuichiro Ando)

> . . .This residence is a place to grow new creative leaders who can lead the creative society coming in the future, from different perspectives. Here is not the place to get lectured by someone else, but the place to develop yourself . . . People who are known as creative know well about their own strengths, abilities and roles. Students in this residence therefore get many opportunities to know about themselves through the <**Dialogue by Extremes**>, <**Mixed with different colours**> and <**Seat-reserved Cafe**>. In a nutshell, this residence is a prototype of an educational system in future, which supports students to become active-lifelong-learners who can develop their abilities by themselves and have confidence in their qualitative works. . . (‘*Student Residence from the perspective of education in future* by Konomi Munakata)

4.2 Results

As the diagram below shows (Fig. 7), we could see some significant changes in the initial set of ideas after two months of continuous story writing. Some future words were integrated, differentiated and removed, whereas new ideas were also added to

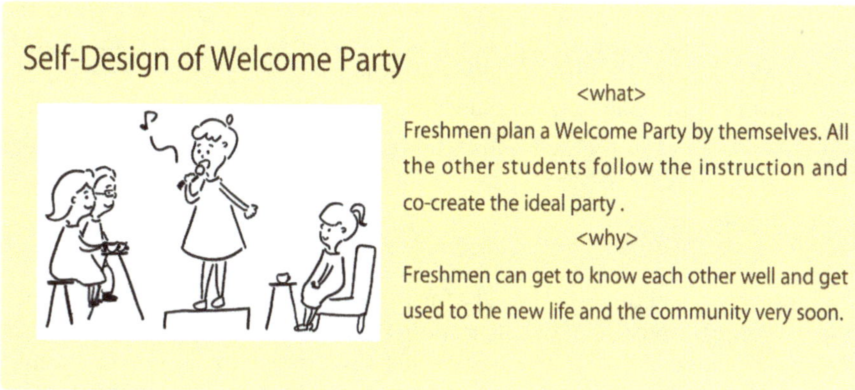

Fig. 6 Future word 'self-design of welcome party'

Fig. 7 Change in future words in story writing

the list. Most importantly, the names of the future words, which symbolised the essence of each idea, have dynamically changed in the continuous process of story writing. These results lead us to the conclusion that story writing enabled the continuous self-reflection of ideas and helped us to re-develop the original ideas.

5 Conclusion

In this paper, we have discussed how the fragments of ideas could be elaborated by the proposer using the process of writing stories. The approach opens up the mechanism of idea elaboration in the creative process and develops a methodology for creative revising with story writing. Although this calls for further investigation, creative revising is evidently a topic which should be further, especially in the field of design.

In fact, there are some areas of design which put a lot of weight on idea revising and which have developed their own ways of creative revising, for example, the concept of a Writers Workshop. This is a collaborative revising process for writers, who gather at one place and make comments on each other's work. There is also a semi-permanent revising project conducted by Alexander (1977). Oregon University was constructed, and it keeps being repaired according to changes in its reality. It is obvious that ideas and designs could keep evolving and becoming more fascinating in an uninterrupted revising process. Therefore, we anticipate that further studies will be conducted to develop the methodologies of the creative revising.

References

Alexander, C. (1977). *The timeless way of building*. New York: Oxford University Press.

Baecker, D. (2002). *Einführung in die Systemtheorie*. Frankfurt: Carl-Auer-Systeme Verlag. (English edition: D. Baecker (2013). *Introduction to systems theory* (P. Gilgen, Trans., p. 172). Cambridge: Polity Press).

Bosch, T. (2012). *Sci-Fi writer Bruce Sterling explains the intriguing new concept of design fiction*. http://www.slate.com/blogs/future_tense/2012/03/02/bruce_sterling_on_design_fictions_.html

Csikszentmihalyi, M. (1996). *Creativity: Flow and the psychology of discovery and invention*. New York: Harper Perennial.

Ellis, J., & Hirabayashi, M. (2005). *In dreams begins responsibility: An interview with Haruki Murakami*. Tokyo: Japan UNI Agency.

Heijden, K., Bradfield, R., Burt, G., Cairns, G., & Wright, G. (2002). *The sixth sense accelerating organizational learning with scenarios*. Chichester: Wiley.

Iba, T. (2016). Future language for collaborative design. *PUARL conference, USA*.

King, S. (2000). *On writing: A memoir of the craft* (p. 213). New York: Scribner.

Luhmann, N. (1984). *Soziale Systeme: Grundriß einer allgemeinen Theorie*. Frankfurt: Suhrkamp. English edition: Luhmann, N. (1995). *Social systems* (J. Bednerz, & D. Baecker, Trans.). California: Stanford University Press.

Murakami, H., & Kawai, H. (2016). *Haruki Murakami goes to meet Hayao Kawai*. Einsiedeln: Daimon Verlag.

Sterling, B. (2009). COVER STORY: Design fiction. *Interactions, 16*(3). https://doi.org/10.1145/2207676.2208279. New York: ACM.

FSC
www.fsc.org
MIX
Papier | Fördert
gute Waldnutzung
FSC® C083411

Kolibri 360 GmbH
Ferdinand-Jühlke-Straße 7
99095 Erfurt, Deutschland
produktsicherheit@kolibri360.de